THE POLITICS OF SANCTUARY

THE POLITICS OF SANCTUARY

THE POLITICS
OF SANCTUARY

Vojislava Filipcevic Cordes

CORNELL UNIVERSITY PRESS   ITHACA AND LONDON

First published 2025 by Cornell University Press

Librarians: A CIP catalog record for this book is available from the Library of Congress.

ISBN 9781501783289 (hardcover)
ISBN 9781501783302 (pdf)
ISBN 9781501783296 (epub)

GPSR EU contact: Sam Thornton, Mare Nostrum Group B.V., Mauritskade 21D, 1091 GC, Amsterdam, NL, gpsr@mare-nostrum.co.uk.

For Danilo and Francis and to the undocumented,
asylum seekers, and refugees

Contents

Preface

This book argues for a more inclusive political life of an expanded urban citizenship for undocumented immigrants, asylum seekers, and refugees through the active urban mechanisms of sanctuary practice. My argument is legal (examining the legality of sanctuary, including the lawsuits in San Francisco), empirical (looking at responses to the criminalization of immigrants), political (analyzing the character of cities as sanctuaries), and normative (arguing for an expansive sense of the rights of the city). Empirical arguments are made on the basis of participant-observation fieldwork with the New Sanctuary Coalition (NSC), New York City, July 2017–June 2018.

The book will make six cumulative arguments in six chapters. The key point of the book (see item 4 below) concerns *the political spaces of sanctuary* and argues for an expansion of urban citizenship for the undocumented, asylum seekers, and refugees via sanctuary practices (to not only supplement the ordinances or designations of sanctuary cities but truly enfranchise the migrants who reside in them). The book is divided into three parts, each of which includes a theoretical chapter followed by a fieldwork chapter: the first explores the politics of immigrant exclusions; the second, the limits of sanctuary as a political space; and the third, rights to sanctuary and rights to the city.

Six main points that the book will make that correspond to the six chapters are as follows:

1. The book argues for planning interventions to shape an inclusive urban polity as an alternative to the restrictive state (drawing from urban planning history and legal contexts).

    Anti-urban sentiments have a long history in American political culture and can be seen as rooted in part in anti-immigrant biases, which have resurfaced in the political context that witnessed the separation of families and caging of children at the US border with Mexico, the planning of a border wall, the Muslim travel ban, and, most recently, border closures, restrictions on asylum claim applications, and plans for mass deportations.

    This chapter, using in its last section the example of San Francisco's lawsuits and policies against the federal government, argues that sanctuary cities can be viewed as an urban social justice intervention in the context of a profound state bias against the undocumented, refugees, and asylum seekers.

2. The book evaluates arguments for an expanded urban sanctuary that would include a broader range of individuals who come in contact with the criminal justice system (drawing from ethnographic research in urban political sociology).

   This point concerns grassroots responses to the criminalization of immigrants. Research findings indicate that the NSC in New York did not screen immigrants to distinguish between the worthy/deserving and the underserving, nor did it create a boundary between the "host" and the "guest" but instead worked actively to disrupt claims of state monopoly on the legal and the political. Difficulties that the NSC encountered in forming coalitions for the purpose of advancing expanded sanctuary policies are discussed.

3. The book focuses on the limits of city sovereignty and argues that cities should be utilizing the powers that they increasingly do possess to substantively address deep urban inequalities (drawing from urban politics and urban theory).

   Mayors may not "rule the world," as Benjamin Barber's (2013) forceful argument would have it, they are in fact failing to sufficiently intervene in eradicating urban inequalities. The argument, which includes a delineation of urban constraints to sovereignty, focuses further on the implications for the sanctuary cities movement as a form of sovereignty from below given the lack of coalitional politics that would link urban pro-immigrant movements with redistributive workplace- and residence-based urban political activism.

4. The book argues for the expansion of urban citizenship (via solidarity of social movements and political activism with immigrant groups) into a fundamentally inclusive category. This is referred to as the political spaces of sanctuary practices (drawing from ethnographic research in urban political sociology).

   This argument makes a distinction between the empty branding rhetoric of sanctuary cities that make public declarations that they will protect the undocumented but nevertheless criminalize immigrants and the substantive sanctuary practices of, for example, the NSC in New York. Based on fieldwork, the argument here emphasizes that the claiming of political spaces of sanctuary could be seen as following four trajectories toward legality, publicness, visibility, and secularization. These four trajectories also expose the limitations of the movement—on the one hand, the emphasis on legal challenges faces the obstacles of restrictive immigration law and places emphasis on individual cases. Public efforts such as Sanctuary Hood are faced with insufficient resources and inadequate civic infrastructure. Visibility places in the foreground the faces of the Dreamers (Deferred Action for Childhood Arrivals (DACA) recipitents) and relies upon selective media coverage, although examples of grassroots documentary filmmaking represent another form of viable resistance. Secularization is, however, indicative of the increasing strength of the movement to resist pressures of religious organizations to select "worthy" cases to support—yet support of churches still appears critical in cases of physical sanctuaries.

5. The book examines the tradition of civil disobedience in sanctuary activism and argues that sanctuary could be seen in a dual manner as a set of solidarity practices and a striving toward an abolitionist movement (drawing from urban political and social theory and interdisciplinary sanctuary research).

    Civil disobedience can be seen as a guardian of the legitimacy of the constitutional state (Habermas 1985, 105) and essentially an appeal to principles of justice (Rawls 2009). The subject of this book concerns in part these acts of noncitizens and of citizens to protect noncitizens, who in essence together, as Rawls (2009, 252) has stated, "must decide on the basis of the principles of justice." The chapter debates pro- and anti-sanctuary arguments developed in legal scholarship and then turns to the subject of urban membership as a normatively expansive category that can be seen in two complementary approaches: (a) urban denizenship and solidarity and (b) grassroots abolitionist strategies, which show how sanctuary practices merge with struggles of other marginalized groups to form a transformative force.

6. The book argues that certain aspects of right to the city arguments do advance the alternative legality of rightful presence, especially given the limitation of the framework of right to difference. Sanctuary practices create legitimate claims to immigrant urban membership and belonging, resisting the hostile, exclusionary, parochial state (drawing from urban theory and ethnographic research in urban political sociology).

    This argument discusses activism concerning the proposals for a different type of governmentality for undocumented immigrants, regarding them as effectively citizens of the city with rights of protection, including immunity from being deported. The argument advanced here is cautiously suggestive of an emancipatory potential of sanctuary practices in the urban environment, although in many aspects of their lives the undocumented must remain in the shadows of the city. Sanctuary practices create legitimate claims to immigrant urban membership and

belonging and forms of rights to urban denizenship that should be supported by governance and social service arrangements.

* * *

Sanctuary can be conceived of as "a small gesture toward alleviating human suffering and preventing humiliation"—a gesture signaling reciprocity and copres-
ence of human beings vis-à-vis one another—asserted Elie Wiesel (1984–85, 390)
in his essay titled "The Refugee." Rejecting the notion of sanctuary as a place,
Wiesel argued instead for "a living sanctuary [of a human being] whom nobody
has a right to invade" (387). This book shares Wiesel's humane, sheltering meaning of sanctuary, and proposes to define it in modest ways as a set of social practices and networks of solidarity that affirm the human dignity of asylum seekers,
refugees, and the undocumented. But the book also endorses a place-based, if not
solely place-defined, understanding of sanctuary by examining migrants' claims
for rightful presence in the city and indeed their attempts at attaining the right
to the city. Sanctuary cities in the United States are defined in chapter 3 as places
where a local government or police department has passed a resolution, a city
ordinance, an executive order, or a departmental policy explicitly banning city or
law enforcement officials from inquiring into immigration status and/or cooperating with the Department of Homeland Security's Immigration and Customs
Enforcement (ICE) agency. Sanctuary is discussed in relationship to municipal
ordinances in chapters 1 and 3 and in relationship to grassroots practices and
processes antithetical to the hostile, parochial, exclusionary state in chapters 2,
4, and 6. Yet still a broader definition of sanctuary is offered in chapter 5, where
it is seen as a resistance struggle and a means of interrupting the violence of the
deportation machinery and its regimes of fear, emphasizing the role of radical
solidarity of "co-citizens" (that is, citizens who partake in sanctuary practices
with noncitizens). Finally, abolitionist conceptions of sanctuary are discussed in
chapters 2 and 5.

Acknowledgments

The Politics of Sanctuary commenced during my research associate appointment at Fordham University, where I worked with the political scientist Benjamin Barber (*Jihad vs. McWorld, Strong Democracy, If Mayors Ruled the World*) until his untimely death in 2017. With Ben's death, I was left with a research task that became an independent research project and quickly grew into a book manuscript.

While the book is in the field of urban studies, it reflects my learning from and long-standing advising by political scientists Ira Katznelson and John Mollenkopf, although numerous scholars from other disciplines including sociology, planning, and law have read and commented on my work as well. None are, of course, responsible for the unsteadiness of my research.

Thus, for helpful comments, discussions, encouragement, and/or simply sharing research, I wish to thank Sheila Foster, Randy Lippert, Saskia Sassen, Ester Fuchs, Yumiko Shimabukuro, Rose Cuison-Villazor, Idil Atak, Nestor Davidson, Thomas Coggin, Annika Hinze, Rosemary Wakeman, Matt Block, Gesche Loft, Diego Renato Azurdia, Jane Guskin, Todd Brown, Dave Brotherton, Henry Pontell, David Green, Daniel Stageman, Father Luis Barrios, Juan Carlos Ruiz, Ravi Ragbir, Sara Gozalo, Goeff Trenchard, Nathan Yaffe, Milena Gomez, Ingrid Olivo, Tom Angotti, Elliott Sclar, Robert Beauregard, Peter Bearman, Bill McAllister, John Krinsky, Weiping Wu, Aaron Passell, Maria Kowalski, Els de Graauw, Debra Klaber, Alan Yaspan, Andre Daughtry, Grace Yukich, Gemma Solimene, Saille Murray, Nihad Bunar, Gordana Rabrenovic, Ryan Mulligan, Andrew Karmen, Serin Houston, Peter Mancina, Jennifer Ridgley, Steve Sacco, Carol Banks, Igor Vojnovic, Sabin Bieri, Christoph Bader, Jelena Milojevic, Cameron Kaufmann, Ivana Kronja, Aysha Khan, Aiyuba Thomas, and Antonie Schmiz, among others. I had a wonderful opportunity to work with my research associate Noelle Amber Shih, a Columbia University political science student who prepared the bibliography and demonstrated her excellence as a researcher.

My fieldwork with the New Sanctuary Coalition in New York coincided with CUNY Graduate Center colleague Matt Block's own extensive fieldwork. This meant sharing research sources as well as ideas, thoughts, and anxieties and included a special memory of a joyful moment of Matt donating his guitar to sanctuary activists. Matt's brilliant dissertation will answer so many questions not examined in my own research and will take discussions of sanctuary further in the direction of citizenship research.

Finally, among friends and exiles, I honor Elvira and Ervin, Tamara and Sergey, Tanja and Davor, Vivian and Charles, Biljana, Suncica, Goran, Olja, Milan, and Lidija and among family members, Milovan and Zagorka; Stephanie and Richard; Kate, Jared, Ada, and Eme; Laura, Minas, and Evan; David, Suzanne, Rebecca, and Sierra; and especially Daniel, Danilo, and Francis.

Many of those I have crossed paths with in my own experience as an immigrant from Belgrade, Serbia, formerly in Yugoslavia, will remain unacknowledged. I began my journey in the early 1990s as an exile with an expiring visa and one suitcase in Stockholm, not knowing exactly where I was going yet suspecting it would be to America, where I eventually obtained an "Extraordinary Ability" visa category designation. I know that my experience, as difficult as it has sometimes been, cannot be compared to the experiences of many who have crossed the Rio Grande on foot or the Mediterranean by boat; the more accomplished sections of this study are dedicated to them.

The following papers that I presented at conferences have been helpful in shaping ideas for book chapters: "Locations of Citizenship: Recognition Claims and Immigrant Inclusion in Global Cities," American Association of Geographers Annual Meeting, April 3–7, 2019, Washington, DC; "Urban Studies Week Discussion on Sanctuary Cities," Fordham University, April 19, 2018, New York (invited participation); "A Sanctuary City's Political Space," International Research Group on Law and Urban Space (IRGLUS) Workshop on the Judiciary and the City, Fordham University's Urban Law Center, June 14–15, 2017, New York.

Finally, the chapters of the book are revisions of the following published articles (and I thank the editors and the anonymous peer reviewers for their thoughtful comments):

"Right to the City, Right to Sanctuary: Sanctuary Practices, Urban Inequality, and Immigrant Political Subjectivities in New York," in *Sustainable Development Goals* book series: *Transitioning to Reduced Equalities* (February 2023), edited by Sabin Bieri and Christoph Bader.

"'She Can't Even See Her Shadow': The New Sanctuary Coalition's Response to the Criminalization of Immigrants in New York," *Journal of Urban Affairs*, August 2021.

"(Mis)recognition, Faltering Cosmopolitanism: Theories of Social Diversity and the City," *Critical Issues in Justice and Politics* Volume 11, Number 1, March 2019.

"Aquí estamos: The Sanctuary City's Political Space," *Critical Planning Journal*, Volume 24, Fall 2018/Spring 2019.

"Planning Interventions: Urban Bias, Social Reform, and the City," *Planning Practice and Research*, Volume 34, Issue 1, December 2018.

"City Sovereignty: Urban Resistance and Rebel Cities Reconsidered," *Urban Science* Volume 1, Issue 3, Number 22, 2017.

Op-ed: "It's Time for Cities to Extend and Expand Sanctuary," *Next City*, September 6, 2023.

I am deeply grateful to Jim Lance, Bethany Wasik, Ellen Labbate, Jennifer Crane, book peer reviewers, and Cornell University Press for their interest in the manuscript.

THE POLITICS OF SANCTUARY

THE POLITICS OF SANCTUARY

Introduction

MIGRATION AND THE LIMITS OF URBAN POLICY

Refuting the ultimately successful 2024 presidential campaign rhetoric of President Donald Trump, who routinely referred to an "invasion" of "illegal immigrants" on the southern border and promised mass deportations if reelected, then-President Joe Biden declared on June 4, 2024, "I will never demonize immigrants. I will never refer to immigrants as 'poisoning the blood' of a country. And further, I'll never separate children from their families at the border. I will not ban people from this country because of their religious beliefs. I will not use the U.S. military to go into neighborhoods all across the country to pull millions of people out of their homes and away from their families to put [into] detention camps . . . while awaiting deportation, as my predecessor says he will do if he . . . occupies this office again" (White House, June 4, 2024). Yet President Biden spoke on the occasion of issuing an executive order to close the southern border if a daily average of 2,500 arrests was exceeded for any week and to instruct border agents to refrain from posing outright "manifest fear" (for their lives) questions to asylum seekers. The executive action still allowed for exceptions, including for asylum claims for victims of torture and for unaccompanied children, and allowed for the reopening of the border if the daily arrest average for a week subsequently dropped below 1,500 and remained below that level for another week.

President Biden went on to propose policies for granting amnesty to undocumented spouses of American citizens, for providing work permits for Deferred Action of Childhood Arrivals (DACA) recipients, and, in January 2025, for extending the Temporary Protected Status for migrants from Sudan, Ukraine, El Salvador, and Venezuela. Following failed bipartisan legislation in Congress, and facing political pressures during an election year, unfavorable polls on migration based in part on fears of community and demographic change, and discontent from local Democratic leadership in overwhelmed sanctuary cities, President Biden still continued to rely on the same Immigration and Nationality Act section 212(f) law invoked by President Trump in 2017 to ban migrants from predominantly Muslim countries and in 2018 to limit asylum claims on the border (Martinez-Beltrán 2024). In fiscal year 2024, under President Biden, the US Immigration and Customs Enforcement (ICE) deported 271,484 migrants (of which 180,476 were "border security arrests")—the highest figure since 2014—although President Obama holds the record of 3,066,457 removals during the eight years of his presidency, with an average of 383,307 deportations per year (Miroff and Sacchetti 2024; Nowrasteh 2019a; US ICE 2024, 14).

While protecting human rights is a moral obligation, states may limit their own action and policies regarding the human rights that they accept (Carens 2013, 7), albeit respecting the minimum standard set by human rights and flowing from democratic principles, but ultimately ethical questions are unavoidable in the context of citizenship and migration (8). This is especially the case given that the control that democratic states exercise over immigration serves to maintain global inequality and limit freedom (230). This idea of state control over migration has also been criticized from the frameworks of justice, equality, liberty, and international and human rights laws (Bauder 2022, 3). By "constructing vulnerabilities" for migrants (Anderson, Sharma, and Wright 2009, cited in Bauder 2022, 6) who are denied legal status and rights, states are further economically excluding and socially marginalizing this population (Bauder 2022, 6). But migration is also a thornier policy issue as the anxieties of social cohesion; fears of cultural dissolution; and material concerns regarding resources, jobs, and services shape anti-immigrant public opinion and are not mere prejudices and animosities (Miller 2016, 163–64). (In chap. 1, this book will take up a historical discussion of anti-immigrant biases in an urban polity that, as has been noted, have resurfaced in the recent political debate on migration in the United States. This book will discuss in chap. 2 forms of resistance to the pervasive criminalization of migrants by the sanctuary movement and, in chap. 5, similar ideas of resistance by the modern abolitionist movement.)

The political theorist Benjamin Barber offers a critique of the powers of the state rooted in exclusions such as those cited above. Calling for simultaneously global and local ("glocal") interdependent democratic movements, Barber (2017, 65) avers, "We confront [the] brutally interdependent challenges with antiquated nation-states, wrapped in the very sovereignty and independence that leave them incapable of meeting the new perils. We have HIV without borders, war without borders, immigration without borders, a digital web without borders, but we do not have citizens without borders or democracy without borders. . . . Unless we find ways to globalize democracy or to democratize globalization, humankind will be in ever greater peril." The chief argument that Barber advances is that under these borderless conditions, a special place opens up for the role of cities as opposed to the nation-states: "Where once nations advocated for civic, social, and economic rights while supposedly parochial states and cities opposed them, more often nowadays it is cities that promote universal claims concerning gender rights, gay marriage, higher wages, and environmental sustainability—cosmopolitanism in its true meaning—while states grow small-minded, mean, and parochial" (29). Appealing to democracy and seeing citizens as the ultimate source of sovereignty, Barber (2017, 18) seems to argue for the right of cities to govern themselves in the context where federal authorities fail in their responsibilities. It is not clear from Barber's argument whether cities should pressure federal authorities to act more responsibly and redistribute greater amounts of resources to cities or what the role of state and regional authorities should be. Citing Schragger's *City Power*, Barber notes that "we should *want* cities to govern" and emphasizes the "*desirability* of city power" (Schragger, cited in Barber 2017, 23). But Barber (2017, 25) warns that nations will not passively stand by as cities assert their rights and claims. Urban collaboration should be based on rights arguments fundamentally responding to an abusive authority, addressing challenges that cross frontiers (rendering them meaningless), and highlighting the "rightfulness" and also "righteousness" of cities (28). And while Barber underscores the role of the courts (e.g., in the case of environmental politics, the *Juliana v. United States* climate change lawsuit filed in 2015) and the role of social movements, he does not discuss the great variation across cities regarding which movements succeed and which fail. This error is made in the earlier urban sociological literature. As Ira Katznelson (1981, 211) points out, theorists such as Manuel Castells make it seem that urban movements will emerge automatically, but "not all structural possibilities find historical expression." We need to understand nationally distinctive working-class traditions and cultures in order to understand why movements occur in some places and not in others. Urban movements take place in articulation with other movements, in particular working-class movements and political class struggles. "Urban struggles in this view, even though they are about 'secondary structural issues, that is to say, ones not directly challenging the production methods of society nor the political domination of the ruling classes' need not be relegated always to a peripheral or merely reformist role in the quest for social change. . . . The importance of urban movements is thus an open, contingent matter, hinging principally on the 'effects it has upon the power relations between social classes in concrete situations'" (Katznelson 1981, 212).

Without elaborating on urban social movements, however, Barber venerates the role of cities, eschewing the question of the resources needed to undertake substantive urban reforms and lionizing mayoral leadership ("Mayors must manifest the rights of cities, fight for those rights, and if necessary, go to court or jail for them" [Barber 2017, 28]). Yet in spite of the theory's limitations, Barber's hope for mayoral leadership and deliberation across borders is less significant than the arguments in which the author hints at the role of global-scale collective action by directly engaged citizens (and, presumably, noncitizens as well), offering kernels for a theory of urban dimensions of rooted cosmopolitanism. (This book will take up this discussion further in chap. 3, which probes the limits of city sovereignty in the context of deep urban inequalities.)

The Urban Prospect of Grounded Cosmopolitanism

Urban cosmopolitanism, in a closely related view, would thus allow us to "look to the city, rather than to the state" (Derrida 2001, 4) and ask the questions that French theorist Jacques Derrida posed in the context of French asylum policies but that are now particularly applicable to the new role of cities as sanctuary spaces under the increasingly restrictive national regime in the United States (applicable not just to Republican presidential candidates but to mainstream Democratic representatives as well). Derrida writes, "I also imagine the experience of cities of refuge as giving rise to a place [*lieu*] for reflection—for reflection on the questions of asylum and hospitality—and for a new order of law and a democracy to come to be put to the test [*expérimentation*]. Being on the threshold of these cities, of these new cities that would be something other than 'new cities', a certain idea of cosmopolitanism, an other, has not yet arrived, perhaps. . . . If it has (indeed) arrived . . . then, one has perhaps not yet recognised it" (Derrida 2001, 23). Probing the limits of hospitality and openness toward new immigrants, Derrida calls for cities of refuge as a new form of solidarity. "They must, if they are to succeed in so doing, make an audacious call for a genuine innovation in the history of the right to asylum or the duty to hospitality" (4). Hospitality ought to be seen in the broadest sense, including material, legal, political, and spiritual support and advocacy for migrants (see Vitiello 2022, 29–30). As ancient Greek notions of hospitality (*xenia*) and asylum appeared in the crucial transformative moment of the fifth-century polis, so too can sanctuary activism in a moment of heightened exclusionary state actions contest them in discourse and shape public policy (Isayev 2018, 11, 18). This view, exemplified here by Derrida's writing, does not respond to, and indeed fails to address, the rise of the political right, fueled by anti-immigrant rhetoric, in EU countries.

Derrida (2001, 7–8) poses the question central to this inquiry: "Could the City, equipped with new rights and greater sovereignty, open up new horizons of possibility previously undreamt of by international state law?" To answer this question, we need to first probe the scale, scope, and, of course, limits of urban cosmopolitanism. And while fundamental aspects of equality are not resolved on the local level but are dependent on broader state and international protections and larger institutional contexts set up to uphold them, it is in the local sphere that that the consequences of those actions can be felt most fully—in the neighborhood, in the workplace, and on the street where discriminatory effect against immigrants of color is compounded by their low socioeconomic status. Furthermore, the neighborhood as the locus of contact and encounter represents a focal point of social life for immigrants and importantly a key space for the development of bridging ties; while the neighborhood is thus a significant field for socialization (even if immigrants may have interethnic contacts elsewhere), it may only partially be of importance for the shaping of strong interethnic ties (Pratsinakis et al. 2015, 4, 6). Indeed, if ethnic rifts are heightened by a class divide, hopeful scenarios cannot be assumed based merely on interethnic contacts or neighborhood encounters, and these cannot be equated with substantive social practices of inclusion (Blockland and Eijk, cited in Pratsinakis et al. 2015, 14). The significance of a neighborhood is nevertheless perhaps greater in the earlier stages of incorporation, as social networks expand beyond the place of residence in subsequent phases (Pratsinakis et al. 2015, 14).

A cosmopolitan life more broadly defined displays "kaleidoscopic tension and variety" (Waldron 1995, 94); a cosmopolitan is one "conscious of living in a mixed-up world and having a mixed-up self" (and the former can reinforce the latter). These notions encompass the idea of variety, diversity, and mélange, and the cosmopolitan self is constituted through a sense of consciousness about this "kaleidoscopic tension." In the urban context (distinct from the exclusionary spaces of community and citizenship [Muller 2011, 3416]), the cosmopolis can be seen as "a city . . . in which there is genuine acceptance of, connection with, and respect and space for the cultural other, and . . . the possibility of a togetherness in difference" (Sandercock, cited in Young, Diep, and Drabble 2006, 1689). Muller refers to this as "urban alchemy"—"the belief that the diverse and divided population of a city can be transformed into one harmonious community of cosmopolitan citizen" (Muller 2011, 3416)—but warns that urban cosmopolitanism should not be celebrated that much (3429). Cosmopolitanism can be seen as a discursive social practice in which people attempt to overcome the parochialisms of their own ethnic, national, or religious identities to form a shared community of equals with others without compromising cultural differences (3418). While a compatibility of immigrant cultures with liberal values cannot be assumed, what is critical here is the emancipatory potential of grounded urban cosmopolitanism that would (a) overcome parochialisms and particularisms and (b) be dependent on active processes of reshaping of the national citizenship in a more inclusive direction. These two processes would move concurrently and be open to dialogue, interaction, and negotiation—an enriched, strengthened polity emerging especially from the conflictual arenas of urbanity, including as well in this ideal case scenario active interaction with and synergic enfranchisement of native-born minority cultures.

But urban cosmopolitanism cannot escape the "ways in which urban reimagining creates a geography of difference in which certain forms of difference are valued or pathologised and fixed in space" (Young, Diep, and Drabble 2006, 1687) and otherwise commodified (1689, 1691), upholding hegemonies of urban regeneration (1688). "Place-marketing" stereotypes places, reproduces sameness, represents powerful groups' views of the city, reinforces social exclusion, enhances privatized images that limit publicness, and "denies [the] play of difference" and the unacceptable forms of difference that disrupt the city's regeneration strategies (1692), which may involve exclusion of the homeless and the poor from public spaces, for example. Young, Diep, and Drabble show how real estate agents and those engaged in the marketing of place "reinterpret and represent 'class aesthetics' of this process, tapping into the subtleties of taste differences and the deployment of cultural capital by potential purchasers, a process which can exclude other tastes" (2006, 1697), thus marketing a "narrow cosmopolitanism" (1698) produced with the engagement with promotional media in which the new cosmopolitan city that excludes the marginalized groups is "marked out as different, but this is a form of difference which is planned, legitimized, regulated and commodified as a part of marketing the city" (1698, 1700). And where research finds as locations where cosmopolitanism is tolerated and welcomed (1709), these processes are often harmed by commodification and gentrification.[1] Thus, in terms of class difference, cities include, on the one hand, diverse yet impoverished neighborhoods, and on the other, privatized, exclusionary and, mostly (although not solely) homogeneous areas as well as the refurbished, gentrified downtowns, where diversity can be safely consumed without genuine social interaction with migrants and minorities. The living multiculture (in this case, voluntary and in part involuntary enclaves), situated amidst tremendous inequality, contributes to the shaping of the fragmented city in which not only class, but also ethnic and racial, conflicts persist (Judd and Hinze 2019, 445).

These descriptive accounts contrast with liberal multiculturalists who have challenged the notions of universal citizenship by pointing out that by including difference we can achieve true equality even if this proposal may be challenged on many grounds. Nevertheless, it could be argued further that the frequency with which individuals (e.g., second/third generation immigrants) in cosmopolitan cities break away from a group to embrace other identities mitigates the threat that the ethnic particularism of communities would be internally oppressive (e.g., a redefinition of what it means to be, for example, a Bangladeshi, a Dominican, or a Turk in the context of a large global city like London, New York, or Berlin). We can note this process of formation of multicultural citizenship in metropolitan areas where geographic identity does not merely feature a return to the older, geographically smaller (regional) container for citizenship but serves as a bridge to a broader multiethnic and cosmopolitan identity (e.g., a Dominican New Yorker, a Turkish Berliner, a Bengali Londoner, etc., rather than a Dominican American, etc.) and can also expand to include racial identifications with native-born minority groups.

This is further compatible with the social theorist Saskia Sassen's (2019) argument that an "unmooring" of identities takes place in global cities that allows for the shaping of new notions of community or membership. Sassen's research places particular emphasis on migration as "one of the constitutive processes of globalization" (77) emphasizing, for example, the role of women in neighborhood economies as a part of transnational networks. Sassen hints at a new politics that arises from actual participation in the global economy that involves workers who are disadvantaged and who lack recognition (78). This is in agreement with Muller's view that "some people feel that their urban identity offers them a way to claim local belonging where they feel excluded on national or ethnic grounds" and that "such an urban identification implies a community that is open to the membership of others who are nationally, ethnically, and religiously different" (Muller 2011, 3419). In a related example, immigrants in Canadian cities increasingly seek residences in multicultural neighborhoods and not necessarily in their own enclaves (Hiebert, quoted in Binnie 2006, 20); thus, the urban identities are also created through interactions with other groups. There are also, it should be noted, examples of groups that have rejected the notion of urban cosmopolitanism, as with the Bangladeshi community in north London, due to the diasporic trajectory and the labor market position (Muller 2011, 3420).

Grounded urban cosmopolitanism (see also Young, Diep, and Drabble 2006, 1688) tries to rescue cosmopolitanism from the elitist inclinations associated with the term and from "consumers with middle or high incomes who find the multicultural theme appealing and want to experience the difference of the 'other'" (van der Horst and Ouwehand 2012, 871) but perhaps refrain from genuine socializing with immigrant groups (Crul and Lelie 2024); from those who try to reinvent themselves by performing new cosmopolitan lifestyles (Young,

Diep, and Drabble 2006, 1700) or by engaging in "fun-filled, flavoursome and exciting" multicultural planning (van der Horst and Ouwehand 2012, 872);[2] from the notions of the "togetherness of strangers" (Young 1990, 237); and from the tolerance of difference that hides indifference (Sennett 2002). This can be accomplished "by questioning the 'predefined' categories of identity"—"the multiplicity of identities together with everyday life interactions in multicultural neighborhoods create a cosmopolitan practice (elite as well as vernacular) that strengthens co-existence and relations among difference groups" (Koutrolikou 2012, 2052). Thus, we return to the promise of urbanity as an arena for potentially altered, unmoored identities through substantive everyday practices in which a living multiethnic society takes shape. This idea should not be taken so far as to argue that improved relations will result from increased contact and interaction given the realities of intergroup conflict and competition for resources and of the presence of "homogeneous micro enclaves ([created] through gentrification)" (Koutrolikou 2012, 2062) that can displace locals and diminish diversity (2058). Moreover, researchers in Quebec found that immigrants identified patterns of discrimination as more influential than citizenship policy (which balanced the specificity of Quebec's French community's demands with Canada's multiethnic society and diverse cities) and saw "the coexistence of diverse loyalties and multidimensional identities as far less problematic than either the Canadian or the Quebec governments have" (Aleinikoff and Klusmeyer 2001, 11). Evidence from Canada (see Wright and Bloemraad 2012, 88) further questions the thesis that diverse urban areas might complicate or fragment participation (Putnam 2007). This is suggestive of the emancipatory aspects of hybrid belonging, shaped by urban diversity and actively embraced as a category of identification and citizenship practice by immigrant groups.[3] But this argument also warns that immigrant inclusion and related multicultural arrangements are critically tied to issues of racial discrimination in both native-born and foreign-born communities insufficiently addressed by the new assimilationist policies. This includes further "segregation that went beyond housing, separating facilities, education and forms of social interaction . . . leading to polarized communities that lived 'parallel lives'" (Koutrolikou 2012, 2053); this particularly affected minority youth (2057). Thus, the mainstream discourse that insists upon the distinctness of migrant cultures in contrast can lead to social exclusion, racialization, perception of alien culture (language, religion, and so on), and doubt about possibilities for social cohesion (especially, in the case of European cities, for Muslim groups). The global city literature is suggestive of possible connections between the exclusions of immigrants of color and vestiges of racial discrimination[4] (e.g., the riots in the racialized spaces of British and French cities in 2011 and 2005, respectively), although the connections are left undeveloped. For example, the "rioters [in Britain] were

young Britons who were bi-lingual [and] perfectly at home with British modernity and Islamic tradition, politicised and unequivocal about their identities as
British Muslims . . . [their anger] aimed at the lack of economic opportunity,
negligence by the public authorities and community elders, racism and racialized
institutional practices, and enduring history of taunt and intimidation, and material deprivation and maginalisation. . . . They were civic riots by a group wanting
to claim the public turf as full British citizens and not the riots of cultural aliens"
(Bennett et al. 2016, 1018).

Modood has argued that immigrant groups can benefit from the political
environment created by the native-born minorities whose mobilization creates
institutional opportunities and increases influence beyond the inclusion of their
own group (Modood 2009). This argument is discussed further in chapter 2,
which analyzes fieldwork research results regarding abolitionist trajectories of the
sanctuary movement in New York; a theory of abolitionist strategies that shape
transformative sanctuary practices is also discussed in chapter 5. Modood (2009),
however, goes as far as to conclude that forms of conflict (such as the Brixton riots
and the Rushdie affair) can have positive effects reflecting a recognition-based
strategy that would foster "integration for marginal groups" (246), although
evidence suggests that the legacy of institutional reform following the riots is
among the most significant benefits of this conflict-based strategy (see Jones-
Correa 2009), indicating that misrecognition that can trigger conflict may result
in limited institutional reforms (e.g., increased minority hiring by the police or
city administration rather than educational or criminal justice system reform).

Urban institutional and noninstitutional structures (informal organizations,
non-governmental organizations) may offer space for democratic action and thus
also perhaps for transforming recognition struggles.[5] One argument in political
theory is that we cannot impose on immigrants more than what is necessary for
the sustaining of the republic, but at the same time we can impose more on immigrants than on birthright citizens (Appiah in Pickus 1998, 44). This argument can
be extended to suggest the necessity of participatory commitments on the part of
new immigrants, although these obligations ought not to be seen as a mandatory
draft into community participation. While Appiah is correct in that requirements
imposed on immigrants reveal fears of disunity and even territorial disintegra-
tion, the multiculturalism debate has shown further that accommodation of
numerous particularistic recognition claims in many cases also leads to disunity.
Participation per se cannot ensure unity, secure the inclusion of all groups, or
preserve the republic. But if understood as "recognition of the need for special
laws, institutions and social policies to overcome barriers to full participation"
(Castles 1995, 303), an inclusive grounded urban cosmopolitan paradigm would
in essence assume active action leading toward citizenship, the action that would

empower groups to fully participate. This would align with Miller's (2016, 155) argument that a balance ought to be struck between the claims of migrants and the responsibilities they might assume. This would also respond to Sassen's challenge of forging a new politics of migration from the ground up, focusing on the neighborhoods, on coalitions with native-born minority groups, and on mobilizations to protest urban inequalities, building on social practices and participatory activism. Yet even this sketch of possible scenarios of how urban cosmopolitanism might play out reveals limitations not just because of the discriminatory structures but because of the questions of resources and urban policy constraints more broadly. Nevertheless, while migrants need representatives and advocates, the shaping of a bottom-up urban cosmopolitanism would crucially depend on inclusion within participatory structures in neighborhoods, workplaces, and educational and social institutions as well as within social movements. This point regarding participation of migrants will prove crucial in the discussions of sanctuary movements in this book, which concludes with a chapter on the "right to the city"—a form of participatory enactment of politics of "rightful presence" of immigrants in urban public spaces. Before turning to the questions of urban policy specific to sanctuary in New York City, global cities, local participation, and political opportunity structures should be examined.

Global Cities and Political Opportunity Structures

Before examining sanctuaries as spaces of politics it is important to tackle at least briefly the subjects of (anti-immigrant) counter mobilization and the nexus between economic and political incorporation in global cities. Theorist Bonnie Honig (2003) argues that "the co-presence in American political culture of xenophilia and xenophobia comes right out of America's fundamental liberal commitments, which map a normatively and materially privileged national citizenship onto an idealized immigrant trajectory to membership" (97). This mapping of the political imagination of the national citizenship with the (initially, white, after the 1965 reform, multiethnic) immigrant ideal existed concurrently with anti-immigrant policies (King 2000). Historian Donna Gabaccia (2008), similarly, has argued that the very construct of citizenship in the United States is framed though a lens of immigration, based on the assumption of both a history of immigration and a (contested) premise of social inclusion; yet tracing the acceptance of immigration to the Civil War era, Gabaccia notes that the notion of "the nation of immigrants" was not initially embraced by the population but was in fact used by those who favored the exclusion of immigrants.

Both Sassen (2007) and Honig (2003) argue for an expanded practice of demo-cratic cosmopolitanism (urban vs. national, respectively) in the case of immi-grant groups via empowerment though claims-making—in Honig's case these are "illegitimate demands made by people with no standing to make them, a story of people so far outside the circle of who 'counts' that they cannot make claims within the existing frames of claim making" (Honig 2003, 101), which parallels Sassen's (2007) emphasis on the informal economy and claims on the city. Both authors, however, tend to focus more on the civic than the ethnic and eschew the question of formal citizenship or institutional arrangements needed to support the practice of citizenship. The key issue concerning the polarization of, on the one hand, the expanded scope to claim rights, and, on the other hand, the unwill-ingness and the inability of institutions to formalize or respond to these claims (as can be seen in the increasingly "silent" sanctuary cities at the beginning of the sec-ond Trump administration) can fruitfully be examined in the case of global cities.

Global cities such as New York have become "political spaces where the con-centration of different groups and their identities are intertwined with the articu-lation of various claims to citizenship rights" (Sassen, cited in Isin 2000, 13; see also Keith 2005) that would grant access to social, economic, and political rights. Global cities in the US and the EU are thus political spaces for demands for the new entitlements and the equality of citizenship ranging from antidiscrimination measures to forms of reasonable accommodation and consist as well of claims "for differentiated visibility" (Saint-Blancat 2008) in the case of religious groups and the sanctuary movement activism. Global city theories add transnational variables to urban research and prompt an inquiry into the embeddedness of citi-zenship in urban power structures as well as in less formal participatory move-ments or affiliations, but they do not define the type of immigrant empowerment that can occur. These theories miss the critical point that the racialization of the citizenship of the excluded migrants cannot be understood through the study of localized or transnational practices alone but requires examination of national-level group arrangements and histories of immigration policies. This argument further neglects to investigate specific state accommodations that have made this challenge possible or impossible (changes in citizenship preferences, laws, party openings, institutional reforms). Rather than merely the search for a politics that is outside the boundaries of the formal polity (see Sassen 2005, 92), localities could also be seen as arenas and points of engagement with formal and informal polities under transnational economic and sociopolitical conditions. For exam-ple, in Los Angeles, undocumented youth lobbied in recent years for education access and also for a broader consideration of immigrant rights as human rights, taking advantage of institutional openings made by Latino political mobilization and the successes of campaigns such as opposition to Proposition 187 (Burciaga and Martinez 2017, 465–466). Research on the undocumented shows that their institutional exclusion cannot be explained by a politics that escapes the formal political domain. "Groups with higher proportions of undocumented parents in New York City (e.g., Mexicans compared to Dominicans) reported lower levels of access to checking accounts, savings accounts, credit, and drivers' licenses. Lack of access to such resources, in turn, was associated with higher economic hardship and psychological distress among parents, and lower levels of cognitive ability in their 24-month-old children" (Yoshikawa, Godfrey, and Rivera, 2008).

Global cities do not offer the highest prospects for either the economic or the political inclusion of those lowest-income groups who comprise, in Sassen's terms, the infrastructure of jobs in the postindustrial economy (Sassen 2007, 109). The global economy devalues the work culture of immigrants and low-income women, raising further questions regarding the legitimacy of that devalorization (Sassen 2007, 119). Further, while urban economic conditions are likely to reinforce "ethnic segregation of work" (Tilly 1998, 165) in places where chain migration persists, these conditions are not simply shaped by the networks or enclave ties they have access to, but reinforced by institutional arrangements regarding schooling and social services, and so on. available for the new immigrants and their children. Thus, while the economic conditions in global cities are likely to strengthen the structures resulting in durable inequalities, the latter are in the case of immigrant and minority groups not simply shaped by the networks they have access to, but rather reinforced by institutional arrangements and citizenship structures. The findings that lower-skilled, often new immigrant and minority workers fare less well in diverse global cities (compared to suburbs and smaller, less heterogenous cities) pose questions not only regarding both their class and racialized identities, but also the ways in which they may be pressed to use sociocultural and political resources to advance economic inclusion and obtain the full benefits of citizenship, which increasingly emphasizes legality and citizenship obligations over rights for the lowest income groups who need these benefits the most. Struggles for urban citizenship in global city enclaves further depend on the extent to which ethnic resilience becomes a transformative force, linking to bridging social capital and forging broader multiethnic political alliances. Groups lobby on the basis of ethnicity for political inclusion of their own, which can compromise panethnic or multiethnic identifications and face obstacles in forming alliances with other races or ethnicities, especially in the initial stages of inclusion. Mayer (2009) has argued for a reemphasis on the Lefebvreian political domain of the right-to-the-city concept, which would politicize social movements, although the applicability of this concept remains limited to cases where alliances would not be impaired by the group-specific claims. An argument that the immigrant labor movement can be seen as a "form of citizenship movement" (Aleinikoff and Klusmeyer 2001, 10) allows for a connection between political dimensions of immigrant citizenship and economic inclusion. In contrast, it could be argued that the presence of immigrants allows for political coalitions and new electoral alliances (see also Sassen 2007), even if this does not necessarily imply that these alliances will be inclusive to other groups or broadly redistributive. To what extent is this the case for sanctuary organizing in New York City? The following section addresses the subject of migration, sanctuary, and urban policy in New York City.

"No More Room at the Inn"?: Urban Policy and the Hope of Sanctuary in New York City

Ellis Island was once the border of New York City, a gated drawbridge for millions of immigrants to what would become their new homeland. But today, when New York's border is at the Rio Grande, that checkpoint is beyond its control. Therefore, the argument that we can advance, based also on Barber's and Derrida's noted rights arguments for the renewed purposes of cities, is that New York ought to, from the perspective of necessity, prudence, and even justice, expand its policies of welcome to match its extended borders.

And yet more than a year has passed since Mayor Eric Adams declared that there was "no more room at the inn" (De Frank and Fitzsimmons 2023) for asylum seekers arriving in the city. Invoking, perhaps inadvertently, a biblical metaphor, the mayor suggested that New York City's shelter system was at capacity. The city has been struggling to shelter the more than one hundred thousand migrants who have arrived since 2022—mostly via buses from states led by Republican governors, who in a controversial political ploy have encouraged the migrants to travel to self-proclaimed sanctuary cities. On May 21, 2023, the mayor's former chief of staff Frank Carone was busy justifying the mayor's increasingly harsh criticism of President Biden, arguing that the United States is facing a "humanitarian crisis" that is "falling squarely on the shoulders of New York City" (Epstein, Rubinstein, and Kanno-Youngs 2023).

In May 2023, the city was housing 42,400 migrants and had run out of shelter space (Epstein, Rubinstein, and Kanno-Youngs 2023). By June 2024, it had already spent $1 billion of the $4.3 billion that had been earlier estimated as the cost of feeding and housing migrants (Mays 2023). In addition to the limited capacity of 140 hotels already filled by migrants, the city said it had explored "other options" for housing migrants, each of which faced local challenges: tents on Orchard Beach in the Bronx (proved prone to flooding and abandoned), gym spaces in public schools (resulted in protests from public school parents and abandoned), suburban communities (in Rockland County, the municipality blocked the relocation of migrants), tents on Randall's Island (opposed by petitions with more than three thousand signatures), and a cruise ship terminal in Brooklyn (objected to by immigrants themselves for inadequate living conditions). The city had also considered setting up tents in Central Park, and in August 2023 hundreds of migrants slept on the streets near Roosevelt Hotel in Midtown Manhattan before the city relocated them to shelters.

According to the Coalition for the Homeless, 147,518 people, including 48,298 children, slept in the main shelter system in New York City in April 2024. Arguing that the city lacked the resources and capacity to maintain adequate shelter for migrants, Mayor Adams requested in 2023 that New York's right to shelter be suspended. The request ignited strong opposition from the Coalition for the Homeless and the Legal Aid Society, which had filed a historic lawsuit in 1981 that resulted in the right-to-shelter rules. The migrant condition in New York exposed not just the failure of federal immigration policies and the difficulties of undertaking immigration reform or the failures of federal urban policies in investing in housing and needed resources in cities, as Mayor Adams appeared to be suggesting. It also exposed the failures of city policies.

Of course, city politics, as the political scientist Paul Peterson (1981) showed in his book *City Limits*, is fundamentally limited, unlike national politics. Arguing that national policies limit the range of city policies and not the internal struggles for power within cities, Peterson concluded that the place of the city within a national political economy fundamentally affected urban policy (1981, 4).[6] While Peterson's book was written in 1981, its conclusion is echoed more recently in the urban political theorist Susan Fainstein's (2010) *Just City*. In her research on diversity and public policy, Fainstein asserts that "without a national regime that is committed to equity, heightened competitiveness of a particular city will likely only produce polarization, and diversity may result in rivalry rather than tolerance" (2010, 16). Fainstein argues for political consciousness that supports progressive policies at the national and local levels and cites as an example the city of Amsterdam, where there is "a national housing policy that equalizes access to housing among different income and ethnic groups." The policy does not prevent the clustering of ethnic groups (still avoiding homogeneity) but also eschews isolated social housing projects (15).

Even if cities are limited in what they can do, city politics is not necessarily always a limited politics—we could argue that it is a politics within bounds, or bounded politics (Frug and Barron 2008). While legal rules limit cities' exercises of power, cities have instead pursued global and tourist policies that defer to private development interests. The arguments here join Fainstein's (2010, 19) aim

to move the discussion in the field of planning away from economic development and in the direction of social equity. The critique of planning in the 1960s
is particularly influential for the planning of today—scholars of urban politics
have especially condemned planning focused on downtown revitalization that
ignored the needs of neighborhoods and emphasized the building of tourist and
sports facilities rather than schools, affordable housing, labor-intensive indus-
tries, or public spaces (Fainstein 2010, 3). Fainstein's (2010, 8) argument is against
the rise of neoliberal policies and instead for an expanded government intervention. I will come back to these points related to urban inequality in chapter 3. It
is sufficient here to chart the limits of urban policies by using a reference from
Pierre and Peters (2012, 79), who, discussing the positioning of market forces in
relationship to collective needs and objectives, drive home the point that market
forces generate urban growth, provide jobs, and pay taxes, presenting the relationship of the city-business sector as asymmetrical: "Cities do not bite the hand
that feeds them and tend to avoid enforcing tough regulation on local business."
If we focus on what is being governed, local policies are embedded in a web of
institutional (cities as creatures of the state), economic, and political constraints,
thus urban policies would be seen as constrained, if not entirely limited (Pierre
and Peters 2012). (Chap. 3 will discuss how city power has been used in New
York to develop public-private partnerships and mega-project planning authorities that have skewed the balance toward the market, luxury city developments
that have heightened inequality, and regulatory policies that have pushed the visible homeless from public spaces and the subway and train stations.)

But cities, Pierre and Peters (2012) also argue, have a responsibility to the
broader urban community: Citing the example of public spaces as sites for democratic debate, the authors stress the loss of these spaces in the context of privatization. Pierre and Peters point out that urban governance is more society-centric
than state-centric, with urban institutions more constrained and contingent on
state resources. This all depends, however, upon the objectives of governance.
If the chief objective is economic growth, other urban-policy objectives such as
redistributive problems are sidelined. *The Politics of Sanctuary* also makes an
argument that historically, the role of planning has been complacent in allowing
the legitimization of interventions in the urban environment that favor economic
growth and, in its avoidance, devalued and undermined social planning. Bluntly
stated here, albeit not solely motivated by long-standing anti-urban biases, planners used the "rational" methods of the profession to conceal discrimination
against poor neighborhoods, often comprising minorities and immigrants. This
topic is discussed extensively in chapter 1.

The prioritization of the key issues of "transparency, accountability, and popular input" (Peirre and Peters 2012, 83) remains while in this narrative the hope

gradually fades for a participatory and democratic governance given local government's collaboration with powerful economic players. Governance emphasizes that government is not alone in the process of steering but involves a variety of actors (83). Pierre and Peters (2012, 83) underscore seeking coalitions and cooperation with powerful players on the local level, but it is as if the authors relegate to secondary consideration the issues of "transparency, accountability, and popular input." The question remains of how, then, governance can be participatory and democratic, as the authors note that the role of political leaders is critical in large urban regeneration projects, but holding them politically accountable is not an easy task, as it cannot be ascertained that they were in fact in control of these projects.

Seen in this light, the city's migration policy is perhaps all of the above—limited, bound, and constrained. Yet even within that constraint there are opportunities to improve strategies of engagement: Redistributional policies, in particular those involving housing, education, and social services, should share a commitment to equity and inclusion. It cannot be overemphasized that cities blindly focused on growth are not utilizing the powers they already possess to substantively address myriad urban inequalities, powers that have grown in recent decades as the federal government has increasingly exited from urban policymaking—this point is discussed extensively in chapter 3. If we agree that urban governance is society-centric and that there is a need for social responsibility to a broader community, then we must argue for the building of (no matter how fragile) coalitional politics to address the needs of migrants and marginalized groups. In other words, one understanding of urban citizenship is that it offers avenues for expanding local belonging to include a range of "unmoored" identities; another, complementary notion is that of urban solidarity, which expands to include broader marginalized groups (Bauder 2021b). Thus, a critical argument of this study links urban migration policy to key questions of inequality in urban policy and politics, arguing that the two cannot be separated. Thus the point here is that it is not simply unethical but utterly unsatisfactory policywise, to fall back on the new mayoral (supposedly nonideological) pragmatism of simply "cleaning up the streets" to appease constituencies displeased with the presence of the homeless, drug-users, and low-income migrants on the sidewalks of American cities. While improvement of urban conditions is a pragmatic necessity, the abandonment of urban values of inclusiveness and equity weakens policy and undermines urbanity.

Misconstruing this, Nicole Gelinas (2023) of the *City Journal* challenged readers to consider the death of Jordan Neely, a homeless street performer who died in an altercation on the New York subway. "Why wasn't *he*"—a New Yorker in need rather than a newly arrived asylum seeker—"in a private hotel room, with round-the-clock 'welcoming' care?" Gelinas, who reproachfully focused her discussion on how asylum seekers were taking space from paying tourists in New York hotels, was in a sense correct to link the urban conditions of homelessness and migration. Indeed, the city *should have* provided health care and supportive housing to Jordan Neely, who struggled with mental illness while homeless. But how should the city have prioritized the seemingly competing needs of a migrant influx and the homelessness crisis?

To answer this question, we need a new urban theory embedded in urban struggles (see Slater 2021, 189) and a reconceptualization of the role of urban policy in resolving urban problems, from racism to affordable housing. In terms of affordable housing, the crisis needs to be viewed as a national issue. Research on the subject offers staggering figures: Over 30 percent of US households are spending more than 30 percent of their income on rent; 17.6 million households paid more than 50 percent of their income on rent, which is affecting more younger and older households and households of people of color. Between 2001 and 2017, the number of households with worst-case housing needs (inadequate conditions and paying more than 50 percent of income for rent) rose by 54 percent, representing 7.7 million renter households (Mueller and Tighe 2022, 72–74). According to the Joint Center for Housing, for every unit of affordable housing constructed, two are lost. Regarding race and housing, New York City is the second most segregated city for Latino and Asian Americans and the third most segregated city for Black people. According to the January 2020 New York City Council report on homelessness, while 20 percent of the city's population is Black, 60 percent of single adults and children in the main shelter system of the Department of Homeless Services are Black. Latino are 29 percent of the population and 30 percent of the single adult and 40 percent of families with children in the shelter system (21).

On February 3, 2023, *Gothamist* (Sundaram 2023) reported the exodus of 125,000 non-Hispanic Black residents from New York City, according to an analysis of the 2000 and 2020 Census data, especially affecting gentrifying neighborhoods such as Bedford-Stuyvesant. Arya Sundaram (2023) of *Gothamist* cites L. Joy Williams, president of the Brooklyn chapter of NAACP, who noted that "these [are] not just issues that are persistent in the Black community in Brooklyn. They are issues of working class and poor people across the city."

Cities have a responsibility to this broader urban community, and the objectives of participatory and democratic governance should shift in that direction of equity, inclusivity, sustainability, and right to the city and away from recent decades' emphases on economic growth, zoning, tax subsidies, and tourist policies that serve private development interests. We also need a new understanding of sanctuary from below, focused on robust community-based initiatives. Similar to Domenic Vitiello's research on sanctuary practices in Philadelphia (2022, 225–26), this study also finds civil society efforts "more enduring and more meaningful" and agrees that these offer a window into understanding various dimensions of sanctuary and solidarity. The New Sanctuary Coalition (NSC)—whose work to assist migrants and asylum seekers continues through several channels of secular and faith-based activism including the Good Shepherd Lutheran Church in Brooklyn (under the leadership of Juan Carlos Ruiz)—attempted to build an expanded sanctuary movement linking immigrant rights to the struggles of a broader group of individuals who have come in contact with the criminal justice system. This book will address coalition building in chapter 2 and will expand upon the notion of urban citizenship as a fundamentally inclusive category in chapter 4, which focuses on sanctuary's political space and its limitations. It should be stated at the outset that these limitations are significant in addressing the cause of marginalized, disenfranchised, and exploited migrants. As Harald Bauder stresses, "Urban sanctuary policies and practices do not eliminate illegalization; they merely enable illegalized migrants to better cope with their circumstances of living in illegality. Thus, sanctuary cities fail to tackle the root problem caused by Westphalian statehood" (2022, 96). In turn, while documenting the insufficiently funded resettlement of Southeast Asians, Domenic Vitiello found unjust, degrading, and inadequate responses to migrants in destitute circumstances in decaying inner-city neighborhoods that were also sites of racial violence (2022, 63–64, 65) and showed how acts of kindness and compassion were insufficient to "overcome the fundamental structural limits and violence of the resettlement system nor the deeper economic and social problems of American cities" (69; see also 81–82). These subjects will be discussed extensively in chapters 3, 4, and 5, which examine grassroots challenges to the constraints of urban policy. But it should be noted as well that sanctuary ordinances are not always the empty proclamations that grassroots activists sometimes purport them to be: They can offer important institutional openings for an expanded sanctuary struggle, such as sanctuary campuses involving university protection of undocumented students; police reform policies involving noncooperation with ICE; and civil bureaucracies involving municipal IDs, which can help immigrants open bank accounts and access services.

At the grassroots level, however, notwithstanding Bauder's and Vitello's arguments, as this book will show, the New Sanctuary Coalition in New York did not try to distinguish between "worthy" immigrants and "undeserving" immigrants, nor did it draw a boundary between the "host" and the "guest." Instead, through its accompaniment program (in which citizens and permanent residents engage in solidarity networks with migrants) and its radical practices of empowerment, it actively worked to disrupt claims of state monopoly on the legal and the political. The sanctuary movement exposed the political subjectivities of sanctuary participants, who challenged the state to recognize their right to have rights. The key point here is that the shaping of a grounded urban cosmopolitan environment thus depends upon the acts of disempowered migrants who claim their rights (including right to asylum, right to work, etc.) and assume local participatory rights *and* responsibilities, which in turn have the potential to grant them power. For this to occur, alliances are necessary, including with citizens and permanent residents who enact solidarity practices, legal advocacy groups, selected local political representatives, and, at times, local institutional structures that might support sanctuary ordinances (see Lovrich, Pierce, and Simon 2021).

Yet this endorsement of sanctuary comes with a warning expanded upon in chapter 4—indeed, sanctuary declarations may purport safety for immigrants but offer little real protection. At the same time, one cannot argue that grassroots practices of sanctuary are sufficient either. For to the extent that it can be argued, as this book does, that grassroots practices construe sanctuary as an emancipatory space through empowered subjectivities and the grassroots rhetoric of social justice during fieldwork, these practices nevertheless did not entail institutional responses to addressing urban inequalities that immigrants encounter.

Above all, migrants are not merely voiceless entities in the shadows of the city; rather, migrants call on us to listen and to act. (Indeed, the condition of voicelessness has been associated with, in Carney et al.'s words, resource scarcity, underdevelopment, and disempowerment while the reclamation of the voice entails emancipation [Carney et al. 2017]). And, indeed, some undocumented have refused to stay silent, speaking out against dehumanization of policing, asking for dignity and recognition, demanding humane treatment (Beltrán, cited in Dowling and Inda 2013, 27). Dowling and Inda refer to these as "migrant counter-conducts," which have included labor and hunger strikes, advocacy, physical sanctuary in churches, public demonstrations, street protests and marches, and legal actions for payment of withheld wages (McNevin, cited in Dowling and Inda 2013, 3; see also 28). Cities can enter these conversations with migrants right now, engaging with those who have crossed that distant border and drawing them into the life of the city of which they are already a part. And in chapter 6, this book will precisely examine sanctuary practices that create legitimate claims to urban belonging and gesture toward a right to the city. This humanizing policy, in which the city is chosen as the chief site of enactment, would mean a direct opposition to what restrictionists are proposing—that is, to "prevent illegals from being able to embed themselves in our society" (McNevin, cited in Dowling and Inda 2013, 23) in order to prompt "self-deportation" (Dowling and Inda 2013, 23) as a form of removal. The supposedly neutral term *removal* hides the violence that deportation enacts not just on families and communities but also on the law itself (Coutin 2013, 234).

This argument may ring familiar to scholars of sanctuary cities as it calls upon the role of direct participatory democracy to engage in the urban environment (as highlighted above regarding a new bottom-up urban politics of migration). Here migrants join the squatter movement as they have done in Amsterdam; engage in urban protests and civil disobedience as they have done in New York; and form shared networks to provide food and housing as they have done in Paris. But these projects also highlight the absence of federal and local policies to aid migrants and render hollow the official proclamations of sanctuary cities via mere ordinances as discussed in chapter 4.

Still, a counterargument here may be that what is missing in these accounts is the role of the public sector. Despite Barber's and Derrida's theories, the transformational opportunity may well be at the national level, which could authorize accelerated processing of work permits for migrants with credible claims awaiting asylum decisions and where a federal resettlement agency could be created for the direction of aid toward cities to provide social housing, health and social services, and educational and employment opportunities. Thus, contrary to President Trump's plan at the beginning of his second term to seek a public health justification to authorize mass deportations (for which he would also deploy military), *The Politics of Sanctuary* envisions an alternate path. The agency could direct local government offices and coordinate with legal aid and community-based nonprofit organizations to supplement existing grassroots practices. It could aid immigrants, both the undocumented and asylum seekers as well as refugees, temporary protection status immigrants, and permanent residents. This would not be a program created in the place of other policies for poorer citizens, including public housing for example, but one in synergy with those urban redistributive strategies. Finally, a transformational possibility lies as well at the global level, where grassroots sanctuary efforts would connect into networks extending beyond cities and beyond borders to chart transnational geographies of international migrant solidarities.

In the end, this book makes a call for an *expanded* "strong democracy": Barber's (1984/2003) vision of a participatory democracy is here widened to include not just citizens but also noncitizens in diverse cities such as New York, although this participatory vision is also more broadly applicable. Importantly, Barber further stresses the role of dissent in "strong democracy," arguing that citizens should "bear witness to another point of view" (192), because citizens cannot ever afford to cease political talk (193). For the deliberative, the participatory politics of expanded "strong democracy" is not illusory though it is fragile, occurring in "a rag and bone shop of the practical and the concrete, the everyday and the ambiguous, the malleable and the evanescent" (130). It is in this political space of sanctuary, in this political talk and political listening, that citizens and noncitizens together rediscover their "common humanity" (311).

Part 1

THE POLITICS OF IMMIGRANT EXCLUSION

PLANNING INTERVENTIONS AND SOCIAL BIASES AGAINST IMMIGRANTS

Peter Marcuse (2011, 643–644) has delineated three trajectories of urban planning that can be broadly classified as (1) technical (concerned with inefficiencies, embodied in the work of engineers), (2) social reform (concerned with addressing social welfare and the externalities of industrialization), and (3) social justice (focused on the human costs of urbanization and industrialization) approaches to the profession. The task of this chapter is to demonstrate not only how the first two approaches are laden with social biases but also how the third approach, exemplified in the contemporary example of sanctuary cities' ordinances, grapples with a profound social bias against the undocumented, refugees, and asylum seekers. I thus focus on two periods—first, the era of industrialization and second, the contemporary crisis in planning—and offer an argument regarding the prevalence of social biases in the profession. Behind many planning interventions and urban discourses of the industrial city, a class-based perspective emerges along with an assumed undesirable behavioral pattern or immoral composure typically attributed to low-income immigrant and minority groups as well as urban women.

The 2009 APA Urban Planning Centennial reminded us that the mainstream profession emerged as an organized discipline possessing tools and strategies that would ameliorate the conditions of the industrial city and control its growth while distancing itself both from the social reform movements and, gradually, from the elite pressures for civic beautification. Solidifying this view, Frederick Law Olmsted Jr. argued in 1911 at the National Conference on City Planning that a plan should be a "piece of administrative machinery for preparing and keeping constantly up to date, a unified forecast and definition of all the important changes, additions and extensions of the physical equipment and arrangement of the city" (Peterson 2009, 129). In a well-known contrast that bears restating, Benjamin Marsh, the executive secretary of the New York Committee on Congestion of Population (CCP) (see Wirka 1996) and a social planner, argued that neighborhood overcrowding, location of industrial firms, housing conditions, family composition, and public health issues including reproductive concerns could all be resolved through physical planning and spatial decentralization. In spite of the ethos of social reform, Marsh's view endorsed a physical determinism that would create desirable social results, including altered behavior among the poor.[1] Rejecting visionary and end-goal oriented planning, and marginalizing Marsh's advocacy, Olmsted Jr. instead promoted orderly growth, zoning, public administration, and physical planning.[2] Olmsted's rhetoric became the dominant current of the early twentieth-century planning, during which period less than 50 percent of the country was urbanized. Both Olmsted and Marsh, however, emphasized the influence of the physical environment on what were complex social and political change processes. At the same time that the business elites exerted the highest influence on the shape of American cities and on their planning practices and zoning ordinances, urbanism became an autonomous profession "increasingly dominated by very pragmatic questions about professional city planning" in which civic activism and social reform had a more limited role (Chabard 2009, 202, 222; Abu-Lughod 1999, 90). Mainstream planning's choice to ignore the problems of the poorest neighborhoods and avoid confrontation with the interests of real estate and industrial capital (including banking and the factory ownership) exacerbated the profession's complacent and selective management of urban externalities and its diminished capacity to be an intervening force in the urban realm (e.g., the crisis of planning agency).

The Industrial City and Anti-urban Biases

First, it should be noted that in broader urban studies and sociological discourses, critiques of cities rest on several grounds: moral (cities corrupt virtue and destroy the feminine character), cultural (cities dissolve traditions and religion), psychological (cities cause depression, anxiety, and suicide), democratic (cities cannot be governed or policed; as Jefferson has argued, democracy is impossible in the city), political (cities are places of perpetual conflict; masses in the city pose a threat as they may start an uprising), accommodation (cities are overcrowded), and public health (diseases spread in the city) (see Lees 1985).

Synthesizing the literature in urbanism, planning, and sociology, the urban biases that characterize the era of industrialization can be classified in three subsets.[3] The first sees a social degradation and moral corrosion accompanying urbanization and reveals biases against urban women and youth. The industrial city, in contrast to the countryside, was "intrinsically immoral. . . . [In it] religion lost its grip and people's values atrophied. Intemperance, crime, prostitution, and other vices thrived." Moreover, "The inhabitants of cities were driven by selfish motives, distrust of others, and a severing of ties to the basic human value that anchors a moral existence" (Beauregard 1993, 13–14, 13). (It should be noted that these discourses were not based on a systematic study of rural versus urban conditions and that the argument is here in part complicit in this stereotyping given that sources on rural life were not examined for the purpose of this chapter, only sources on urbanization. Thus, the rural-urban divide ought to be approached with caution.)

The second set of urban biases is related to the unsanitary conditions and public health hazards of poor, often immigrant, neighborhoods. In a well-known account, in 1845, Friedrich Engels walked out of the Manchester working-class neighborhoods with a "true impression of filth, ruin and uninhabitableness, the defiance of all considerations of cleanliness, ventilation and health" (Engels [1845] 1996, 53). As Engels ([1845] 1996, 53) stated, "Everything which here arouses horror and indignation is of recent origin, belongs to the industrial epoch." Industrialism produced the Coketown of Dickens's *Hard Times* (1854), "the most degraded urban environment the world had yet seen" (Mumford 1961, 447). Industrial housing for the workers meant "dreary streets, the same shadowed, rubbish-filled alleys, the same absence of open spaces for children's play and gardens; the same lack of coherence and individuality to the local neighborhood" (465). While Benevolo (1967, 21) cautioned that these conditions were "probably no worse, taken individually, that the country dwellings [workers] inhabited," late nineteenth-century social reformers tended to associate these conditions, in particular dirt, filth, and unsanitary conditions of habitation, exclusively with the urban environment. Although these are mid- and late nineteenth-century examples, a reporter's 1908 quest to document the overcrowded sections of the Lower East Side of Manhattan "led up and down Canal, Hester, Baxter, Chrystie, Mott, Mulberry, and Elizabeth Streets . . . into wretched overcrowded, filthy homes of all manner of wretched beings, laborers, street cleaners, ragpickers, pushcart peddlers, bootblacks, hod carriers, tailors, sweatshop workers, shoemakers, all herded with their miserable families into close, foul, ill-smelling quarters, and most all of these being 'brothers hedged with alien speech'" (*New York Times* 1908b, SM4).

Another example is evident in an article titled "Immigration: Three Interesting Books on an Important Problem," published on November 1, 1914 (BR5) in the *New York Times*, which offers an extensive review of the study titled *The Old World in the New* by Edward A. Ross (a book critical of the open-door policy) and appears to be in disagreement with it, although the other books cited that are in favor of immigration do not seem to be seen as valuable sources. Ross holds the immigrant "responsible" for the "high cost of living and in the same breath for the low standard of living" (*New York Times*, November 1, 1914, BR5). Furthermore, "To his fault must be laid our increasing illiteracy, yellow journalism, peonage, caste spirit, the social evil, city congestion, pauperism, and above all, a disheartening confusion of our political ideals. It is the later immigrant who has weakened the splendid pioneer stock of America" (BR5). As Thomas Bender wrote, when, in 1916 in the journal *The Atlantic*, Randolph Bourne argued that "American culture 'lies in the future' [and] 'it shall be what the immigrant will have a hand in making it,'" the Boston-based editor Ellery Sedgwick published the article but was nevertheless outraged. Sedgwick wrote, "You speak as if the last immigrant should have as great an effect upon determination of our history as the first band of Englishmen," insisting further that "the United States has neither political nor literary lessons to learn from Eastern Europe," and he bridled at Bourne's equation of an old Englander with a recent Czech as "equally characteristic of America" (cited in Bender 2002, 195). Bender (2002) linked urban biases to the fears of a culturally diverse polity in the city, but these biases were further marked by class, status, and religious differences among immigrant and native-born groups.

These late nineteenth- and early twentieth-century examples are also tied to the third group of biases related to perceptions of class and ethnic/racial heterogeneity and ungovernable cities. "Class-segregated city became quite a terrifying object," Katznelson (1992, 281–282) observed, for the dominant strata that "understood the explosive potentialities of concentrated and disaffected urban working class." The profound changes that took place from 1820 to 1890 made, according to Mumford (1961, 447), "the destruction and the disorder within great cities like that of a battlefield." In Mumford's (1961) account (as in Engels's [1845] 1996) text), industrialization almost resembles warfare and the horrors of destruction associated with it, recalling further a possible threat of revolt of the disenfranchised. This set of biases can also entail a fear on the part of the elite strata of a possible revolt of the working classes, as noted by Katznelson (1992), and further anxiety regarding the prospect of democracy in highly diverse urban environments, as demonstrated by Bender's (2002) evidence.

The Emergence of Modern Planning and Responses to Social Conditions

The conditions of urban turmoil and contestation in the industrial city of the late nineteenth and the early twentieth century provided the crucial impetus for the emergence, and a clear demarcation of limits, of the planning intervention in the capitalist city. As is evident in Olmsted Jr.'s dominance over the national urbanist agenda, planners devised programs and policy documents that related, translated, and legitimized the interventions limited by economic and political mandates as structural conditions shaped the transformation of the industrial city into the metropolis and of the metropolis into the megalopolis.

The ways in which these plans resonated with broader cultural discourses about the metropolis are best examined through the depictions of poor areas. The urban biases discussed in the previous section are discernable in the framing of urban social problems in planning documents. Planners promoted a specific vision of the metropolis and used scientific methods and the rhetoric of rational intervention in space to overcome but also to conceal prejudice, discrimination, and biases against poor areas. Even if the planning documents were not single-handedly motivated by socially biased impulses, nor could they be solely reduced to a reflection of economic interests, they nevertheless demonstrate the profound influence of economic forces on urban form as well as show how the social and cultural discourses that accompanied the industrial transformation were adopted by select strata—and indeed by planners—to justify or uphold these transitions.

This can be seen in the grid pattern of American cities and the creation of subdivisions in smaller lots (Krueckeberg 1983, 3). The 1811 grid pattern for Manhattan was created in an attempt to maximize profits from each lot: "The city plan was designed to encourage commerce and to facilitate the transaction of business" (Boyer 1983, 79). The increase in industrialization meant faster urbanization, and as the two forces were almost directly proportional (Mumford 1961, 448), and as a result of this "unregulated and uncoordinated" private and public development, the industrial city "became a vast discriminatory apparatus" (Benevolo 1980, 786), resulting in disastrous living conditions that particularly affected the lowest classes. Once these conditions affected other strata of society, the upper class and its reform-oriented members of the elite began to call for intervention. The reformers realized that "to achieve political equity and personal freedom, strong economic limitations and political restraint were necessary" (Mumford 1961, 453). According to Peter Hall (1995, 14), "Quite suddenly, between 1880 and 1890, the respectable bourgeois urban world discovered the slum city." However, a study of industrialization,[4] economic expansion, and population growth makes it clear that the slum city of the 1880s did not emerge suddenly; rather, the elite strata paid attention to the conditions of disenfranchisement when conditions became so devastating and prevalent as to threaten their economic and political interests and the social order. Mearns's *The Bitter Cry of Outcast London* and Riis's *How the Other Half Lives* aroused widespread moral dismay, which at least in Riis's case seems to have been precisely the intent as his photographs highlight the most appalling conditions of immigrant tenements. The reformers were, however, able to mobilize moral outrage to influence housing and public health policies.

In England, as the establishment and the political elite started to perceive the slum dwellers as "dangerous classes" and "an ominous threat to civilization" (Hall 1995, 25) and feared insurrection followed by the spread of socialism, reformers quickly moved into action. The threat of political agitation worked as a propeller for reform, and the strong working-class consciousness played an important role in causing the city bureaucracy to undertake housing reform. In New York City, which was growing faster and absorbing immigrants at a higher rate (Abu-Lughod 1999, 90), social reformers similarly identified the slum as a threat to American democracy, one characterized by "poverty, crime, socialism and corruption, immigration, Catholics" (Hall 1995, 34). Burdened by the machine politics graft, American cities were seen not only as disorderly but, as noted, also ungovernable. Weaker class consciousness and antagonisms among different immigrant groups brought less weight to bear on the government than in England, and reformers attempted to solve urban problems by offering incentives to the market, zoning, or select physical beautification, even if New York played a pioneering role in tenement reform.[5] An important distinction thus needs to be made between the reformers such as Mearns and Riis, who mobilized discourses or visual imagery of the slums for the purpose of advocacy for social reform, and the reformers or members of the upper-class strata who mobilized anti-urban biases: a sense that the poorer quarters of the industrial city itself possessed a moral and social deviance that also needed to be reformed. Thus, decaying slum areas became notorious not only for their physically repulsive appearance but also as symbols of "evil vices, loose morals, bad habits, intemperance," sites of environmental chaos that became "in the minds of the improvers [linked to] the social pathologies of urban life" (Boyer 1983, 17). The argument here does not deny that in cities diseases can spread more rapidly due to close living quarters and the density of the population.[6] But these descriptions assume a strongly class-based perspective as they are often accompanied by characterizations of undesirable behavioral patterns or immoral composure typically attributed to low-income foreign, immigrant, or minority groups. They evoke the disgust with the slums of Manchester expressed by Engels: "The very turmoil of streets has something repulsive, something against which human nature rebels. The hundreds of thousands of all classes and ranks crowding past each other" (Engels [1845] 1996, 47), although, importantly, this repulsion had more to do with class inequality. The first example cited identifies the corrosive urban pathologies identified as the causes of urban problems; in Engels's quote, the turmoil, the crowding, and the mixing of classes appropriate the same characteristics. Presumptions of immorality, spatially concentrated supposedly in low-income areas, can be found at the roots of many accounts of modern anti-urbanism. Other sources cite even more explicitly pejorative depictions of the poor as "strange beings and alien worlds . . . [who] inhabited a domestic 'Dark Continent' whose denizens were effectively a primitive and 'unknown race,' as social gospel leader Walter Rauschenbusch called them. Perhaps such creatures were not even entirely human" (cited in Pittenger 1997, 48).

While social reformers cannot be placed in the same vein as the physical planners who pursued economic development in the interest of capital, they do not represent a mere contrast to the rational, administrative, or physical planners; rather, their attempts at planning can be seen as laden with social biases and ethnic stereotyping that were also present in the sociological, cultural, and popular press discourses of their time. The social reformers did little to challenge these biases although they did critique the role of planning focused merely on economic development.

Newspaper archives reveal the ways in which social reformers presented their cause to the mainstream media audiences, and while this source cannot be substituted for original documents issued by the reformers, it does point to the relationship between the reformers' understandings of the city and the ways to ameliorate it via planning or housing interventions laden with social biases. In most of the historical articles, the reformers term population congestion an evil and blame it for a range of social problems and health conditions. None of the articles note the racial and ethnic segregation of groups, nor do they discuss classes of immigrants; the reformers further do not present any concern for gender.

In an article titled "Plans to Relieve Congestion Menace" (*New York Times*, April 23, 1911, XX16), Benjamin C. Marsh (1911) describes the "menace" in the following manner:

> About ten thousand deaths a year from consumption is a fearful toll from the city's army of producers. Sixteen thousand children, one out of every eight born, die annually, under one year of age. Nearly three hundred thousand rooms which are legally occupiable but morally a menace and physically murder dens are occupied by from two to three or four sufferers each. The tenement house law of 1901 attempted to remedy these conditions and to close these dark rooms, in which animals could hardly survive, [and which] are now occupied legally by human beings. Not only are these dark rooms responsible for consumption, but also for cripples and for hunchbacks and for other manifestations of the great white plague.[7]

In a *New York Times* (1908c) article titled "The Growing Evil of Congestion in New York," which discusses an exhibit on congestion at the American Museum of Natural History organized by a committee of city departments and "various public-spirited organizations," immigration is presented as the cause of urban congestion, and although the article does suggest that the roots of the problem lie in the economic system, it assumes an alarmist tone in discussing the increase of population in the San Juan district of New York (a part of the area later cleared for the construction of Lincoln Center). The article links congestion with "crime and immorality, accidents and violence" (42).

Another article titled "Death Rate and Congestion" (*New York Times* 1908a) finds a high death rate in the San Juan neighborhood, blaming it also on congestion, which is referred to in the article as one of the "the evils incident to cramping the foreign elements in Manhattan" (8). Using evidence from Dr. W. H. Guilfoy, the chief of the Bureau of Vital Statistics in the Board of Health, the article aims to debunk the evils of congestion, noting, "One 'native American' section of negroes, with a mortality of 38.56 a thousand in a block on San Juan Hill, near Eleventh Avenue and Sixty-first street, contributes to the evils [Guilfoy] deplores. Here in one block 5,100 people are packed, with a death rate from consumption three and one-half times average for the city, and only exceeded by that of the Chinese section" (8). The article then shows that congestion "need not be in itself evil" by citing the low rate of mortality in the Jewish block attributing it to "his [*sic*] temperate habits and his [*sic*] inherited vitality" (8).

In an article titled "Relief of Congestion" (David 1911, 10), social reformer Otto David notes the "bad effects of morbidity and mortality, crime and delinquency" that, he argues, are "caused by the inability of wage earners to pay high rents," although he notes the "capitalized congestion in land values." David (1911, 10) proposes a new tax on land values and also physical planning measures such as the limitation of the heights of buildings and the locations and sizes of factories; the extension of transit lines; proper construction of tenements to improve fire safety; and improvement in sanitary conditions of the poor, which he thought should be done with the support of charitable organizations. Furthermore, David (10) recommends that the federal government "exercises close supervision over immigrants" adopting the Canadian model and that a National Labor Department be created "reporting on labor conditions throughout the country."

As we have seen, in these discourses moral concerns and behavioral stereotypes associated with low-income urban dwellers are further connected to segregated areas. Focusing on the nexus of urban and gender research, Hazel V. Carby (1992) identifies the anxieties about interracial, cross-class contact associated with New York's seedy sections of amusement districts within its low-income minority neighborhoods. Dangerous or illicit transgressions and urban temptations mask the contexts of racism, segregation, and housing conditions, Black family composition, reproductive health issues, and migration conditions. Reformers, outraged over behavioral patterns, failed to aid low-income women in part because of racial prejudices but also because they faltered in understanding the socioeconomic conditions of this population as well as women's emergent urban identities that questioned mainstream social norms. In other contexts as well, the reformers "often saw the poor both as more vital and alive than themselves, and as a devolving, degenerating threat to civilized order" (Pittenger 1997, 29).

Elizabeth Wilson, furthermore, identified women as a problem of order in these narratives because women symbolize sexual adventure ("sexuality was only one source of threatening ambiguity and disorder in the city") and represent a general moral and political threat. "The city offers untrammelled sexual experience; in the city the forbidden—what is most feared and desired—becomes possible. Woman is present in cities as temptress, as whore, as fallen woman, as lesbian, but also as virtuous womanhood in danger, as heroic womanhood who triumphs over temptation and tribulation" (Wilson 1992, 6). Wilson describes nineteenth-century planning as a campaign to exclude from the city disruptive elements that included women, children, working classes, the poor, and minorities. Moreover, the link between women and the masses also pervades these anti-urban discourses. And as the mob became a revolutionary threat, the crowd was invested with female characteristics while retaining associations with criminals and minorities. "The threatening masses were described in feminine terms: as hysterical or in images of feminine instability and sexuality, as a flood or swamp. Like women, crowds were liable to rush to extremes of emotion" (7).

In spite of the emphasis on decongestion of the metropolis and the element of physical determinism in their policies, the importance of the CCP and the housing activism of the settlement house movement cannot be underestimated. "The city social" movement, "primarily concerned with social and economic injustices underlying urban problems" (Wirka 1996, 55), arose from the work of women like Florence Kelly and Mary Simkhovich of the CCP. Women played an important role in the cooperative social settlement movement that benefited low-income tenants in New York, as much as additional research evidence suggests that race and class differences among women reformers were significant in the social programs that the reformers supported. The barriers that social reformers faced in placing concerns of low-income neighborhoods on the national planning agenda further diminished the profession's capacity to deal with both anti-urban biases and social inequalities. This is important to note given that this takes place during the first part of the era (1898–1945), which Ken Jackson has termed "the golden age" of New York, "a time when [the] wealth of America was concentrated in its coffers and the talents of its citizens [were] selectively concentrated there as well' (cited in Abu-Lughod, 1999, 76; see also Jackson 1984). And precisely in the year of the inaugural planning conference, big cities were seen by urban geographers as unhealthy, even deadly environments: "Cities are plainly unfavorable to long life and the greater the city the greater the danger" (cited in Newman and Hogan 1981, 277).

In Peter Hall's (1995, 14) fervent terms, the "city pathological" or the "city of the dreadful night"—the social conditions of extremes of poverty and disenfranchisement—presented the strongest impetus for planning intervention. These devastating conditions in the historical period of industrialization intensified especially in large, rapidly growing cities. Indeed, urban historians offer ample evidence of early twentieth-century planners and social reformers who advocated for "corrective intervention" (Benevolo 1967, 21) on the part of government in the market to improve urban conditions for its poor (Hall 1995, 14). Yet this awareness grew gradually as the modern planning profession first emerged from the attempts of good government organizations and civic groups to ameliorate the negative consequences of industrialization as it intersected with demographic changes, ethnic and racial successions, class and labor conflicts, and housing and neighborhood conditions. Some theorists have argued, however, that reforms were planned more for the benefit of the interests of capital than to improve conditions in low-income areas; others claim that even to the extent that the poor did benefit from these reforms, it was ultimately the upper classes who benefited more (see Boyer 1983; Marcuse 1980; Mumford [1938] 1981; Mumford 1961). For example, led by middle-class Protestant merchants and propelled by their revulsion over the assortment of poor moral and health conditions, organizations like AICP (Association for Improving the Condition of the Poor) and other early tenement reformer groups acted both in the broader class interests and in order to prevent further "deterioration of American social virtue" (Foglesong 1986, 67). In a different example, as Peter Marcuse (1980, 33) has argued, even though zoning was promoted as a way of "providing benefit to the tenement population as well as Fifth Avenue merchants," it in fact promoted business interests and even "legislated the poor out of the better houses." In both examples, however, elements of the anti-urban rhetoric were employed in the planning documents in part to motivate the amelioration of the conditions while in fact solidifying the class difference.

According to M. Christine Boyer (1983), diverse parties of social reformers aimed at imposing a "disciplinary order" in order to prevent social unrest (see also Marcuse 1980, 43). In this view, the discursive "quest for order"[8] in the American city at the turn of the century shaped the "apparatus of planning" (Boyer 1983, xi) and included physical, social, and moral forms of reshaping the urban environment (e.g., investments in transportation, housing, and culture in decaying areas served to "articulate and transcend the contradictions embedded in the city" [7]). Cities, for example, invested in parks and recreational facilities in order to sustain the physical endurance of the labor force and to offer zones of escape from the dreary reality of the workday. Thus, reformers saw parks as important factors of health and social stability of the urban working classes. Some scholars argue that in this manner, "the park thus served as an instrument of social control" (Lubove 1967, 5–6).

As Sonia Hirt (2014, 1, 180, 177) has argued recently, planning in the United States is characterized by an "extraordinary sensitiveness of property to its surroundings" (Ernst Freund cited in Hirt 2014, 1), separation of land uses, and "an unusually radical way of guarding the single-family home" (180) and a life of "quiet seclusion" (Lewis Mumford cited in Hirt 2014, 177). Zoning (characterized by segregation of land uses, protection of private property, and the favoring of residential areas) (Hirt 2014, 111), which Hirt (53) argues is "*particularly American*," "imposes spatial constraints on social behavior" and thus "a moral geography on our cities." Further, "while public regulation of private building activities is the core of the United States system, in Western European countries, England included, governments often regulate less rigidly but their level of public intervention in urban development is higher because they plan and construct more" (6). Hirt (134) argues that the zoning rules, shaped by racial and class biases devised to restrain public action and protect private property, "were justified as a public guarantee of the sanctity of America's most idealized housing form: the detached private home." While in 1930 the American City Planning Institute listed "health, safety, morals, convenience, prosperity and the general welfare" as the reason for zoning laws, zoning developed in the United States due to "a strong tradition of private rule-making that sought to protect the housing enclaves of the elite from invasion by working-class and poor people, including racial and ethnic minorities" (133, 110).

The inquiry into anti-urban biases allows us to further question on whose behalf the planners claimed the ideal of a great city and to analyze the ways in which normative understandings were embedded within specific neighborhood or citywide plans. Daniel Burnham's plan for Chicago of 1909, for instance, entailed a cultural aim to "restore to the city a lost visual and aesthetic harmony, thereby creating the physical prerequisite for the emergence of a harmonious social order" (Hall 1988, 179). Wilson (1989, 284, 302, 304) argues that critics failed to see Burnham's plan for Chicago for what it really was—"a typical, if grand, City Beautiful plan"—and failed to understand the City Beautiful as a comprehensive planning, civic activist, and urban political reform movement with its "yearnings for an ideal community and . . . the potential for good in all citizens."[9] It would be a caricature to see the City Beautiful movement as being focused merely on the wealthy and indifferent to the poor; rather, the movement needs to be seen in the context of the changing relationships between urban activism, government, and the rise of professional planning. Importantly, Wilson also describes an impatience, circa 1909, "with the optimism of early progressivism"; he also cites "the panic of 1907, the portentous electoral successes of socialists," along with the "bureaucratic routinization of reform" (Wilson 1989, 288). Further, Burnham's buildings "were a pictorial representation of Burnham's hopes for a dynamic cultural and commercial city where mere individualism was subordinated to the harmony of the greater good" (283). As Peter Hall has argued, the Chicago plan was in part an emulation of Haussmann's project that Burnham particularly appreciated. While the Burnham and Haussmann projects cannot be equated in scale or vision, the two examples from the early twentieth and mid-nineteenth centuries point to the direct (Burnham) or indirect (Haussmann) claims for "cultural" and political acceptance of an urban "ideal" behind the planning projects.[10] Hence an analysis that would—for instance, within most planning movements, from tenement reform to the City Beautiful movement— find an attempt to "organize local political hegemony" (Foglesong 1986, 6) neglects the fact that the City Beautiful movement nevertheless failed to address the economic needs of the business class and was perhaps more of a visual representation of the power that the business class desired to assert its cultural claim on the urban center. Given Olmsted Jr.'s distancing from the Burnham plan and from the City Beautiful movement (see Peterson 2009), he may have in fact seen the emphasis on beautification as a weak tool to address what he thought was at stake for the planning profession—an orderly spatial development and economic growth.

Although many examples given here show important links between planning interventions and the interests of capital, they are less clear regarding the support among the poor and the working classes for the reforms to improve the social conditions of the industrial city or about the patterns of alliances between different social groups and about the formation of values. There is, however, "sufficient evidence to conclude" that the support of the "urban new stock lower class . . . for reforms commonly accepted as characterizing the Progressive Era was nationwide in scope" (Buenker 1973, 205). That is, the call for improvement of the conditions of the "city of the dreadful night" came too from the immigrant "slum dwellers" and tenement residents (see also Wirka 1996). Buenker (1973, 203) offers an insightful critique of studies of the urban reform movement that have "underestimated the reform contribution of the urban foreign-stock masses." Although many immigrants remained faithful to local political machines, this evidence suggests that they also overwhelmingly supported factory laws, welfare legislation, work compensation, pensions, and regulations regarding child and female labor laws.

The most significant outcome of the industrial era was the legacy of the public intervention—"a growing realization that the power of government could be
used to ameliorate the kind of conditions every urban lawmaker had encountered firsthand" (Buenker 1973, 203). "No better witness [exists] to the impoverished or positively evil conditions brought by the industrial town, than the mass
legislation that has accumulated, in the last century, aimed at their correction:
sanitary regulations, health service, free public schools, job security, minimum
wage provisions, workers' housing, slum clearance, along with public parks and
playgrounds, public libraries and museums" (Mumford 1961, 479).

The challenge of undertaking lasting reforms in the United States (in comparison to Western Europe, for example) that would undermine the established economic interests, contradicts the notions of gradual acceptance of the city (Susman
2003), and says little about the interventions to address urban conditions. The
rejection of Benjamin Marsh's proposals at the inaugural planning conference
in 1909 is a case in point. The ameliorative impulse of planning encompassed
an intervention in the physical urban environment to correct economic externalities—indeed, to promote the interests of economic growth and to legitimize
political powers and, within limits, to express pivotal social reform aims. Planning emerged as a profession tied, directly and indirectly, to broader social and
cultural urban discourses[11] but a profession that sought its legitimacy by distancing itself from these discourses, as can be seen in Olmsted Jr.'s and subsequent
staunch attempts to create a rational discourse about the autonomous field that
would seemingly avoid the connection with social perceptions of urban problems.

The notions of cultural acceptance and cultural ambivalence toward American cities[12] were not solely determined by social conditions, demographic change,
the shape of the built environment, or technological revolutions, but neither were
they shaped by long-standing projections of the late nineteenth-century anti-
urban biases. Anti-urban discourses have to be distinguished from the mobilization of critique of the conditions of disenfranchisement. This, however, did not
absolve the reformers or early social and physical planners from their biases or
from moral panic about the poor, immigrant, and minority residents to which
they often unwittingly contributed.

Sanctuary Cities and the New Crises
of Social Planning

Along with the rise of homelessness in American cities, among the greatest contemporary crises in planning for the poor in the United States is the challenge of
sanctuary cities—the movement that has been growing in response to a federal

policy profoundly shaped by social biases against migrants. President Trump's executive order of January 25, 2017, titled "Enhancing Public Safety in the Interior of the United States," notes that "sanctuary jurisdictions across the United States willfully violate Federal law in an attempt to shield aliens from removal from the United States" and "have caused immeasurable harm to the American people and to the very fabric of our Republic" and proposes defunding sanctuary cities (White House 2017). This policy targets the undocumented, asylum seekers, and refugees—all three categories of immigrants that have become victims of the discourses and policies of criminalization.[13]

Lai and Lasch (2017) view sanctuary defunding as a larger issue, one that goes beyond federalism-based arguments but is related to questions of immigration and crime control (542), especially given that DOJ law enforcement grants would be impacted by the defunding. Sanctuary defunding is more broadly the site of crimmigration resistance (543). Although the DOJ lawyers representing the Trump administration in federal court (where arguments were heard on the preliminary injunction motions filed by Santa Clara and San Francisco) argued that the executive order applied only to DOJ and DHS grants (which in fact involve local law enforcement in immigration enforcement, expand the carceral state, and include discriminatory policing tactics [602]), Santa Clara and San Francisco argued that the order was a "weapon to deprive jurisdictions of the money they need to operate . . . a weapon to cancel all funding to sanctuary cities," which the court found persuasive (Lai and Lasch 2018, 558–59). Lai and Lasch (2018) argue even further that sanctuary cities failed to articulate a stronger argument that "immigration enforcement does not have a sufficient nexus to criminal law enforcement" (581) and did not make nondiscrimination the critical aspect of litigation (603).

The 1980s origins of the sanctuary movement specifically point to biases in federal immigration and refugee policy. The Central American Sanctuary Movement was formed to protect immigrants escaping political violence in El Salvador and Guatemala from deportation.[14]

Houston and Morse (2017, 31) attribute to the SM (Sanctuary Movement) the passage of the Temporary Protected Status legislation in the US Congress in 1990 and the 1991 settlement of the class-action lawsuit *American Baptist Churches v. Thornburg* (which granted impartial interview and adjudication to Salvadorian and Guatemalan immigrants), although these did not entail political asylum. Created in response to this crisis, the city and county of San Francisco's City of Refuge Ordinance, for example, states that "the people of the United States owe a particular responsibility to political refugees from El Salvador and Guatemala because of the role that the United States military and other war related aid has played in prolonging the political conflicts in those countries" (cited in Ridgley 2008, 70;

see also Ridgley 2008, 55). Sanctuary resolutions thus represented a tool of public discourse given the political conditions in El Salvador and Guatemala and the US foreign policy[15] and further included a limiting of the use of city resources related to policing for the purpose of federal enforcement. City sanctuary policies offered substantive support for congregations and organizations that provided sanctuary to Central American refugees; these policies in effect endorsed sanctuary activism at a critical time when members of the movement faced criminal convictions for sanctuary work (Coutin, cited in Ridgley 2008, 66–67).

San Francisco's Sanctuary City: Right to the City and Social Justice Planning

Strengthened by the nonprofit sector and community activism (de Graauw 2016), San Francisco's challenge to the biased federal policies outlined above provides an example of social justice planning and is suggestive of an inclusive urban polity as an alternative to the restrictive state. According to Marcuse (2011, 644), social justice planning is "broadly critical of existing urban social and institutional relationships, proposing sweeping alternatives, and seeing the physical as ancillary to broader social change. It saw social issues from the point of view of those suffering from them, from below, and had broad but varying levels of support from the poor and the oppressed."

San Francisco sued the federal government over its order to withhold funding ($1.2 billion in this case) from sanctuary cities, arguing that the order was unconstitutional and that it represented "a severe invasion of San Francisco's sovereignty" (*Wall Street Journal* 2017). The city won a legal challenge during the first Trump administration, although the legal victory may be tentative given remaining statutory challenges.

The San Francisco example further represents a striving toward the right to the city movement for the undocumented, refugees, and asylum seekers, which started as a symbolic struggle to defend the rights of immigrants, grew into a political movement, and, as a result of community organizing and public protest, became a policy that is formally a part of the city's administrative code (Ridgley 2008, 67).[16] San Francisco, importantly, extended the right to vote in school board elections to noncitizens in 2016. Classifying sanctuary policies in San Francisco as substantive and confrontational, Bazurli and de Graauw (2023) demonstrate how sanctuary policies featured a wide range of programs. These included providing comprehensive health service to seventy-three thousand uninsured city residents through the Healthy San Francisco program launched in 2007 and legal services to migrants facing deportation, expanding minimum wage laws and local voting rights to noncitizens, and including not only voting in school board elections but in participatory budgeting as well (3658–3659).

David Harvey (2006, 102) argues that "we must imagine a more inclusive city, even if it is a continuously fractious one, based not only upon a different ordering of rights but upon different political and economic practices." According to Harvey (2006), the right to access the city should also entail a right to change the city. Harvey (2006, 83) follows Lefebvre's argument that the right to the city can be formulated as "transformed and renewed right to urban life," arguing that the right to remake ourselves while we remake the city is "one of the most precious of all human rights." "If the right to the city is a cry and a demand, then it is only a cry that is heard and a demand that has force to the degree that there is space from and within which this cry and demand is visible. . . . By claiming space in public, by creating public spaces, social groups themselves become public" (Harvey 2006, 103). This represents a demand for public spaces for protest and contestation, spaces that can be seized by political movement, catalytic sites from which "new conceptions and configurations of urban living can be devised" (103). Harvey (103) concludes, "If our urban worlds have been imagined and made, then it can be reimagined and remade. . . . That inalienable right to the city is worth fighting for," and it is the space in which the undocumented, the refugees, and the asylum seekers often limited by the restrictive and biased state policies must be included.

In San Francisco, "the city government became a key ally of the [sanctuary] movement, proving venues from which the movement could amplify the voices of the refugees and counter the discourse and policing practices of the INS" as even government officials acted as sanctuary activists (Mancina 2013, 205). Inclusionary planning measures such as sanctuary policies—which encompass "the right not to be reported to federal officials (unless the immigrant in question is an adult who has committed a felony crime)" (Villazor 2010, 593)—municipal IDs,[17] low-cost banking, and opposition to immigrant raids characterize the city in which the undocumented "are presumed to belong to the city and, thus, treated as if their lack of valid immigration status is irrelevant" (591).

Ridgley (2008, 71) reports that "in September 1989, the San Francisco Board of Supervisors unanimously adopted a revised City of Refuge Ordinance, which is now Chapter 12H of the city's Administrative Code. Under the 1989 City of Refuge Ordinance, local police, city, and county staff could not inquire or disseminate information about a person's immigration status unless affirmatively required by federal or state statute, regulation, or court decision." Furthermore, according to 2017 data, San Francisco had lower crime rates when compared to similar non-sanctuary cities and crime in the city had been falling in spite of its sanctuary status (cited in O'Brien, Collingwood, and El-Khatib 2017).

Expanding from the policies of defending Central American refugees to include the development of a more comprehensive civil rights policy (see Gonzalez, Collingwood, and El-Khatib 2017), the category of urban citizenship in San Francisco has been broadened by challenging the exclusion of noncitizens from housing, health care, education, police services, employment, and social assistance (Ridgley 2008, 55). Advocacy planning in this case went beyond social planning prerogatives "articulat[ing] a more inclusive vision of political belonging, based on the idea that all people in the city should have access to the same fundamental rights, regardless of their immigration status" (Ridgley 2008, 56). The city "set the example for the entire country to do the same, for ultimately a more humane immigration policy will come about only through the gallant efforts of both community and local governments working together to defend the human and civil rights of all persons in the community" (Romero, cited in Ridgley 2008, 69–70). As Mancina (2013, 216) concludes, "By forbidding city employees from engaging in intrusive surveillance, information gathering, and distributing the details of refugee legal status, the municipal government was able to provide life-sustaining municipal services to undocumented refugees and to advocate on their behalf in public arenas." The sanctuary movement in San Francisco has, moreover, been "legal, routine, institutional, and sustained" and has reflected an alliance between grassroots activists (including LGBTQ member organizations [Mancina 2016, 363–65]) and municipal government (Mancina 2013, 206, 216) as the "government apparatus" evolved into "a network of departments, commissions, agencies, officials, and front-line employees, to manage and improve precarious situation of undocumented immigrants" (cited in Lippert and Rehaag 2013, 11). San Francisco's example, which extends social obligations and legal protections to those without full legal status, further shows that the benefits of sanctuary cities include making places more inclusive for all residents, as the undocumented are more likely to report crimes and to express trust in local government.

But the San Francisco ordinance is also an example of a contested law. The city's former mayor, Gavin Newsom (subsequently governor of California), argued "that immigrants who have committed crimes, regardless of their age, should not be able to benefit from the sanctuary policy" (Villazor 2010, 578). The mayor opposed the city's board of supervisors' December 2009 amendment to the sanctuary city law "to delay the reporting of accused juvenile offenders' immigration information until after the immigrants have [been] proven guilty of alleged crimes" (591); the board argued that juvenile offenders should have the same rights as citizens according to the law, including due process and presumption of innocence. Furthermore, "local residents and their supporters actively fought for and against the passage of the amendment to the city's sanctuary ordinance that ultimately delays the reporting of immigration information to federal officials for some undocumented juvenile immigrants" (597).

Freeland (2010) illustrates political support for sanctuary by citing San Francisco Mayor Newsom's and Los Angeles Mayor Antonio Villaraigosa's policies (497, 502). However, while Newsom argued in 2008 for reporting undocumented minors with felonies to federal authorities, which was opposed by the San Francisco Board of Supervisors, Villaraigosa "supported a Council resolution opposing the Secure America with Verification and Enforcement (SAVE) Act" (502).

Importantly, both the California Trust Act and the San Francisco sanctuary ordinance did not preclude cooperating with ICE in apprehending violent criminals (Kagan 2018, 402). But the city and county of San Francisco have also withdrawn from the FBI's Joint Terrorism Task Force, in part based on "concerns that participation in the task force might violate local laws protecting immigrants and religious minorities" (Lasch et al. 2018, 1768).

In spite of criticism, San Francisco's Board of Supervisors passed a unanimous resolution rejecting the federal government's Priority Enforcement Program, thus limiting the degree to which the city could provide information to federal authorities regarding the impending release of noncitizen inmates (Lasch 2016, 171).

The federal immigration backlash against San Francisco has been significant. "Alameda, Contra Costa, Marin and San Francisco Counties have been the sites of some of the largest and most consistent raids on undocumented immigrants in California, ranging from the 63 'illegal' workers detained by ICE on 2 May 2008, when the agency raided a chain of taquerias across the East Bay and San Francisco, to 22 May 2008, when 17 undocumented workers were arrested in San Rafael" (Freeland 2010, 498).

Moreover, an examination of urban economic development and planning in San Francisco shows it to be a city of economic inequality and income segregation with policies reflecting inequities in the housing sector. San Francisco's planning process itself is dominated by NIMBY ("not in my back yard") groups of older, whiter, and more affluent residents, mostly homeowners (McNee and Pojani 2022). While homelessness increased by 17 percent in San Francisco between 2017 and 2019, there was simultaneously an erosion of affordable housing stock (in part due to gentrification) not outpaced by the limited construction of new low-income housing (McNee and Pojani 2022, 558). Low-income households can no longer afford to live in moderate-to high income areas due to price increases and displacement pressures, this particularly affecting Latino residents (Chapple 2017, 88). Under these conditions, virulent NIMBYism dominates the planning process in which first generation migrants, poorer and younger residents, are underrepresented (McNee and Pojani 2022, 569, 564).

In 2025, San Francisco's mayor, Daniel Lurie, furthermore promised a departure from the city's progressive values to offer a pragmatic, nonideological approach to governance, emulating former mayor of New York Michael Bloomberg (Knight 2025). The pragmatic efforts of mayors to clear sidewalks of drug users and the homeless align with critiques of the progressive values of San Francisco that call on city political leaders and bureaucracies to accept their share of responsibility in deepening urban problems (Shellenberger 2021). While Mayor Lurie emphasized the support of immigrant, transgender, and women's rights, he also argued against a confrontational approach to the second Trump administration, seeking a way to merely administer results for voters demanding urban amelioration (see Knight 2025).

* * *

It is a regrettable shortcoming of many planning documents of the early twentieth century that they say little about democracy, the prospect of social equality, and the integration of immigrants (many of whom, it bears repeating, came to the United States in the late nineteenth and early twentieth centuries as "illegal" migrants and refugees) and minority groups, leaving the depictions of the promise of the city to be defined by economic forces or imagined through cultural discourses. Further, the industrial city's faults figured more prominently as an impetus for the planning profession, but the scope and the limit of the planning intervention in relationship to urban problems was in fact what was at stake. At the nexus of the perceived and actual urban problems and the city's prospects, the nascent modern urban planning profession emerged through the accomplishments of social reform in perfecting the city in the fields of housing, sanitation, health, school systems, job security, and so on. This represents the most significant but, as we have seen, limited challenge to the social problems and the anti-urban biases in this era in which segregation persisted. This is important to remember given the boosterism and varied celebrations of city life in our current political crisis, amid a lack of substantive, sustained, and sustainable urban policy.

The San Francisco sanctuary city case examined here can be seen as a contrasting example of social justice planning in response to federal biases that strives toward but does not quite achieve the Lefebvrian right to the city. The right to the city is an empty promise without a right to difference, but neither can a right to difference exist without full rights to the city—city leaders cannot thus simply abandon substantive policies on urban inequality and progressive values while symbolically supporting women and migrants. If we agree with Bazurli and de Graauw (2023) that sanctuary policies in San Francisco are themselves substantive, their taking place amidst profound social and economic inequality necessarily marginalizes their ability to expand the rights to the city.

San Francisco's policies are suggestive of "an alternative legality grounded in 'rightful presence'" (Squire and Darling, cited in Vrasti and Dayal 2016, 998) for the undocumented, the asylum seeker, and the refugee. These fragile yet substantive policies, advanced perhaps most profoundly at the level of grassroots sanctuary movement, which have to be distinguished from the empty rhetoric of merely declaring sanctuary cities, represent further examples of radical or critical planning. With its "insistence on pressing its underlying analysis to confront the functioning of the social, economic and/or political system that gives rise to the particular issues a planning effort confronts" (Marcuse 2011, 651), radical or critical planning in this case addresses the exclusion encountered by the undocumented, refugees, and asylum seekers.

A moral vision of a more inclusive community is at stake in sanctuary: Who counts as a member? Who can be included in the community? Who deserves to be cared for by policy markers? (Ayers 2021, 477–78). Ayers correctly points to the avoidance of concern for the well-being of noncitizens in "welcoming" ordinances (473), showing how the undocumented are so often left out (535) unless instrumentalized for economic benefit, for example (481). But the benefit to the overall community of both citizens and noncitizens from sanctuary policies need not always be limited to Ayers's sense that the undocumented only count to the extent that the broader community benefits (contra Ayers 2021, 480), as we have seen in the case of San Francisco. Critiquing the reluctance of policy-makers to endorse membership for the undocumented (rather than seeing the undocumented as "constituents" (530), for example), Ayers (2021) further points to the limitations of membership for noncitizens: "Noncitizens are not members in the way that citizens are; they exist in a legally circumscribed, federalized, and separate space. In a sense, they carry the border with them wherever they go" (528). Indeed, courts have struck down local laws expanding the franchise in local elections to permanent residents—the New York Court of Appeals ruled 6 to 1 in March 2025 that the state constitution mandates citizenship as a condition of voting (Oreskes 2025). Yet the undocumented, asylum seekers, and refugees should not be seen as entirely outside the realm of representative democracy nor should the role of sympathetic elected representatives be diminished (contra Barber 1984/2003, 145–47). But what is missing in many of these accounts and what is in turn central to the conceptualization of the political space of sanctuary is the key role of grassroots activism, as will be discussed in chapters 2 and 4.

2

RESISTING THE CRIMINALIZATION OF IMMIGRANTS

As the previous chapter noted, although the rise of the crimmigration regime can be traced to the 1980s and the 1990s as well as the government's post-9/11 immigration enforcement strategies (Lasch 2016, 159–60), these policies have only intensified in the early twenty-first century. While the previous chapter considered the San Francisco sanctuary ordinances as a social justice policy in response to federal policy biases against migrants, this chapter will probe the scope of grassroots sanctuary practices in New York in the context of the criminalization of migration and examine the biases that sanctuary literature argues are present on the ground even among the advocacy groups that claim to represent migrants. The focus of this chapter is thus on *sanctuary practices* as opposed to the emphasis on the links between municipal sanctuary ordinances and immigrant organizing considered in the previous chapter.

The criminalization of migration gave an essential impetus to forming the New Sanctuary Movement (NSM) given that the bill passed by the US House of Representatives at the end of 2005 declared illegal immigration a felony and aiding and abetting undocumented migrants a crime (Vitiello 2022, 188). As the border has turned inward in the twenty-first century, there has been an increase in the criminalization of migrants and an enlarged space for policing, including the involvement of state and local levels, leading to a deterioration in the living and working conditions of migrants; an increase in criminal prosecutions for immigration violations; an increase in the numbers of the undocumented in county jails, federal prisons, and privately run immigration centers; increased difficulties in obtaining drivers' licenses for unauthorized migrants; and increases in

ICE raids (Dowling and Inda 2013, 2–3). These processes are bound to intensify. In January 2025, the Laken Riley Act passed the House with bipartisan support and was on its way to being signed into law. The Act mandated federal detention without bail for migrants (including minors, Dreamers, or those with Temporary Protected Status) arrested or accused of any theft-related crimes (the Act arose in the wake of the murder of Georgia nursing student Laken Riley by Jose Ibarra, an undocumented Venezuelan immigrant who had previously been apprehended for shoplifting and child endangerment) (Demirjian 2025; Goldberg 2025). Seeing the United States as a "fortified enclave" and a "carceral space" (18), Dowling and Inda (2013) find that the number of removals doubled after 9/11 and has "increased more than sevenfold since the mid 1990s" (15); noncitizens deported are more often than not nonviolent offenders who committed low-level offenses (15).

The New Sanctuary Movement set out to actively oppose what it saw as the unfair, unjust, gratuitously cruel actions of a restrictive national regime that criminalizes undocumented immigrants. It proposed a different type of governmentality for such immigrants, regarding them as effectively citizens of the city with rights of protection, including the immunity that "no one should be deported." As this chapter's fieldwork results will show, New York's New Sanctuary Coalition (NSC) sought to counter the criminalization of migration and upend the false binary of deserving/undeserving migrants through tactical, inclusive efforts such as accompaniment and a variety of sanctuary practices that build solidarity networks. As the fieldwork was being completed, the author witnessed the NSC struggling toward abolitionist practices, embracing the notion of *expanded sanctuary*, which would include a broader range of individuals who encounter the criminal justice system.

"The Duty to Rescue" and "Deserving/Undeserving" Immigrants

As Betts and Collier (2017) forcefully argue, refuge should be about "the duty to rescue," about our shared commitments toward fellow human beings who have attempted to migrate and who deserve better than a broken refugee system (6). The refugee label can, however, constrain and limit migrant lives (Perla and Coutin cited in Houston and Morse 2017, 31); the emphasis in migrant stories on extraordinary hardship and extraordinary acts of Christianity likewise limit migrant repertoires (Houston and Morse 2017). These narratives of otherwise silent, hidden migrants as "traumatized others" (33, 32) often seem to have an enlightening and even faith-deepening impact on US citizen church parishioners, providing "'traumatic awakening' to the brutalities of . . . wars and the U.S. government's involvement in such violence primarily through hearing migrants' stories" (Pirie cited in Houston and Morse 2017, 32). Evidence of excluding migrants whose narratives do not conform to the traumas of political violence (e.g., Mayan teenage migrants excluded from the Chicago sanctuary) points to an unevenness between "host" and "guest" (Houston and Morse 2017, 35). Yukich (2013a) similarly details a familiar distinction between "good/deserving" and "bad/undeserving" immigrants in immigration scholarship and notes that it goes beyond the legal/undocumented divide to create distinctions among different categories of the undocumented (305)—a categorization that pro-immigrant groups engage in as well. (See also Paik 2017 on "good immigrants" and Chicago's exclusionary Welcoming City ordinance [14–15].) Based on fieldwork from 2007 to 2009 in New York and Los Angeles, Yukich (2013a) found that the NSM tried to counter negative stereotypes associated with the undocumented in the media by selecting model immigrants (308) with credible claims, in particular Latino or Asian mixed-status families, who were heterosexual and law abiding and had good work records and community connections, among other characteristics (309), and intentionally excluded other immigrants, especially singles, LGBTQ individuals, Blacks, Muslims, those with criminal records, and so on (311). In turn, Vitiello (2022, 18) describes a similar process in selecting the 1980s' beneficiaries of sanctuary in Philadelphia, where the host Sanctuary Committee at First United Methodist Church of Germantown sought "articulate people" with a personal story that illuminated the larger political dimensions of the struggle of Guatemalans. But Vitiello (2022) also shows how Central American refugees challenged the paternalism, in some cases tinged with racism and classism, of some participants of the sanctuary movement and struggled to make the movement their own (29). These examples are important to bear in mind as the research findings presented below in the case of the NSC in New York challenge the Houston and Morse (2017) and Yukich (2013a, 2013c) conclusions.

Criminalization of Immigrants and Hyperincarceration

First, criminalization, along with a range of negative stereotypes, has featured prominently as a characterization of Latino (in particular Mexican) immigrants. Ngai (2004) demonstrates how US immigration law and citizenship policies helped to create the Mexican agricultural proletariat as a racialized, subordinated workforce, constituting modern, imported colonialism—a legacy of the nineteenth-century United States conquest of northern parts of Mexico (128–29).

Agricultural business demanded large numbers of low-paid, disposable Mexican workers; exclusion from the polity and the economic and social segregation maintained Euro-American dominance, imposing "foreignness" as a racialized concept on Mexicans (131, 132). Mexican workers organized strikes in California in the early 1930s, with 18,000 cotton pickers striking in the San Joaquin Valley in 1933; New Deal policies that provided limited relief did not substantively improve labor conditions, however (135–36). During the Bracero Program, from 1942 to 1947, the United States imported 215,000 Mexican nationals to work as agricultural laborers and 75,000 to work on the South Pacific railroad, and from 1948 to 1964 an additional 200,000 braceros per year were imported (138–39). The Bracero Program guaranteed transportation, housing, food, and repatriation for the commonly underpaid workers, who were exempt from military service (139–40), with the federal government acting as the labor contractor, delivering workers to agricultural industry (140). Arguing that the Bracero Program in fact generated more illegal migration, Ngai (148) turns to the discussion of "wetbacks" being labeled as "criminal types from Mexico," showing how the construction of the wetback as a dangerous criminal became associated with a general racial stereotype of Mexicans (149), and points to the fluid boundaries between the wetbacks and the braceros (151). In an attempt to curb illegal migration that ultimately did not succeed, INS, during Operation Wetback, which commenced in 1954, apprehended 3,000 undocumented workers a day and about 170,000 in the first three months (156). The Bracero Program ended in 1964 due to pressure from organized labor (AFL-CIO) amid the growing Civil Rights Movement while the exploitation of undocumented laborers only increased and continues to this day. De Genova similarly outlines Mexican immigrants' spatialized sociopolitical condition of "illegality" supported by a legal apparatus that sustains migrants' vulnerability and traceability, rendering them deportable and their labor thus a disposable commodity (De Genova 2013, 42; see also De Genova 2013, 49).

Second, as Rumbaut, Dingeman, and Robles (2019) demonstrate, periods of large-scale migration, such as in the late nineteenth and early twentieth centuries, have been accompanied by moral panics that have included perceptions of the threat of the criminality of immigrants—stereotypes that characterize the Trump administration's restrictive regime and his 2024 presidential campaign and that have persisted in spite of empirical evidence of a drop in crime rates (in categories ranging from violent to serious property crime) and lower incarceration rates for immigrants, and the fact that a significant percentage of immigrants deported have committed minor crimes (Sharpless 2016, 697, 705). Noncitizens with a criminal record are overwhelmingly people of low-income status and people of color (691), with Latinos being the largest group and including a significant percentage of non-Latino Black immigrants (694–95). Connecting the issue of criminalization of immigrants to the racial critique of hyperincarceration, Sharpless (2016) finds that "convicted noncitizens are typically regarded as foils for more deserving immigrants" (692), which heightens social and economic inequality (702). Criticizing the Obama administration's Immigration Accountability Executive Actions of November 20, 2014 (Cházaro 2016, 596) and the immigration enforcement action against "felons, not families" (600), Cházaro (2016) likewise unmasks the logic that pits "the worthy (hardworking, family-oriented) immigrants against unworthy (criminal alien) immigrants" (599) or the policy that argues for amnesty for certain populations (e.g., Deferred Action for Childhood Arrivals [DACA]) while hypercriminalizing the rest of the population (601). While Cházaro is correct, it should be noted that the Obama administration indeed targeted people with criminal records, and Trump's ICE broadened this range, increased the length of detentions in immigration prisons, and targeted children and families (see Vitiello 2022, 218) as well as Dreamers for deportation (Carney et al. 2017). Houston and Lawrence-Weilmann (2016) likewise uncover the neoliberal logic behind the positioning of the hardworking tax-paying migrant in contrast to the "criminal" alien and show the dynamics of neoliberal multiculturalism behind the branding arguments for the benefits of diversity (103). In sum, narratives of political respectability comply with hegemonic norms, legitimizing them and heightening inequality (Sharpless 2016, 707–08).[1] The stark contrast between the undeserving and deserving immigrants (703), evident also in the portrayal of the Dreamers (who themselves have, however, aligned with their parents [761]) as deserving immigrants, has its political uses and has resulted in an immigration policy closely tethered to crime control (705). Cházaro (2016, 613) highlights in particular the category of "significant misdemeanor" (e.g., DUI), which did not exist prior to the June 2012 establishment of the DACA program, noting that in this case "the act of curbing deportation becomes directly linked to the expansion of the categorical criminalization of immigrants" (605).

The research findings presented here uphold Sharpless's (2016) conclusions regarding the intertwining of the immigration enforcement regime and the incarceration regime (718) and show how sanctuary efforts contributed to the undoing of the deserving/undeserving immigrant or, more broadly, the deviant/respectable narrative as a racialized system of control of Blacks and marginalized groups (see also 735). This is further a critique of the racialized incarceration regime in a society that seemingly rejects otherwise present racism although not necessarily an overt anti-immigrant sentiment but encourages hatred of criminals (see Alexander cited in Sharpless 2016, 732). In the context of the criminal justice system, racism and anti-immigrant sentiment are linked (737); "our criminal system . . . is a mechanism for controlling the inevitable social deviancy that flows from the marginalization of poor people under neoliberal social and economic policies" (733). Thus, beyond the account of the NSC's rejection of the deserving/undeserving categorization presented in this chapter, the secondary subject here is the capacity of the sanctuary movement in New York to shape the political subjectivities of migrants to mobilize and to challenge these forms of marginalization and disempowerment.

Finally, as Richard Alba (2020) has recently noted, definitions of mainstream society are expanding to accommodate increased diversity beyond exclusive whiteness; yet Alba also emphasizes the significance of the pathways to legalization, stressing that even if born in the United States, children of undocumented immigrants in particular face barriers to incorporation. The roles of grassroots social movements and of local political responses to immigrant incorporation are particularly significant given that localities make a crucial difference in the integration of immigrants by determining the implementation of federal immigration reforms (Mollenkopf and Pastor 2016, 2–3)—which is itself influenced by local political dynamics (Varsanyi et al. 2012, 24). Motomura (2011) argues that, according to *Gonzales v. The City of Peoria*, "faith in the neutrality of arrest rests on faith in the civil-criminal line, which is an unsound conceptual tool in immigration federalism because its apparent clarity hides a vast realm of enforcement discretion" (1858). Under these conditions, even when the federal government exercises greater post-arrest discretion, such action will be reactive as state and local authorities become gatekeepers (1858). In effect, the Secure Communities program, which, from its inception in 2008 through FY 2014 and since its reactivation on January 25, 2017 through the end of FY 2017, led to the removal of over 363,400 "criminal aliens"[2] allowed state and local governments to act as gatekeepers and to expose a much larger number of noncitizens to federal immigration enforcement than in the past (1852).

Historical traditions of sanctuary city movements point as well to the unfairness of the criminal justice policies. In spite of the rituals of supplication that Bagelman details (2016, 79–80), sanctuaries offered alternate hearings, granted due process, and took into account probable cause and presumption of innocence. Medieval sanctuaries offered protection for a limited amount of time (forty days), however, and requested that those claiming sanctuary settle accounts of wrongdoing or "abjure the realm" (Czajka 2013, 48). According to Bauder (2016a), although the term *sanctuary* was associated with neither migration nor the urban environment in medieval Europe, numerous European cities at that time offered the prospect of freedom to serfs fleeing from the land to which they were bonded, reflected in the medieval saying "city air makes you free," which further resonates with the aims of contemporary sanctuaries. Additionally, while the historical focus of sanctuaries has shifted from criminals to illegalized migrants and refugees (Bauder 2016a), what is important is the linkage between the two categories evident in the increasing criminalization of immigrants. Furthermore, Shoemaker argues that kings supported sanctuaries to prove their power, not that sanctuary practices resulted from weak forms of medieval authority or flaws in existing criminal law procedures (Shoemaker discussed in Lippert and Rehaag 2013, 6). This may be similar to legal and political representatives from San Francisco and New York who sued, or argued powerfully against, the federal government during the first Trump administration. It should be noted, however, that criticism of medieval sanctuary law was extensive and perceived sanctuary as an "error . . . costly to the civilized community, in that wrongdoing was protected"; "by the early modern period, not only had sanctuary come to be identified with injustice, but it was also credited with encouraging more crimes" (Shoemaker 2013, 17)—a criticism that is similar to the former attorney general Jeff Sessions' charges against contemporary sanctuary cities, associating them with the protection of criminals. Medieval sanctuaries were also charged with creating multiple mini-sovereignties (17). Shoemaker argues based on historical sources that where due process and a free trial was guaranteed, there was no need for sanctuary. Sanctuaries were necessary prescriptions for a barbarous society; they "substituted impartiality for prejudice" and "mitigated . . . ferocious punishment" (18). (Although it should be noted that sanctuaries flourished not only in times of conflict and violence but also in times of stability, thus suggesting that they were not just an expression of a just legal order but also of good, strong, devout kingship [18].) According to Shoemaker, "twelfth-century English monks and legal compilers . . . emphasized to English kings that giving homicides and thieves a place to claim sanctuary was a pious and noble act, an expression of a particular form of kingly power that proved to be incredibly persistent" until at least the fourteenth century, when it was seen as a nuisance; Henry VIII further restricted the sanctuary in churches to lesser offences and by seventeenth century sanctuaries for "murder and theft were all but gone" from England (20, 25). Thus, even though scholars make a distinction between the contemporary and the medieval sanctuaries that were "protecting persons alleged to have committed criminal acts, rather than immigrants facing expulsion" (Lippert and Rehaag 2013, 3), recent federal policies in the United States make an explicit connection between criminality and immigration.

Furthermore, these historical examples are suggestive of the greater sovereignty of cities as sites of refuge—examples of a practice of social inclusion and welcoming in contrast to the practices of more restrictive states (Derrida cited in Bagelman 2016, 79). These historical examples of sanctuaries are further suggestive of the errors that states make, either by rejecting divine law or a higher authority or by various forms of transgression or feudal practice. The chief implication of this historical overview concerns the extent to which sanctuaries can further be seen as sites of legal and political contestation over limits of state power over the undocumented, asylum seekers, and refugees, especially those seeking criminal justice.

The Purposes of Sanctuary Practices in the New Sanctuary Movement (NSM)

The subject here is not the sanctuary city per se but the notion that the city can also be viewed as a site of *sanctuary practices* and crucial networks of solidarity with the undocumented, asylum seekers, and refugees that hold the potential to resist crimmigration policies. Sanctuary practices can be seen as a form of local resistance to the state, offering secular and religious responses that are antithetical to a hostile, parochial, repressive regime—a response fueled by local legal and political reactions and the solidarity of social movements and political activism.[3] Similarly, querying reciprocity in an interconnected world, Vitiello (2022, 9) situates sanctuary—"a term activists use as both a noun and a verb" (9)—as a set of practices involving in particular under-resourced migrant civil society organizations (11).

Leyro and Stageman (2018) have argued that crimmigration strategies rely on building up the fear of deportation, which immigrants internalize;[4] avoiding the use of public services and public spaces; evading political participation; and enduring forms of exploitation. But similar to the work of Peter Nyers (2017, 6, 2), who argues that sanctuary cities represent a form of democratization of borders, this research challenges the notion that the precarious legal status of undocumented immigrants, refugees, and asylum seekers[5] means necessarily that they lack agency or capacity for social and political action (in spite of being under-resourced; see also Bauder in Darling and Bauder 2019, 38), as is also, for example, evident in "Day without an Immigrant" strikes (Vitiello 2022, 202; Paik 2017, 11).

It is important, however, not to conflate refugees and the undocumented, and precisely this distinction prompts a brief historical reference to the evolution of sanctuary as a movement. In contrast to the 1980s' Central American Sanctuary Movement (SM), which responded specifically to the condition of refugees fleeing political violence in El Salvador and Guatemala (as discussed in the previous chapter), the New Sanctuary Movement (NSM), launched in 2007, switched its focus to illegalized migrants who have resided in and adjusted to quotidian life in the United States (Caminero-Santangelo 2013, 96). Importantly, Vitiello (2022, 32, 36) likewise cites the white middle-class backgrounds of sanctuary hosts in Philadelphia who assisted refugees of the early Central American Sanctuary Movement, enabling access to decent housing and work. While 1980s' migrants from Guatemala were able to settle in middle-class neighborhoods and locate decent jobs there, mostly in construction, landscaping, and housekeeping, migrants who arrived in subsequent decades tended to settle in working-class and poor neighborhoods and did not achieve the same high wages, benefits, or workplace conditions as the 1980s' migrants in similar occupations (54–55).

The SM's moral imperative to support refugees was rooted not merely in the symbolic rhetoric of urban justice but was based on the First Amendment's clause for religious protection, the United States Refugee Act of 1980, and the Geneva conventions. One of the aims of the SM was to change the Reagan administration's Central American refugee treatment and foreign policies, perceived as violating national and international laws (Collingwood and O'Brien 2019, 23, 26). Wild (2010) presents evidence that sees NSM as the extension of SM and a continuation of the early movement's efforts, with the significant difference that NSM focuses on economic migrants (996), aiding primarily mixed-status families (Yukich 2013c, 6). While SM's efforts to aid refugees received public support, NSM is forced to confront a political climate particularly hostile to the undocumented.[6] Comparing the SM and the NSM, Collingwood and O'Brien (2019) discuss the shift in public opinion from an emphasis on the moral imperative to support refugees to an increasingly partisan media, a framing that linked undocumented migration to criminality (67). This shift started taking place during the 1990s, which saw a decrease in the number of Central American refugees (10, 4), and in the years following 9/11, which saw increased measures of federal surveillance and criminalization of immigrants through the Secure Communities program (41, 121). While these measures did not decrease undocumented migration, they garnered populist support for a renewed emphasis on militarization and enforcement (121).

Yukich (2013b) found reluctance among native-born citizens to join the NSM movement because of their fear that providing shelter for immigrants would count as an illegal activity (115). The movement lacks resources and networks (114) and has, in recent years, encountered an even more hostile political climate—so much so that leadership in New York, for example, feared a federal crackdown (see Offenhartz 2016); yet President Trump's rhetoric during his first term in office also "inspired" a significant increase in immigrant rights organizations and growth of the sanctuary movement (Vitiello 2022, 220). The NSM was not an antiwar movement aiming at altering foreign policy but rather a movement focused on broader human rights and more specific city and state policies, along with policies such as neighborhood safety (220, 222). What is critical here, in contrast to the SM of the 1980s' attempt to merely shield or conceal immigrants, is the visibility and publicness of the NSM (see Michels & Blaikie 2013, 32; see also Caminero-Santangelo 2013, 92). Caminero-Santangelo (2013) writes that the NSM might be seen as an effort to challenge the exclusion of the undocumented, partially by demanding that the noncitizens represent themselves via individual first-person accounts that narrate the trauma of migration, family separation, and life in fear of deportation (93). NSM uses stories of immigrants in sanctuary to increase awareness and strengthen activism (Freeland 2010, 492–93). Critiquing rational choice theory, Freeland (2010) stresses the spiritual and emotional inspiration and the significance of the narratives by the undocumented (504) and finds that the movement "continues to . . . take advantage of political opportunities for political activism as a result of cultivating legislative relationships" (503). The argument here is thus that sanctuary practices, even if symbolic, may hold the potential to challenge the exclusion, marginalization, and dehumanization of the undocumented, asylum seekers, and refugees, overcoming their social isolation and even providing a critical link toward incorporation through empowerment and political participation in social movements.

New York's New Sanctuary Coalition Fieldwork: Methods

Participant observation fieldwork in the field of political sociology was conducted in New York with the New Sanctuary Coalition (NSC) July 2017–June 2018 to study resistance to exclusionary statist regimes and the criminalization of immigrants. During the fieldwork, I attended dozens of weekly community meetings known as the Assembly and dozens of vigils at the Varick Immigration Court and Jericho Walks (a symbolic prayer walk) (see figs. 2 and 3 later in this chapter) in front of 26 Federal Plaza (location of the US Citizenship and Immigration district office), participated in several Sanctuary Hood efforts, and conducted numerous unstructured discussions with the participants of the sanctuary movement. I opted for participant observation rather than interviewing to avoid scripted, formal responses and to observe the NSC as if I were merely one of the participants of the movement, notwithstanding the possibility that this could have appeared as a performance, aware of its own observation, not able to have been taken at face value.[7] But the statements made and cited here were shared with other participants of the movement while I stood by and were not directed solely (or at all) to me, nor were they meant to confirm or deny any prior conceptions I may have had, to count on my approval, or to attempt a connection with my own immigrant experience. At the risk of ending up with a string of citations from fieldwork, and worried about selectivity, I sensed nevertheless the absence of voices of immigrants in prior research on sanctuary, reaffirming their exclusion as silent, hidden witnesses. I wanted instead to let the immigrant activists speak in their own voices as they struggled for empowerment and social inclusion and indeed as they struggled *through* their own sanctuary efforts to escape deportation. The citations from fieldwork shared here attempt, moreover, to convey a sense of the insecurity and precariousness of the social condition of migration, especially undocumented, and the unsteady knowledge of that condition.

The methodology applied in this research is similar to that of Mitchell Duneier's *Sidewalk* (Duneier 1999), keeping in mind Duneier's emphasis elsewhere on the reflexive and ethical aspects of qualitative research (Duneier 2012), given that, even as I told informants my own immigrant story, I encountered that same sense of suspicion that lingered over many encounters I too have had, even if at the same time I also felt welcome in spite of my racial, linguistic, and religious (secular) differences from many of the immigrants and sanctuary practices' volunteers. The fieldwork results that follow take into account reflexive and ethical aspects of research and are intended to convey ambiguities and losses amid the empowering potential of sanctuary practices. The primary focus of the research is resistance to criminalization while, as a secondary point, fieldwork findings are suggestive of immigrant narratives becoming a source of empowerment by revealing the hidden script of injustice, yet this did not appear to this researcher to be tied to a prophetic narrative or to faith-based leadership grooming (contra Yukich 2013a, 313) but appeared to be gained by social and political activism in the context of legal struggles. It is also instructive to see the sanctuary practices analyzed here in relationship to Vitiello's (2022) evidence from the welcoming practices in Philadelphia, which show how the movement struggled to move from charity to solidarity, from adoption of refugees into "wholesome host communities" (44) to true inclusiveness, outlying the limits of civil society's involvement in sanctuary practices (58).

Observation included active participation as a volunteer assisting with meetings, sharing my own immigration story, helping the efforts of the coalition, participating in vigils and Jericho Walks, and sharing my previous research with the coalition. All meetings were conducted in English and in Spanish given the presence of mostly, although not solely, immigrants from Latin American countries (in contrast to the NSM meetings observed by Yukich [2013c], which were held in English [155, 156]); I participated in both languages and received support and encouragement when speaking Spanish. Attendance at the meetings ranged from a few to over thirty participants; Jericho Walks included at times a few participants to hundreds of participants. Vigils were smaller and included from a few to up to twenty participants. The NSC is based in the Greenwich Village neighborhood of New York but holds a monthly assembly in outer boroughs and includes the Sanctuary Hood effort in Brooklyn and Queens. The NSC works to prevent deportations and boasts one thousand volunteers who accompany immigrants to court and ICE check-in appointments (fieldwork notes, August 10, 2017). The NSC organizes a legal clinic in addition to accompaniments, bond funds, and weekly community meetings (fieldwork notes, August 10, 2017). It should be noted, however, that I have not investigated the internal dynamics of the NSC, the hiring of organizers, their compensation, their dynamic with volunteers, nor the gender or power dimensions within the NSC movement or among its organizers that eventually resulted in leadership and organizational challenges.[8]

New York's New Sanctuary Coalition Fieldwork: Results

Resisting the Criminalization of Immigrants

Although the rise of the crimmigration regime dates to the 1980s, it is crucial here to view a key background element of the more recent criminalizing narratives of sanctuary cities. These often begin with the death of Kathryn "Kate" Steinle on July 1, 2015, on Pier 14 in San Francisco as a result of an accidental shooting on the part of José Ines Garcia Zárate, an undocumented immigrant with prior deportation and criminal records (Lasch 2016, 165). Collingwood and O'Brien (2019) demonstrate how Donald Trump's frequent references to the Steinle shooting used this tragic event for anti-sanctuary rhetoric that would become the core of Trump's successful 2016 presidential campaign,[9] with 77 percent of his campaign speeches featuring immigration policy, 26 percent of which included references to sanctuary cities (1–2, 16–17, 36, 38, 42). Linking sanctuary policies to violent crime, the Trump administration sought to discredit sanctuary cities as sites that attract criminals, breed crime, and cause "so many needless deaths" (5, 39, 68, 102). As the then attorney general Jeff Sessions proclaimed in January 2018, "I continue to urge all jurisdictions under review to reconsider policies that place the safety of their communities and their residents at risk. . . . Protecting criminal aliens from federal immigration authorities defies common sense and undermines the rule of law."[10] Using the example of President Trump's discourses, Lasch argues that the absence of an overt reliance on race in the retelling of Kathryn Steinle's tale is unsurprising given that "'dogwhistle politics' relies on coded racial appeals to inject race into political debate" (Lasch 2016, 173).[11] According to Lasch (2016), the smooth accomplishment of this agenda was supposed to convey the profound identification of immigrants with criminality (186). These and similar cases shape a social perception of San Francisco's Sanctuary City ordinance as awarding rights to undocumented immigrants at the price of the rights of citizens and other lawful members of the community (Villazor 2010, 590). O'Brien et al. (2019) argue that following the Steinle shooting, the media frame changed to target undocumented immigrants (in contrast to refugees—humanized or perceived sympathetically through a victimization frame [761]), emphasizing crime and the partisan divide (758; see also 769). Examining media stories from 1990 to 2017, O'Brien et al. (2019) find a movement away from the victimization frame placing emphases on fleeing conflict/war and toward increased emphases on crime, the partisan divide, and references to President Trump (768–69). In their research based on the print media outlets of five national news publications (excluding network and cable TV news), O'Brien et al. (2019) find increasingly negative coverage of undocumented migration with recurrent references to immigrant criminality[12] and "threats to American culture and identity, public safety, health, or economic well-being" (761–62).

It is important to place this in context with the perspective of rising nativism, echoed in President Trump's 2024 campaign speeches calling on the "Congress to pass a law outlawing sanctuary cities nationwide" (Trump, cited in Vakil 2024). Douglas Massey (2020) noted that two factors predict nativist responses—an increase in economic insecurity, especially felt by the lowest classes, and rapid demographic change. In the circumstance of mass immigration illegality, the response to which has been increasingly stringent immigration enforcement, we are encountering a profound racialization threat evident, for example, in the demonization of Central American caravans (see Buff 2019, 16–17). The field-work presented below is indicative of forms of resistance to this criminalization and demonization of the undocumented. For this reason, it is important to examine the evidence that links migration to crime.

Sharpless (2016) reports that the United States held 6,600 people in immigration detention on any given day in 1996 while in 2013 the United States detained 440,000 in over 250 facilities (713); the conditions of detention can be described "often abysmal" (723). Based on ICE data, of the 240,255 ICE removals in 2016, less than 1 percent could be classified as suspected or confirmed gang members (as cited in Rumbaut, Dingeman, and Robles 2019, 8). Longitudinal analysis of the macro-level relationship between undocumented immigration and violence in the United States 1990–2014 shows that undocumented immigration does not increase violence (Light and Miller 2018), which is consistent with Cato Institute findings that undocumented immigrants have lower incarceration rates than the native-born population (Nowrasteh 2019b). A 2017 source based on the statistical examination of sanctuary policies[13] found that they do not lead to either net increases or decreases in crime, even when cities are matched to isolate the effect that sanctuary status has[14]—types of crimes examined included violent crime, property crime, and rape (O'Brien, Collingwood, and El-Khatib 2017).[15] Comparing sanctuary and non-sanctuary cities, Collingwood and O'Brien (2019) find no difference in crime rates and likewise find no increase in crime in areas whose policy responses aim at noncompliance with ICE-detainer requests. Collingwood and O'Brien (2019) similarly identify no changes in crime patterns following pro- or anti-sanctuary legislative activity; their data thus shows no clear connection between sanctuary statuses and crime. Additionally, analyzing the impact of Texas SB-4 anti-sanctuary legislation, Collingwood and O'Brien (2019) find a drop in 911 calls among foreign-born noncitizens in El Paso—thus a positive correlation between an increased difficulty in fighting crime and anti-sanctuary legislation (14–15, 118–19, 125–45). Instead, the authors find an additional positive correlation between, on the one hand, increased Latino voter turnout (with Latinos three percentage points more likely to vote in sanctuary cities) and slightly greater Latino representation in the police force (a 2.54 percent increase) and, on the other hand, sanctuary status (Collingwood and O'Brien 2019, 15, 119, 147–49).

Since Madison, Wisconsin, first declared itself a sanctuary city in 1983, city-level sanctuary ordinances proliferated in response to support from the Democratic Party (Collingwood and O'Brien 2019, 28), and indeed, partisanship reappeared as the key factor in enacting sanctuary policies, with the rise in both pro-sanctuary (e.g., California's SB-54) and anti-sanctuary (e.g., Texas's SB-4) legislations during the first Trump presidency (36, 40–41). Democratic representatives, however, most strongly defended sanctuary cities in stronghold states with large Latino populations such as California, New Jersey, New York, and Illinois (117). According to Collingwood and O'Brien (2019), Democratic mayors and immigration activists saw attacks on sanctuary cities as attacks on Latinos (68); studying opposition to sanctuary policies in Texas, the authors find that the size and the growth of local Latino populations increases opposition to sanctuary policies rather than the crime rates (88). The authors explain the conflating of crime and sanctuary cities by media coverage that creates "illusory and inaccurate correlations between Latinos and crime" (Collingwood and O'Brien 2019, 94). Elsewhere, O'Brien (2018) asserts that these erroneous perceptions of immigrant criminality increase political support for restrictive policies that result precisely in the criminalization of immigrants (152), restarting a vicious cycle. Studying sanctuary and anti-sanctuary bills introduced in 2017, Collingwood and O'Brien (2019) find that these are determined by "racial threat," ideology, and the structure of state political institutions, dismissing arguments that economic anxiety or crime rates drive sanctuary legislation (115–16) and concluding that behind the narrative of criminality lies an attempt to protect racial hierarchy (158).

Wadsworth's (2010) research findings indicate that the cities that experienced the greatest increase in immigrant population between 1990 and 2000 also reported the largest decreases in homicide and robbery during that decade. Wadsworth (2010) suggests that immigration might be one of the factors responsible for the 1990s' drop in crime rates, and although other factors such as the waning of the crack epidemic, the improved economy, and increased policing may have further contributed (Mitchell 2003, 227), credit should also be given to community-building nonprofits that helped to combat violence. Data seems to show that "the addition of 10 community nonprofits per 100,000 residents leads to a 9% decline in the murder rate, a 6% decline in the violent crime rate, and a 4% decline in the property crime rate" (Sharkey, Torrats-Espinosa, and Takyar 2017, 1234). Further consistent with the Wadsworth research evidence is Martinez, Stowell, and Lee's (2010) findings that San Diego neighborhoods with a larger percentage of immigrants experienced lower homicide rates. Moreover, a majority of immigrants who have in fact committed crimes did so only after having lived in the United States, and the length of residence is correlated with incarceration rates (Sharpless 2016, 725, 748). According to 2014 ICE data, approximately half of the convicted noncitizens who were deported were Level 2 (they had committed one felony or three or more misdemeanors) or Level 3 (they had committed one misdemeanor) offenders; about half of the latter group had been convicted of only a single misdemeanor (as cited in Sharpless 2016, 730). According to Cházaro (2016), who highlights how crime is used as a tool of immigration enforcement, "young Latino men, the group that disproportionately bears the brunt of the immigration detention and removal apparatus are among the young men of color most likely to be subject to misdemeanor arrests without probable cause, particularly when they reside in poor communities where high-volume policing is the norm" (610). In New York, the NYPD reduced stop and frisk policies in recent years (following the high of 70,000 stops for African American and Latino men in 2011, according to NYPD first deputy commissioner Benjamin Tucker [2020]) and has included new policies of neighborhood policing, de-escalation training, and body cameras (Tucker 2020). Kenneth Montgomery (2020) argued, however, that the legal system worked to maintain the status quo by protecting egregious police conduct, and cameras have not changed police conduct and will not do so in effect unless officers with prior violent conduct are held accountable or lose their pensions. An argument can be made here for the reduction of the necessity of policing in neighborhoods and for an abolitionist movement that would depart from the paradigm of the carceral state (Hoag 2020). The related concept of defunding of the police would in theory shrink the footprint of police power and legitimacy and in practice would channel funding into communities (Hoag 2020). Whether this is in fact practicable is beyond the scope of this chapter; it suffices to say that this change would require a fundamental urban restructuring in advancing the goals of access to racial and economic justice in the domains of affordable housing, living wage jobs, mental health and social services, homeless services, domestic violence victims' services, and so on.

The sanctuary practices of the NSC examined here provide empirical evidence for the claims of Rumbaut, Dingeman, and Robles (2019) and Ridgley (2008) that the criminalization of immigrants legitimizes the removal of basic and even constitutional rights from noncitizens (see also Lasch 2016). Through their sanctuary practices and within their legal clinic, the NSC does not screen immigrants and refuses to play the preference card that underlies the legal definition of the "deserving refugee"[16] as a very limited understanding of the kind of immigrant who is entitled to support (although this may differ for cases of physical sanctuary for which "model" immigrants are more likely to be selected).[17] As an organizer claimed, "We do not distinguish between the good and the bad immigrants. All of our immigrants are 'criminals,'" although the discussion quickly turned to an immigrant leader who was arrested in Vermont because he was merely riding in a vehicle driven by his cousin, who was speeding.[18] The organizer further emphasized, "The pressure we receive is not from ICE but from other religious organizations who pressure us to screen immigrants" (fieldwork notes, August 10, 2017), acknowledging the prior history of screening processes on the part of faith-based leaders detailed at length by Yukich (2013a, 2013c). In contrast to this history, sanctuary participants construe the space of sanctuary as an open, safe environment that, according to Father Luis Barrios of Holyrood Church in Washington Heights, New York, is intended to shelter not merely immigrants but also members of the LGBTQ community, heroin users, the homeless, sex workers, alcoholics, and members of street gangs (fieldwork notes, October 20, 2017). Furthermore, this space facilitates a process of healing from the traumas of criminalization by providing a place where identity, culture, and parts of the self can be shared with others (fieldwork notes, October 20, 2017).[19] The NSC exits the entrapment of screening immigrants by acknowledging sanctuary as a transgressive space. This contrasts with Freeland's (2010) account, which describes conditions under which a deserving immigrant can claim sanctuary (494)[20] and with the evidence presented by Houston and Morse (2017).[21] The unique findings of this research (contra Freeland 2010; contra Yukich 2013a, 2013c; contra Houston and Morse 2017) are thus that the NSM in New York contests the undeserving/deserving distinctions and attempts to offer sanctuary to a broader range of individuals affected by the criminal justice system. Although Houston and Morse (2017) cite 2007 data from the NSM emphasizing the importance of clean legal records for gaining a stay of removal, my evidence (again, with the exception of the cases of physical sanctuary) contests this. The increasing politicization and secularization of the movement in a federal climate that is hostile toward immigrants may have accounted for the change in rejecting the screening processes to demonstrate a growing solidarity with undocumented immigrants.

Acts of Sanctuary by Citizens and Noncitizens

The accompaniment program is the NSC's chief act of sanctuary and its main tactical response to the exclusionary regime of President Trump's first term, an "act of citizenship" that disrupts the state monopoly on the political as well as the legal. During my fieldwork, one of the members of the sanctuary coalition explained to me that there were two types of accompaniments: (1) accompaniment in front of a judge and (2) ICE check-in. An organizer with NSC stated, "With judges, our presence makes a difference. We showed up to support our Friend (the term for the undocumented used by the NSC) and we stood in front of a judge. It is a small influence, but it helps a lot. ICE is, however, inscrutable—they can decide to deport, detain or order house arrest" (fieldwork notes, July 13, 2017). During fieldwork, I walked with members of the sanctuary movement to the ICE check-in inside 26 Federal Plaza, passing through security, which allowed only one of the faith-based leaders with a Friend inside. One of the organizers explained, "It crosses a line to just be vicious and not to let a faith leader in" (fieldwork notes, July 13, 2017). Another member of the coalition, who has participated in the March on Washington and has been involved with the sanctuary coalition since January 2017, explained, "We protested in front of Varick Street. We brought blocks of ice to melt. A person was here for 31 years and he was being deported. [It is suggestive of] the meanness of the administration" (fieldwork notes, July 13, 2017). She recounted encounters with immigration security guards, often immigrants themselves. She noted what she referred to as absolutely absurd criminal records that are brought up, affecting, in her view, mostly Blacks and Hispanics. She suspected that the system was more open in New York City but added that the "city is catching up with the rest of the country" (fieldwork notes, July 13, 2017). Another member of the coalition noted, "New York is not Texas, but the city cannot stop ICE; it is even worse in other places. ICE has gotten into a couple of schools, but they have not been let in" (fieldwork notes, July 13, 2017). A rabbi added that her synagogue has been involved due to a sense of urgency—"We are always immigrants, immigration is a recent story, my grandmother came here in the 1930s. Even very secular people have immigrant sympathies. My synagogue hosted the accompaniment training. I offered assistance to my child's day care teacher who is in the DACA program" (fieldwork notes, July 13, 2017). Another member of the coalition noted, "One of the effects of sanctuary city is that all judges are very sympathetic. The judiciary system is a part of the city" (fieldwork notes, July 13, 2017).

These examples are suggestive of the active involvement of NSC members in a variety of forms of sanctuary organizing that aim to disrupt the state monopoly on the political and distort the boundary between the "host" and the "guest", the helper and those being helped, the organizer/member of the coalition and the undocumented immigrant or asylum seeker / member of the coalition. This is apparent in the citizens' mistrust of the political establishment and official immigration policies, in the citizens' identification with immigrants and the immigrant community, and in the citizens' pressure on local institutions not to implement federal immigration policies.

These fieldwork findings further contest the results of field research on sanctuaries in the UK (Bagelman 2016; Darling and Squire 2013), which show limits of sanctuary practice; the findings nevertheless do not entirely succeed in demonstrating Nyers's (2017) emphasis on noncitizens' political agency as much as they seem to convey the political agency of citizens advocating for noncitizens and searching for institutional openings on the local level. The findings on accompaniment affirm Freeland's (2010, 499) noted goal of this program as respect for human and legal rights.[22] Following Coutin, Freeland (2010) cites personal transformation and change in consciousness as significant for social movements such as the NSM (504), and this can be seen, as noted, in the rising political consciousness of citizens who distrust the state, assist noncitizens in their immigration struggles, and appear to grow in identity as political activists through the process of aiding noncitizens.

Enforcing Immigrant Rights

The NSC has, furthermore, gone beyond the accompaniment program and has engaged the security officers guarding the entrances to ICE check-ins even without accompanying a Friend. A volunteer explained about a recent meeting, "We discussed the change in the immigration court proceedings which in the past couple of weeks has banned presence in the courtroom of coalition members supporting Friends. We discussed strategies of resisting this new policy. One strategy is to approach politicians, another to work with faith-based leaders. The other strategy is working with lawmakers. An additional strategy was to appear in the courtroom in spite of the ban" (fieldwork notes, August 3, 2017). Another volunteer explained the latter: "Our strategy is to go to the 9th floor of 26 Federal Plaza in groups of 3–4 without accompaniment and simply try to talk to the guards in a controlled, calm manner, trying to understand why we cannot accompany Friends. We did this, and this worked" (fieldwork notes, August 3, 2017).

This example is suggestive of the NSC's successful attempts to disrupt the state monopoly on the legal, which an organizer referred to in another context as enforcing the line of rights, stating, "We are literally standing at that line and making sure that we hold that line and enforce [immigrant] rights" (fieldwork notes, October 19, 2017). These research findings are consistent with Czajka's (2013) argument regarding the political potential of sanctuary practices and with Bauder's notion of the sanctuary city as a strategic site of immigrant political solidarity (Bauder 2016a). Moreover, these immigrant rights, as Attoh (2011) argues, can be seen as at once collective rights and rights against unjust collectivity—a critique of urban democracy from a grassroots perspective. And indeed, perhaps the right to the city can become a symbolic emancipatory claim in sites of complex urban diversity where sanctuary cities might complement other grassroots movements—from anti–mass incarceration to youth and squatter movements and urban commons. Fieldwork findings, moreover, suggest that ordinances that facilitate governmental sanctuary (such as in San Francisco) may be necessary but insufficient to further enable conditions for the city as "a place where all residents, including the undocumented, could thrive free from discriminatory treatment and fear" (Mancina 2013, 212), and that these ordinances ought to be complemented with NSM sanctuary practices with the aim of creating safe(r) places within cities.

Immigrant Suffering and Empowerment

Fear and discriminatory treatment as well as trauma and the suffering of immigrants were apparent in the New York fieldwork. In an assembly themed ¿Como podemos contar nuestra historia? (How can we tell our history?), a Friend added, "We need to wake up. We can't keep waiting for the laws to change. We need to lose our fear. We need to join groups, we need community support." Another Friend noted, "I was invited to this group by a Friend. I didn't suddenly open my eyes last year. I *lived* through this process [with my Friend], this suffering, I *experienced* it every day." And further, "Sanctuary space is a safe place where one could place oneself in the shoes of those who suffer—being able to see people in the same situation builds that confidence." Another Friend asserted, "Todos somos seres humanos [We are all human beings]. Solo pedimos la inclusión social después de la migración forzada. . . . como esclavos modernos [We ask only for social inclusion following forced migration . . . like modern slaves]" (fieldwork notes, July 20, 2017).

From the standpoint of the undocumented who rely on the NSC to represent them, narrative reconstructions of the self that are often a part of the meetings seem necessary but insufficient, community activism is seen as indispensable, and incorporation emerges as a key goal (also consistent with the conclusions made by Ridgley [2008, 2013]). These findings, revealing collective traumas of immigration and narratives demanding inclusion, are also suggestive of the political consciousness and social agency of the undocumented, thus coming in this instance closer to Nyers's (2017) conclusions. While the statements cited here by the undocumented may appear too broad, they nevertheless capture the messy sentiments of social empowerment through sanctuary practices.

This further contradicts the evidence in Houston and Morse (2017), who, citing Yukich, state that few immigrants or people of color participate in the sanctuary movement (43). This claim did not appear accurate from the standpoint of the NSC in New York; as noted, the meetings attended were marked by the presence of both currently and formerly undocumented immigrants as well as citizens, in contrast to the findings by Yukich (2013c), who pointed out that the movement encountered difficulty in recruiting "the essential group of single-institutional actors—immigrants themselves" (141). Houston and Morse (2017) charge that the sanctuary movement minimizes the "space available for articulating a plurality of identities (beyond heterosexual, married, employed and parent)" (42), which is in stark contrast to the finding of this research; during fieldwork, one of the sanctuary leaders tried to recruit this researcher to assist members of the Ukrainian LGBTQ community fearing the threat of deportation from New York, although intersections with queer sanctuaries were not the subject of the sanctuary meetings, assemblies, and vigils that I attended (in contrast, see Ellison's [2019] account of gay and lesbian police-reform activism as a political form of sanctuary in Los Angeles). This research further finds a redefinition of the sanctuary identity along political goals rather than those of religious conversion (contra Yukich 2013c, 145), with the state being the primary target of activism.

Community Activism and Political Strategies

Another Friend responded by recounting the trauma of family separation and emphasized the role of the community and not just the government. A Friend, for example, emphasized that immigrants feel criminalized ("Nos acusan de hacer un crimen si estamos sin papeles") but that they feel the separation of families as a real crime (fieldwork notes, July 6, 2017). This point is also emphasized by Carmen de la Rosa, then Assembly member for the 72nd District (Hamilton Heights, Harlem, Inwood, and Washington Heights), who defended Amanda Morales Guerra, a Guatemalan mother of three seeking a physical

FIGURE 1.   Amanda Morales Guerra, a Guatemalan immigrant, claiming physical sanctuary in Holyrood Church in Washington Heights, New York. Source: Fieldwork, August 18, 2017.

sanctuary in the Holyrood Episcopal Church in Washington Heights (see fig. 1) and called for the creation of "un verdadero sanctuario" (a real sanctuary) and emphasized the rights of immigrants who believe in the American dream, arguing, "No podemos ser una verdadera ciudad santuario y un estado santuario si dejamos atrás las familias que están divididas . . . y denunciar el odio que está teniendo lugar en esta nación. . . . Necesitamos actuar y hoy día estamos actuando [We cannot become a real sanctuary city and sanctuary state if we leave behind the families which are divided . . . and denounce the hatred which is taking place in this nation. . . . We need to act, and today we are acting]" (fieldwork notes, August 17, 2017). In support of this case, City Council Member Ydanis Rodriguez, stressing struggles for social justice and the common immigrant background of New Yorkers, asked members of the sanctuary movement, faith-based leaders, and political representatives to go to ICE offices to submit a "stay of removal" form to allow the mother to stay in the United States (fieldwork notes, August 17, 2017). Congressmen Adriano Espaillat emphasized in all of his examples of sanctuary movements the gendered aspects of sanctuary, suggestive of the caring, perhaps less intimidating characteristics of the female victims of violence (both domestic violence and political violence in their home countries, even if it is commonly young male victims escaping gang violence who seek sanctuary) (fieldwork notes, August 17, 2017). In spite of the publicness and the visibility of traumas of family separation and cases of physical sanctuary (often in the spotlight of the media), and in spite of the collaboration between the NSM and the local political leadership, the NSM was unable to ensure the "stay of removal" for Amanda Morales Guerra, who eventually abandoned the sanctuary.

This and the following examples are indicative of the limitations of the NSM's political strategies: On July 13, 2017, the protest outside 26 Federal Plaza, in which about fifty people participated, included several faith-based leaders and members of the coalition. One of the members of the coalition noted, "The case of the Friend who is now detained suggests that we may not have the strength that we hope to have. Jean's [Jean Montevil, Haitian immigrant rights leader, recently deported] case is the case of the family trying to stay together. We bear witness, we help with action and prayer. We are creating a lot of noise for Jean. He has us and a thousand letters. We know ICE is watching what we are doing. Not being able to go upstairs to the accompaniment [only one faith-based leader was allowed] is very bad news. People just disappear. I went to sleep last night praying for [the Friend], praying for Jean. I had this enormous feeling how much I trust the community, how much I distrust the state." One of the priests explained, "We walk now in silence [around 26 Federal Plaza]—7 times or 5 times [in the end it was 3 times because of the weather]. We stop and put our hands on the door and pray in silence. We pray together in Spanish and in English" (fieldwork notes, July 13, 2017). In a flyer in support of the July 13, 2017, Jericho Walk in support of Jean Montevil, the Coalition noted, "Millions have faced mandatory detention and deportation for decades, leaving whole communities ravaged by the absence of breadwinners, fathers, mothers, sons and daughters. Deportation touches not just the person at risk, but their entire family and community."

The research findings suggest that the city can be seen as a site of sanctuary practices—the locus of crucial networks of solidarity with the undocumented, asylum seekers, refugees, and permanent residents who have become deportable, which are antithetical to a hostile, parochial, repressive state regime. These sentiments, shared by the sanctuary participants cited above, validate Derrida's (2001) and Barber's (2017) claims about the special role of cities as sites of struggle for immigrant rights, as stated in the introduction of this book. These are fragile acts and practices by and in solidarity with these groups, yet this research has argued that, in contrast to the informants in Yukich's studies, sanctuary practice participants were not engaged in religious conversion but were rather carving political spaces in the city (in spite of the active role of the faith-based leadership).

Furthermore, this set of strategies applied by the NSC, emphasizing on the one hand distrust of the state and on the other linkages with political leadership, shows ambiguity regarding the role of political leadership who appear as eager supporters of the sanctuary movement once the media places provocative aspects of sanctuary into the limelight. It should be noted that one of the leaders of the coalition argued repeatedly that he did not have faith in either the political leadership or the legal strategies but that he was banking on the community (fieldwork notes, 2017–18).[23] The examples cited here are not meant to offer a definitive conclusion regarding the traumas of family separation or fear and discriminatory treatment but are merely suggestive of the politicization of the movement and the limits of community participation in the face of deportation.

Expanded Sanctuary and the Abolitionist Project

The final point regarding the work of the NSC concerns precisely the limits of empowerment of the undocumented in the face of criminalization and the notion of *expanded sanctuary* further tied to the criminalization of both immigrants and minority native-born citizens. One of the Friends of the New Sanctuary Coalition argued strongly at a meeting regarding the traumas of criminalization, "One does not feel free. How can immigration stop persecuting us? I wear an ankle bracelet and people think that I am a criminal." She recounted the trauma of immigration. Another Friend discussed the difficulty of maintaining the "face of strength" in front of her children while her partner was in detention and scheduled for deportation. She came to the Coalition to express appreciation because her partner would be released from detention soon. A volunteer discussing the case of another Friend and her partner noted that the support of the Coalition had "made her to some extent invincible," but she emphasized "that hurt, that anxiety, that stress" of having her partner's stay in the United States be in jeopardy (fieldwork notes, August 3, 2017). While Yukich (2013a) found that immigrants selected for sanctuary support could and in fact should keep their emotions under control (310), this research found that participants in the meetings were emotional and that people did not seem to exercise restraint under a prescribed script.

The following examples from fieldwork are indicative of how NSM's efforts lean more toward social justice than toward merely faith based efforts. One of the faith-based leaders told the group gathered for a protest at 26 Federal Plaza on July 20, 2017 (see fig. 2), "For the last 4 years we meet here on Thursdays and we walk 7 times around 26 Federal Plaza. It doesn't matter whether you believe or don't believe or you simply [wish to] project positive energy—it is important that we are together. We walk in absolute silence, and we pray." Another member of the faith-based leadership included the following words in the prayer: "We encircle [the building] not with hatred but with love that can perhaps change hearts . . . to do good, to unite families . . . that the walls of injustice that are holding people in waiting can come down . . . so that we can build bridges" (fieldwork notes, July 20, 2017). A similar metaphor was used by a female priest supporting an interfaith effort to offer physical sanctuary to Amanda Morales Guerra; the priest noted at a press conference, "This afternoon we are so grateful to be in support and solidarity with [the mother and her family]. The church unites its arms and hands together with the interfaith coalition of northern Manhattan and with all the other leaders to support this family at this time. It is here during this very critical and pivotal movement that we see that the walls that are being built against those that are marginalized and oppressed [are beginning] to come down. . . . These are the times when we are called to work, we put our hands and hearts into action" (fieldwork notes, August 17, 2017). And a rabbi who supported Amanda Morales Guerra evoked a Hebrew verse to show hospitality to strangers and noted, "What impacts us north of 181st impacts us south of 181st, what impacts us west of Broadway impacts us east of Broadway. What affects any of my neighbors in Washington Heights affects me. We [stand] in solidarity with my neighbors in Washington Heights" (fieldwork notes, August 18, 2017). Carmen de la Rosa, an assemblywoman for Washington Heights, linked Amanda's case with opposition to fascism. This was done as well by Angela Fernandez of the Northern Manhattan Coalition for Immigrant Rights. De la Rosa noted, "We often hear about the shadows—she can't even see her shadow. She can't leave the sanctuary. She has health care needs, educational needs. She must be solely dependent upon what the community can bring in . . . to survive this trauma that she is forced to endure. If we are not on the right side of this, history will look at us in disgust—like Jews fleeing the Holocaust" (fieldwork notes, August 18, 2017). A member of the New Sanctuary Coalition noted, "JCC has a sign, a citation by Elie Wiesel: We must all take sides. Neutrality promotes oppression. Silence encourages tormenters, not the tormented" (fieldwork notes, September 5, 2017).

FIGURE 2.   Jericho Walks around 26 Federal Plaza (location of USCIS offices). Source: Fieldwork, July 20, 2017.

FIGURE 3.   Jericho Walks around 26 Federal Plaza (location of USCIS offices). Source: Fieldwork August 17, 2017.

Fieldwork findings are thus further consistent with the examples of faith-based sanctuary movement in Canada—a movement that has also included secular community groups and had a nondenominational base—as discussed by Lippert (2004). Interfaith efforts represent an important history of the NSM movement. At the first national gathering in Washington, DC, on January 29–30, 2007, the NSM included representatives of Interfaith Worker Justice, United Church of Christ, the Union of Reform Judaism, and members of Lutheran, Roman Catholic, and Evangelical churches and the Muslim faith (Freeland 2010, 490). While the movement appeared to include religious diversity, Yukich (2013c) finds that religious minorities were dominated by the large number of members of mainline Protestant and Catholic churches (172, 190) and describes how the movement struggled to build a genuinely inclusive interfaith movement (198). However, rather than religious actors serving as the primary actors in the movement, as Freeland (2010) argues based on his research in Los Angeles County, the San Francisco Bay Area, and Ventura County, California (486), this research finds an increasing presence of secular actors while still using language and religious institutions to challenge the state. Freeland (2010) argues for NSM's qualitative rather than quantitative (the number of the undocumented in sanctuaries) significance, stressing that it presents a model of political opportunity and mobilization structures (487). However, this research finds a greater emphasis on the commitments of social justice than on religion in the sanctuary model. This does not deny that religious convictions may still serve as a motivator for involvement of some participants, but the movement appears rather to be gaining political emphasis and a political knowledge as well.

While references to Nazi Germany were often made by politicians attending sanctuary events, including by New York City Council representative and current public advocate Jumaane Williams, who spoke eloquently regarding increasing divisions between supposedly deserving and undeserving immigrants (fieldwork notes, March 8, 2018), what emerged as a critical aspect of sanctuary as the fieldwork was being completed was the notion of *expanded sanctuary*, which, according to Ravi Ragbir, an NSC leader, would include an emphasis on not just immigrants but women, the LGBTQ community, Muslims, and people of color and an expansion of sanctuary beyond houses of worship, to include schools, hospitals, and entire communities (fieldwork notes, March 8, 2018). Importantly, Vitiello's book on Philadelphia sanctuaries (2022) refers to this expanded space of sanctuary as one that also transcends specific locations of a congregation or a city (34) to include places and practices as well as United States and transnational sites (7), not merely spanning the geography of migration but also revealing links to unjust foreign policy (8). Thus, expanded sanctuary in this view is a set of relationships among local, national, and transnational policies and practices (8).

My fieldwork conducted in New York found instead expanded sanctuary as a local abolitionist project involving other marginalized and oppressed groups. At the Expanded Sanctuary event held at the New School on March 8, 2018, Janaé E. Bonsu, a Black feminist activist with the Chicago-based Black Youth Project 100, referred to sanctuary as "a praxis of abolition in everyday life," an abolitionist project where resistance can be contemplated and condoned, a project that would go beyond noncooperation with ICE to include people who have had contact with the criminal justice system, which is especially crucial given the heightened moment of criminalization of not just immigrants but native-born Black and Latino youth (fieldwork notes, March 8, 2018). Although Bonsu discussed difficulties in Black youth forming a coalition with immigrant groups and organizing around the very notion of sanctuary, perhaps it bears repeating here Sharpless's (2016) point that the movement for immigrant justice is not free from racism, citing immigrant claims for whiteness (739). Nevertheless, the "Black Youth Project 100 is pairing up with Mijente, a Latino civil rights group, to push to increase the number of sanctuary cities. . . . While the groups had teamed up in 2015 to stage a large protest in the city when the International Association of Chiefs of Police held its annual conference, last month [January 2017] the groups held their first news conference together." They are "aimed [not only] at expanding both the number and the definition of sanctuary cities to protect undocumented immigrants . . . [but also at] curb[ing] police brutality" (Alcindor 2017). Sanctuary spaces would thus make networks and coalitions, impact policies, work on community education, and fight for eliminating the gang database (95 percent of those tracked and targeted are Black and Latino, according to Bonsu (fieldwork notes, March 8, 2018; see also Paik 2020, 110, on racial profiling and the gang database). Paik makes a similar point: "Noting that Black immigrants are three times more likely to be deported for an alleged crime but less likely to obtain deportation relief than other immigrants, the M4BL platform incorporates immigrant justice as central to Black liberation" (2020, 124). In terms of organizational strategies, this concurs with the notion that the New Sanctuary Movement can be seen as a decentralized group of local organizations that will occasionally come together to form an alliance or advocacy coalition (Vitello 2022, 188).

These fieldwork findings are further aligned with the criminal justice reform proposals by García (2016) and are further consistent with Freeland's (2010) recommendation for the NSM to develop transnational networks and partner with other immigrant rights organizations as well as criminal justice reform organizations. And while these conclusions are in full agreement with Sharpless's (2016) account of how the United States immigration enforcement regime has become a punitive system and her call for "reform for convicted noncitizens, including those convicted of more serious crimes" (765), what Sharpless's account lacks is a focus on redistributive strategies; while the emphasis on joblessness in poor Black communities (753) is important, jobs in the global economy do not equal a safety net. Keeping in mind this point on redistribution, the key example here is thus the notion of expanding the limited aspects of sanctuary to include those excluded and marginalized from sanctuaries, making the notion and its political subjectivities truly encompassing.

In broader terms, the notion of expanded sanctuary allows for the redefinition of the notion of sanctuary as an abolitionist project. Roy (2019, 773) calls for a new abolitionist agenda that is attentive to the "deep historical spatial logics of the 'ghetto,' the 'plantation,' the 'colony' and the 'reservation'" in order to understand "uneven urban environments." Roy's (2019, 774) sanctuary as an abolitionist project "grants historical and revolutionary agency to the Black radical subject." What is further relevant for the purposes of this research is the notion of abolition as place-making. Roy (2019, 775) notes that "abolitionism, as a liberation movement, built infrastructures of resistance and refuge, from vigilance committees and the underground railroad to the Bureau of Refugees, Freedmen, and Abandoned Lands, which [are] both precedent and horizon for today's sanctuary spaces." Remaining to be examined is the extent to which the sanctuary movement can in fact follow this trajectory.

Fieldwork results show further that the sanctuary model has turned away from a social emphasis on families (Freeland 2010, 487, 492; Yukich 2013c) as a mobilizational strategy to representing a broader range of individuals affected by the criminal justice system. The research upholds Sharpless's (2016) conclusions that "the ability of reformers to roll back punitive deportation practices and secure legalization for the broadest group of undocumented immigrants as possible depends on the movement for immigrant justice aligning its messaging and politics with those of the racial justice movement to end hyperincarceration" (736), yet this movement is constrained by difficulties in forming coalitions given the competition for jobs, including in the public sector, and for political power (738). A hopeful prospect for the sanctuary movement may, however, be found in indications of a recent decline in group identity politics in New York, which might hold the promise of minority coalitional politics addressing inequality and fairness. The Black Lives Matter movement, as a multiracial protest, can also be seen in the New York context as a neighborhood movement that, while led by African Americans, also included substantive numbers of young whites (Mollenkopf 2020; see also Williams 2020).

Finally, Wild (2010) claims that NSM actions threaten churches' tax-exempt status and finds it likely that "the movement will fail" (999), suggesting that it might be only a matter of time before the government opts for action against the NSM, whose members could face imprisonment, and the undocumented could face deportation (999). Wild (2010) finds that the NSM's activities are "likely illegal under current law" (1006), argues that the movement must end sheltering immigrants in churches (1012), and advises instead the use of the media and spiritual counseling (1012) and engaging in "targeted, specific legal reform" (1015). Wild's (2010) argument to state the goals related to the protection of deserving immigrants to win the appeal for a bipartisan legislation that would pass both houses of Congress may be a pragmatic suggestion (1013) but one that clashes with the strong stance the movement has taken to avoid the distinctions between deserving/undeserving immigrants in the politically polarized landscape left by President Trump's demands during his first term in office for the building of a border wall.

Evidence of lower crime rates for immigrants did not sway the public opinion that supported more punitive anti-immigrant political agendas in the 2024 presidential election. What is apparent from the activism during the first Trump administration discussed in this chapter, however, is that citizens who joined to support noncitizens strongly opposed criminalizing migrants, gaining a type of political consciousness, through demonstrations and protests, that disposed them to uphold the rights of noncitizens through sanctuary practices such as accompaniment. Their vocal identification with, not just the story of migration, but with their role as legitimate claimants within American urban democracy led these citizens to 26 Federal Plaza in Manhattan to support and "represent," as it were, their migrant Friends attending ICE appointments. Their proximity to immigrant neighborhoods, extensive contacts with immigrant Friends, and perception of political opportunity structures residing in New York City's institutions (including the court system) that could be open to migrant claims, all contributed to this support of citizens for noncitizens. For their part, the immigrants tended to see themselves as tentative residents, not criminals to be accused in a court, a perspective of their rights being violated growing from their participatory practices and narrative reconstruction of the self in meetings. One of the immigrants cited above indeed came to see herself as the victim of a criminalizing exploitative economic system that took her labor without giving enough in return, treating her in fact as a modern slave. The immigrants' articulation of the social consciousness of their position, including in the economic system, thus contested the views of migrants as willing pawns in a neoliberal system. Their activism led NSC to consider a variety of coalition partners, from local political and faith-based leaders to groups opposing hyperincarceration, and with them it struggled to expand sanctuary by forging links with criminal justice reform advocates. Rejecting the deserving/undeserving dichotomy, NSC's abolitionist activism could be seen as being on the spectrum of demonstrations against unjust policing, offering an interpretation of American urban

democracy that would be more open to those who strive to possess the right to
have rights.

* * *

The importance of the New Sanctuary Movement can be located in new organizing strategies against what are seen as the unfair, unjust, gratuitously cruel
actions of a restrictive regime that fosters immigration conditions of uncertainty,
instability, and legal liminality (see R. Gonzales 2016, 9). The NSC has not only
redefined the notion of the immigrant as a Friend being helped but has helped to
redefine the notion of the helper as a citizen working to uphold democracy in a
country in which the marginalized, who include immigrants, the homeless, and
minority youth, are criminalized. The NSC proposes a different type of governmentality regarding what it means to be a citizen in the city by arguing that people have a right to be protected and that "no one should beeported" (fieldwork
notes, January 15, 2018). While the NSC does not go as far in enacting rights
as, for example, nonprofit organizations in San Francisco that Els De Graauw
(2016) documents, including rights such as immigrant language access, labor
activism, and municipal ID cards for disadvantaged communities, it nevertheless presents community struggles that can influence the government to become
more accountable, especially given the rising criminalization of undocumented
immigrants. While Freeland (2010) demonstrates anti-undocumented actions
in Ventura County (496) and Yukich (2013c) describes anti-immigrant political action in New York, this researcher did not witness during fieldwork in New
York such populist actions directed against the NSC (apart from the response
by the state and the city, which is beyond the scope of this chapter), although
it should be noted that during the time of this research the media reported the
appearance of posted signs criticizing illegal immigrants in the super-diverse
borough of Queens. An important contribution of the NSM in New York is that
it has rejected the deserving/undeserving duality and attempted to broaden the
coalition, which is particularly significant given that, as Houston and Lawrence-
Weilmann (2016) warn, the paradigm that posits model migrants against criminal aliens limits prospects for progressive alliances (121).

Having examined the case of New York, we can assert that liberal social
movements have helped to establish sanctuary cities. But while New York's NSC
could be compared to sanctuary movements in other Democratic strongholds
(Collingwood and O'Brien 2019, 157)—for example, Philadelphia (see Vitiello
2022);—its practices appear unique when placed in an international perspective
and compared, for example, to the evidence of sanctuary researchers in Europe
and Canada who demonstrate limited, undermined, deficient, and compromised
sanctuary practices (Bagelman 2016; Georgiou, Hall, and Dajani 2020; Hudson
2019). Thus, New York's sanctuary movement may not be representative interna-

tionally, and the conclusions presented here should be approached with caution when seen against a broader set of cross-national examples.

Sanctuary cities pose a critical question regarding the existence of an alternative to the oppressive state—one that would be more inclusive and offer less of a limbo state for the undocumented and asylum seekers. If sanctuaries can attempt to constitute a reclaiming of "'positive' and 'progressive time'"; if they bring "concrete and beneficial changes in individuals' lives" (Rotter, cited in Bagelman 2016, 36); and if they have the potential to recuperate the agency of the undocumented and asylum seekers, then a whole range of other institutions from federal resources to local government offices, from legal aid to community-based nonprofit organizations, would need to supplement the existing sanctuaries. Sanctuary cities can be alternatives to state hostility, especially in the cases of sanctuaries such as New York that offer legal representation to immigrants in detention, which is positively correlated with the chances of immigrants prevailing in court (Sharpless 2016, 723), all the more acute given the February 2018 Supreme Court ruling affirming the legality of the indefinite detention of immigrants. Sanctuaries can function as these alternatives in spite of the rejection by some cities of sanctuary practices and of accounts that challenge the notion that sanctuary cities "offer a hospitable, even sacred, remedy" to "hostile, top-down explicitly punitive politics" (De Genova, cited in Bagelman 2016, ix).

Importantly, Houston and Morse (2017) warn not to typecast migrants as making solely economic contributions to the city or embodying multiculturalism in the city (44); Vitiello (2022) describes migrants from Mexico driving the revitalization of many neighborhoods, including commercial strips deemed "blighted" by the city, and opening up stores and businesses in Philadelphia, their labor serving more affluent residents and visitors (194) while encountering racism, nativism, and xenophobia (195–97). And in her critique of DACA, Cházaro (2016) likewise charges that "DACA recipients emerge as the ideal neoliberal actors: framed as exceptional, required to perform the myth of self-reliance, driven to show that they are self-propelled and can achieve their own economic viability, and exempting the state and private industry from social support" (635); yet this researcher's fieldwork finds emphasis on both solidarity and belonging to the city.

In sum, fieldwork research finds that NSC did not screen immigrants to distinguish between the worthy/deserving and the undeserving, nor did it create a boundary between the host and the guest; instead, it actively worked to disrupt the state monopoly on the legal and the political with its accompaniment program, distrusting the state but also collaborating with local political leadership, advancing strategies for empowerment of the undocumented and asylum seekers even when recognizing defeat in the face of deportation, and struggling toward an *expanded sanctuary* that would include a broader a range of individuals who have come in contact with the criminal justice system.

Fieldwork findings may thus suggest various cultural routes that characterize the sanctuary city movement but ones sharing a commonality found in sanctuary practices' offer of safety from prosecution and opposition to the criminalization of immigrants. The argument here has thus been that sanctuary practices, especially in the form of an *expanded sanctuary*, carry the potential to be broadened to reduce the number of people arrested and incarcerated, as the immigrant rights movement and the movements against mass incarceration might form an alliance to strengthen the rights of immigrants and minorities.[24] The increasing visibility and publicness of the undocumented, asylum seekers, and refugees as new political subjects is of crucial significance for the domain of urban governance and political participation.

The case for the politicized sanctuary should not be overstated, however. In a brilliant account in *Sanctuary in Pieces*, Laura Madokoro (2024) chronicles the two-hundred-year history of sanctuary in Montreal (also known as Mooniyaang/Tiohtià:ke), finding it broken, in pieces, exacting a cost on sanctuary seekers who encountered a hostile, inaccessible city, lacking hospitality and generosity (15, 4, 9). Madokoro's (2024) analysis reveals the complicity of oppressive forces of power and authority, the sanctuary itself emerging as "deeply problematic historically in terms of dashed expectations, questionable motives, the fickle subjectivity of deservedness, the obfuscation of structural precarity, and exposure to public scrutiny and added state controls" (15). In critiquing romanticized notions of fugitive democracy, Haro and Coles (2019) likewise showed how abolitionist public practices, whose "substance and conditions of appearance hinged on vast networks and practices of concealment, largely autonomous community formation, and creative law breaking," could not have "transcended the horrific vulnerability and terror associated with illegality and potential capture" (662). The description of sanctuary practices in this chapter was not meant to deny the carceral aspects of church sanctuary seeking (see Madokoro 2024, 235) or the daily struggles to avoid deportation, to obtain shelter and employment, to access basic services, or to secure schooling for children. The examination here did not seek to glue back the shards of sanctuary—the "broken" accounts properly illuminate the limits of sanctuary—but by stark contrast the *expanded sanctuary* brought into focus the bonds, however fragile, that hold the citizens and noncitizens together in a mosaic of sanctuary practices.

Part 2

THE POLITICS OF
SANCTUARY CITIES

3
THE LIMITS OF CITY SOVEREIGNTY

The subject of the previous chapter was the notion that the city can also be viewed as a site of *sanctuary practices* and of crucial networks of solidarity with the undocumented, asylum seekers, and refugees who can mobilize to resist the criminalization of migrants. The discussion now turns to the role of cities and the role of urban policy more broadly, drawing important implications for cities as sanctuary sites in relationship to questions of sovereignty, democracy, and urban power.

Cities are schoolhouses of democracy, argued Tocqueville, and "can retain their ability to enable people to learn the skills of self-government only if they are given sufficient power to make decisions that have tangible consequences for the quality of local life" (Frug and Barron 2008, 50). Benjamin Barber argues that cities should be empowered "to secure human sustainability, especially when nations fail to do so" (2017, 7). In *If Mayors Ruled the World*, Barber emphasized that "politics cannot be found in (or rescued from) increasingly dysfunctional nation-states or rigidly ideological national parties" (cited in Barber 2017, 10). Defining sovereignty as "the rightful exercise of power by a governing body whose legitimacy depends on its capacity to secure the life, liberty, and property of its citizens" (18), Barber (2017) argues that "the crisis in national governance is a crisis in sovereignty, in the capacity of the nation-state to make good on the terms of social contract on which their founding legitimacy turns" (17).

It is critical that recent protest movements have assumed an urban dimension with cities emerging as chief locations of political action and progressive policies ranging from minimum wage to immigration. This can be seen most poignantly in the example of sanctuary cities in the United States that have posed a challenge to federal rule in the domain of immigration. Cities—their resources, capacities, and institutional infrastructures, by which I mean especially the urban legal apparatus—are becoming "the most important, constructive alternative to a Trump agenda," noted Benjamin Barber (cited in De Haldevang 2017), arguing further for "the necessity for intercity cooperation and networking" in an interdependent cosmopolitan world (Barber 2017, 22). "A national government may think it simple to defeat one city's policies on climate or immigration, but let it try to defeat six hundred cities working together nationally, or six thousand acting together globally" (27).

This chapter probes the limits of an argument for an increase in city sovereignty in a manner de facto already claimed. While Barber's argument is global, this chapter focuses on the United States, starting with the argument that in the face of a hostile sovereign, cities have a significant role to play—a role that shows signs of claiming increasing powers and enfranchising substantive governance (see Howlett and Ramesh 2014).[1]

Importantly, following Michael Blake's (2021) two-part delineation of sanctuary cities, Barber's model might be seen as what Blake calls the "wholesale model" (a persistent refusal on the part of the city to provide assistance to the federal government in apprehending migrants) while what is evaluated here could be in part viewed as a "piecemeal model" of sanctuary (a specific and perhaps intermittent response to a form of injustice caused by a specific policy). But perhaps the distinction between the two models of sanctuary city is more fluid insofar as the argument here is that there are special purposes for cities who cannot *and should not* exclude all of their residents regardless of status to genuinely constitute a welcoming polity. This would thus fit the wholesale model. On the other hand, the piecemeal model stresses the circumstances of unjust federal policy that has contributed to the rise of sanctuary ordinances, presenting a sanctuary policy as a self-reflexive acknowledgment on the part of cities of their purpose. Blake does not include the significance of social movements as a part of the sanctuary policy, which is a striking omission because the argument for sanctuary cities cannot be examined while neglecting sanctuary practices and sanctuary movements. Blake poses the question as to why cities do not engage in outright deception of federal authorities or in providing privileged information to the migrants, and this is precisely where a broader conception of sanctuary *practices*, not mere ordinance policies, is necessary. If, as Blake mentions, a response to injustice might feature active resistance and not just noncompliance (Blake 2021, 27), the role of social movements in their full abolitionist expression as well as in their at times ambivalent interaction with municipal structures and local representatives is necessary to fully embody the city as a site of a wholesale model of resistance.

While cities cannot replace the state's capacity in military, taxation, redistribution, infrastructure and public services, international relations, or trade and
migration policies, they are nevertheless showing signs of leadership in the arenas of land use and development, minimum wage, regional tax sharing, sustainable development planning, climate change, and especially, as will be emphasized
in this chapter, sanctuary practices in the area of immigrant inclusion. Sanctuary
cities in the United States can in this narrow sense be defined as places where
a local government or police department has passed a resolution, a city ordinance, an executive order, or a departmental policy expressly forbidding city or
law enforcement officials from inquiring into immigration status and/or cooperating with the Department of Homeland Security's Immigration and Customs
Enforcement (ICE) agency.

The chapter situates the discussion first in the historical context of city-state
relationships and second in the recent urban crises in the United States tied to
the sanctuary city movement, then examines legal grounds for devolution of
power to cities before discussing the legal concepts of "urban commons" (Foster
and Iaione 2016; Foster and Iaione 2022; see also Harvey 2013) and "city power"
(Schragger 2016), finally outlining constraints facing increasingly sovereign cities. While mayors may not "rule the world," as Barber's (2013) forceful argument
would have it, this chapter reiterates that cities are indeed not utilizing the powers
that they increasingly do possess to sufficiently and substantively address urban
inequalities and to expand urban citizenship into a fundamentally inclusive category. Barber is arguing that expanded city sovereignty ought to be a normative
goal given the crises of the nation-state while this chapter argues that the noted
normative goal should be approached with caution given the persistence of urban
inequalities. The context of the state being hostile to redistributive urban policies, however, opens a social and political space for a special emphasis on urban
sovereignty. Sanctuary practices represent one arena in which cities have begun
to address substantive problems of social inequality; legal mechanisms utilized
for this purpose are reviewed in this context in this chapter. While sanctuary cities and urban crises in the United States provide a contextual framework for the
discussion, the theoretical framework for sovereignty is examined, as noted, in
relationship to the concepts of "city power" and "urban commons." The chapter
argues that current legal literature on urban commons and city power needs a
stronger normative lens and better conceptualization of urban inequality, redistribution, and publicness. Moreover, if cities are to assume greater capacities to
govern and to ensure the life, liberty, and sustainability of their populations, they
have to overcome serious constraints in the four domains outlined in the chapter: (1) surveillance and control of urban space, (2) privatization of public space,

(3) the rise of the luxury city, large-scale developments, and megaprojects, and (4) homelessness, among many other challenges ranging from environmental to criminal justice policies. The linkage between urban constraints and urban sovereignty is further emphasized by suggesting the ways in which cities have attempted to address these problems through, for example, the spaces of commemoration, waterfront access areas, participatory community-based plans (197-a plans in New York City), community benefits agreements, affordable housing, and litigation on behalf of the homeless.

Capital, Coercion, and City-State Relationships

City-state relationships—in particular, the influence of the processes of urbanization on states, the interactions between the state rulers and urban populations, and the correspondences between urban structures and state types—are not well developed in the literature. Diane Davis has studied conflicts between identity politics and sovereignty in divided cities, focusing specifically on urban dimensions of contestation and investigating "how the superimposition of certain sovereignty arrangements on identity-diverse urban locales has affected the built environment of the city or its people in ways that fan the flames of aggression and violent conflict" or "lead to the establishment of a genuinely pluralistic, tolerant, and autonomous form of urban citizenship" (Davis 2011, 228–30). Research compiled in Davis and de Duren's (2011) edited volume finds that conflicts are more likely to arise under "conditions of uncertain or contested sovereignty" and to "emerge in cities where divergent populations are denied access to formal or informal institutions for claim-making, for influencing urban policy, or for advocating for citizenship rights or identity aims" (Davis 2011, 247, 251). The research does not sufficiently question identity-based projects, nor does it take into account the ways in which institutions can be captured and populations manipulated by identity-based claims. Nevertheless, the research outlines "the degree to which unity of division among identity groups is facilitated by urban form—whether through symbolic buildings, iconic architecture, or the development of urban projects" (247) and includes, significantly, Lawrence J. Vale's conclusions that "the urban world has been filled with effort to manipulate citizens through provocative acts of narrow subnational nationalism" (Vale 2011, 207).

Tilly and Blockmans's edited volume *Cities and the Rise of States in Europe, A.D. 1000 to 1800* (1994) and Tilly's *Coercion, Capital, and European States, AD 990–1992* (1992) represent particularly valuable contributions to the study of city-state relationships. First, cities can be defined in relation to "the formation of dense, differentiated populations having extensive outside connections"; this formation is facilitated by the proximity of "trade, warehousing, banking, and production" (Tilly 1992, 17). Second, cities cannot be simply reduced to "expressions of their dominant classes and surrounding economies" (Tilly and Blockmans 1994, 4). Third, it is important to distinguish between city systems and systems of states. "Europe's systems of cities represented the changing relations among concentrations of capital, its systems of states the changing relations among concentrations of coercion. European cities formed a loose hierarchy of commercial and industrial precedence within which at any point in time a few clusters of cities (usually grouped around a single hegemonic center) clearly dominated the rest" (Tilly 1992, 47).

Citing Machiavelli's notion that "a city used to liberty can be more easily held by means of its citizens than in any other way, if you wish to preserve it" (Tilly and Blockmans 1994, 2), Tilly shows how this notion nevertheless proved inaccurate as states developed into large war machines, although the author can be criticized for an overemphasis on the role of coercion and the war-making powers of the state. The author further offers three conclusions: (1) strikingly different types of states emerge in densely populated urban regions versus regions that contain few cities; (2) where distinctive forms of urban organization existed during the period of the formation of major states, they survived the growth of state power and continued to play national influence; (3) urban merchants and financiers played considerably influential roles in the formation of states, including their armed forces (Tilly and Blockmans 1994, 6).

Tilly distinguishes between two periods. In the first, between 1000 and 1500, when cities were rare and states numerous, "the rulers of most cities of 10,000 or more exercised something resembling sovereignty within their own walls and their immediate hinterlands" and "relative to territorial lords, urban oligarchies wielded considerable political power" (Tilly and Blockmans 1994, 15). In the second period, after 1500, however, "the formation of consolidated states coupled with the proliferation of cities to change the city-state relationship both numerically and politically. . . . Politically, the odds that the oligarchy of any single city would dominate a state declined drastically. The proliferation of cities facilitated a state-making strategy of divide and conquer, the gradual monopolization of coercive means by consolidated states weakened the defensive positions of cities vis-a-vis national authorities, the expansion of state administrative apparatus (which was itself largely a consequence of war and the preparation for war) gave those authorities increasing ability to monitor and control the urban population" (15, 16).

In both *Cities and the Rise of States in Europe, A.D. 1000 to 1800* and *Coercion, Capital, and European States, AD 990–1992*, Tilly emphasizes a critical point that cities serve as the chief containers and distribution points for capital, which "gives the urban political authorities access to capital, credit, and control over hinterlands that, if seized or co-opted, can serve the ends of monarchs as well" and can facilitate the aims of the states (e.g., "containers and deployers of coercive means") to develop their armed forces (Tilly and Blockmans 1994, 8; Tilly 1992, 51, 52). While the state represents the chief container of coercion with its central-ized, differentiated, and autonomous structure (Tilly 1992, 131), Tilly also points to the significance of welfare and regulatory states that intervene in economic affairs to obscure and mitigate their coercive aspects (52).

Tilly stresses further "the autonomy of [the cities'] ruling classes with respect to would-be and actual state-makers, and the strength of their representative institutions" and shows how "major trading cities and city-states mounted more effective resistance to the penetration of consolidated states than did cities in mainly agrarian regions" (Tilly and Blockmans 1994, 22). Moreover, "most often consolidated states only gained genuine control over major trading cities when cities had begun to lose their predominant positions in international markets" (22). But the focus of bargaining over the means of war and the fact that "urban institutions themselves seem to have become part of state structure more readily where capitalists predominated" (22) were integral pieces.

Two conclusions are particularly relevant for the contemporary context of this research. First is Tilly's emphasis on the ways in which the states are weak-ened today; for example, "the ability of European states to detect and counteract movements of illegal migrants . . . has declined radically even as capital moves ever more freely from opportunity to opportunity, regardless of state interest" (Tilly and Blockmans 1994, 26). Additionally, Tilly points to the separation of the dynamics of capital and coercion after centuries of their intertwining under state command (26). Thus, increasingly sovereign cities are encountering state sovereigns whose coercion power has been weakened, although the sovereign has in the United States applied threats of defunding and limited redistribution to noncompliant cities during the first Trump administration.

Second, and of particular relevance to rebel cities, Tilly discusses the condi-tions under which rebellions have tended to start—namely, when (1) "the state's demands and actions offended citizens' standards of justice or attacked their primary collective identities, (2) the people touched by offensive state actions were already connected by durable social ties, (3) ordinary people had powerful allies inside or outside the state, and (4) the state's recent actions or interactions revealed that it was vulnerable to attack" (Tilly 1992, 101). Rebel cities during the first Trump administration show that the sovereign has offended urban stan-dards of justice; that the undocumented, refugees, and asylum seekers and their families have started to develop durable ties with the social community of the United States; that urban political leadership—namely, the mayors of American cities—have a stake in at least symbolically defending this population; and that the US national leadership is increasingly vulnerable to the mounting opposition including by the legal system. Resistance and protests on the part of sanctuary cities may thus be the weapons of the weakest.

Rebel Cities

David Harvey has asked whether the city can be "a center of revolution," noting that "political and urban social movements have used the city as an agent of social and political innovation in the search to construct an alternative social order and a different sense of the right to the city" (Harvey 2006, 101). This chapter argues that the city can be theorized as a center of power for the benefit of the excluded if the notions of "urban commons" and "city power" can be expanded and substantiated to address profound inequalities—this possibility is seen in the example of sanctuary cities. And a more inclusive city can indeed be a revolutionary idea, one that depends on increased urban powers and on creating a social and political space to direct resources away from surveillance, privatization, and luxury and toward inclusive and sustainable social planning, thus opening cities for public participatory processes and for enhanced possibilities of a novel poetics, not only politics, of daily urban life. City sovereignty is significant, after all, only if it can be claimed by enfranchised citizens as well as a range of denizens, including those who do not have legal rights but certainly could claim the right of the city.

Referencing the role of migration, Harvey concludes that the right to difference is one of the most precious rights of urban dwellers but warns further that "difference can also result in bigotry and divisions, marginalization and exclusions, sometimes boiling over into violent confrontations" (Harvey 2006, 86). US mayors have recently offered their response to diversity politics in relationship to the recent restrictive state policies. "To anyone who feels threatened today, or vulnerable, you are safe in Boston," noted Martin J. Walsh, the mayor of Boston, adding at a news conference, "We will do everything lawful in our power to protect you. If necessary, we will use City Hall itself to shelter and protect anyone who's targeted unjustly" (Robbins 2017). This remark comes in response to President Trump's executive order that threatened to cut funding to sanctuary cities that refused to cooperate with federal immigration authorities. Moral outrage of diverse groups over the injustice committed by the state galvanized the sanctuary movement in the early months of the first Trump administration (Carney et al. 2017).

In his Cooper Union speech on November 21, 2016, New York's former mayor Bill De Blasio emphasized, "We don't consent to hatred. And we will fight anything we see as undermining our values. And here is my promise to you as your mayor—we will use all the tools at our disposal to stand up for our people. If all Muslims are required to register, we will take legal action to block it. If the federal government wants our police officers to tear immigrant families apart, we will refuse to do it. . . . If the Justice Department orders local police to resume stop and frisk, we will not comply. We won't trade in neighborhood policing for racial profiling. If there are threats to federal funding for Planned Parenthood of New York City, we will ensure women receive the healthcare they need. If Jews, or Muslims, or members of the LGBT community, or any community are victimized and attacked, we will find their attackers, we will arrest them, we will prosecute them. This is New York. Nothing about who we are changed on Election Day." Similarly, Mayor Ed Murray of Seattle (a Democratic-leaning sanctuary city) announced support for sanctuary policies, vowing to "resist President Trump's 'demonstrated outright misogyny, demonstrated xenophobia and homophobia, nationalism, racism and authoritarian tendencies'" (Oskooii, Dreier, and Collingwood 2018, 957).

"The right of cities to govern themselves and to come together with other cities, both within and beyond their national borders, increasingly is being grounded in powerful rights arguments" (Barber 2017, 18). To revitalize democracy today, we must have rebel cities—to borrow David Harvey's notion that is tied to the idea of right to the city, which "primarily rises up from the streets, out from the neighborhoods, as a cry for help and sustenance by oppressed people in desperate times" (Harvey 2013, xiii). Citing Lefebvre, Harvey has in mind "a vigorous anti-capitalist movement that focuses on the transformation of daily urban life as its goal" (xvi). But in the cited speeches by America's mayors, the right to the city is evoked as the right of resistance to federal authority while protests during the first Trump administration focused on the defense of women's, immigrant, and refugee rights.

An important group of protests focused on opposition to President Trump's order to ban refugees and immigrants from several Muslim countries, and it is perhaps not an accident that the first protest against the first Trump administration, the March on Washington, was organized by the feminist movement. At a time when many thought that the feminist agenda had been achieved, women still felt oppressed, especially given the sexism, misogyny, and threats to cut funding to reproductive health support organizations (which precipitated political turmoil regarding further erosion of reproductive rights following the overturning of Roe v. Wade). Cities are logical locations for feminist struggles as they have, as Elizabeth Wilson has argued (Wilson 1992; Wilson 2001), provided a plank in the gradual emancipation of women.

All of these provide examples of how states can construct a stigmatized other. As Koutrolikou has argued in the case of Athens, Greece, the other who is "perceived as a threat faces stigmatisation and exclusions (even criminalisation), while processes of 'othering' may also distinguish the 'rightful' from the 'Others'. It might be the 'terrorist', the 'migrant', the 'rioter' or else, but in any form a group becomes negatively correlated to the emergency while it simultaneously becomes disassociated from the 'deserving', law-abiding citizenry. . . . Legal aspects and ethical/moral representations further intensify such divisions. In this way, we have a differentiation, a de-familiarisation and an enemy-formation tactic, dividing the citizenry between 'us and them' . . . between 'good' citizens and their interests and 'uncivil or threatening others'" (Clarke and Tilly cited in Koutrolikou 2015, 175, 176).

Sanctuary cities in the United States could in this manner be seen as a bulwark against the hostile state and "provide a territorial legal entity at a different scale at which sovereignty is articulated" (Bauder 2016a, 9). Sanctuary cities exemplify what Lippert has termed "sovereignty 'from below'" (Lippert 2004, 547), shaped by local legal and political contexts and the solidarity with social movements. Given the recent federal crackdown on sanctuary jurisdictions during the first Trump administration, some cities were attempting to assert their sovereignty through legal battles while others were seeking alternatives to formal sanctuary city ordinances; the number of sanctuary cities was increasing in defiance of the federal authorities. Powell notes that as of February 6, 2017, there were 39 sanctuary cities and 5 sanctuary states in addition to 633 sanctuary counties (Powell 2017); it is thus important to emphasize that sanctuary cities range from small towns and counties to major cities in the United States. Sanctuary cities have been "incorporated into the legal and institutional spaces of local governments" and have attempted to exert moral and legal authority (see Cunningham 1995; see also Sassen 2013, 69) in cases where, in their view, the federal government had failed, moving away from their roots in faith-based organizing, however, toward "institutionalized mechanisms of local governance" (Ridgley 2013, 219, 223, 228). San Francisco has sued the Trump administration over its order to withhold funding ($1.2 billion in this case of this city) from sanctuary jurisdictions, arguing that the order was unconstitutional (Fuller 2017). San Francisco has been criticized in the legal community for attempting to impose urban liberal values as a nationwide policy.[2] While the judge applied the anticommandeering principle to stop the federal government from coercing San Francisco to undertake the work of the federal entity, an additional hurdle is a section of the federal immigration statute that argues that localities can't withhold information or refuse to cooperate with the federal government.[3] Although this notion should be approached cautiously given the remaining statutory challenges, the argument here is that sanctuary cities show promise in offering an inclusive polity as an alternative to the restrictive state. This argument is applied to cases in the United States in contrast to UK examples (Bagelman 2016; Squire and Darling 2013) in which sanctuary cities "reproduce some dominant discourses that sanctuary practices overtly seek to counter" (Lippert and Rehaag 2013, 4). Thus, the argument here supports the claim that "sanctuary's promise lies in its potential to disrupt the state's attempt to monopolize territorial sovereignty and ways of being political" (Czajka 2013, 44). The role of cities, however, ought to be central to this argument, as they can become sites of crucial networks of solidarity with the undocumented, asylum seekers, and refugees. Sanctuary cities in the United States are more than just "'pockets' of sovereignty, where citizens assert their visions of justice and contact the state when it drifts too far from social realities" (Lippert and Rehaag 2013, 10). The argument here is that sanctuary cities in the United States contest the sovereign power of the nation-state and its exclusionary politics toward asylum seekers, refugees, and the undocumented and, in the face of recent challenges, especially the federal crackdown, include movement into both increasing legality (by challenging the federal government in court) and publicness and visibility (by increasing media exposure in seeking an immigration policy reform—for example, the Dream Act or public reemphasis by Democratic mayors on maintaining sanctuary city policies). This is a critical example of city sovereignty in the contemporary United States while sanctuary cities in other nations such as the UK seem to be replicating state exclusions. Nevertheless, led by a member of the Global Parliament of Mayors (GPM) steering group, Marvin Rees, the mayor of the city of Bristol, is proposing a crowdfunding campaign to "support" counterpart US mayors whose cities have sanctuary city status. The GPM campaign would involve crowdsourcing resources from UK cities (Bristol initially), transferring them to an intermediary body nominated by the GPM secretariat, and providing the funds as a donation to a selected mayor (e.g., Boston, Chicago, Los Angeles, or New York City) representing sanctuary cities in the United States (Global Parliament of Mayors 2017). GPM is an example of translocal urban citizenship that provides representation to cities beyond their nation-states and proposes even forms of redistribution across sanctuary cities. As Barber argues, what is necessary is "cooperation among networked municipalities and a deployment of collective local power that will establish a democratic and public counterweight to private global capital" (Barber 2017, 40). "Glocality is proving that local government works more efficiently and productively when mayors cooperate globally, forging networks for common action" (85), as the Global Parliament of Mayors's call for crowdsourcing resources indicates.

Yet it is important to acknowledge here the challenges that the municipal sanctuary movement has experienced as well, including difficulty in recruiting immigrants, as noted in chapter 2. While Yukich's (2013a) point regarding the absence of immigrants in the New Sanctuary Movement is less valid for the sanctuary practices observed in New York, as the fieldwork chapters of this book detail, her point is particularly valuable for the context of sanctuary cities' legislations. Acording to Houston and Lawrence-Weilmann (2016, 122), "It is reasonably rare for migrants to participate in the creation of sanctuary legislation."

Houston and Lawrence-Weilmann (2016) detail practices of the decentralization of immigration enforcement in which local police contacted ICE instead of assisting tenants in disputes with their landlords in New Haven, Connecticut, and in Berkeley, California, and in which ICE officials conducting a raid posed as local police (104–05). Local legislations such as Resolution LM-2011-0330 in New Haven and Resolution 63,711-N.S. Berkeley counter federal immigration enforcement acts attempting to secure access to services and police protection and to guarantee public safety for the undocumented. But Resolution 07-162 in Davis, California, and Order 16 in Cambridge, Massachusetts, go beyond this scope to refer to public discourses or immigration policies as racist, dehumanizing, criminalizing, and exclusionary (106). Houston and Lawrence-Weilmann (2016) also note, however, cooperation with criminal cases that characterize ordinances such as Hamtramck MI 2008-1, which modified Chapter 38 of the City Code, and New Haven's Police Dept General Order 06-2. But here, again, Houston and Lawrence-Weilmann (2016) find that where support from residents and local politicians existed, the ordinances appear more robust in shielding immigrants from disclosure of immigration status (108), even if the police lack training to support sanctuary ordinances (109) and the immigrants themselves can easily be criminalized for crossing the border illegally.

Similarly, Houston and Lawrence-Weilmann (2016) show how liberal politicians define high-risk or criminal aliens and low-risk (106–7), law-abiding, or model migrants (Yukich cited in Houston and Lawrence-Weilmann 2016, 107). The latter are thus construed by sanctuary legislations as immigrants who deserve sanctuary due to their "moral behavior" and "economic productiv[ity]" (110), the latter evident, for example, in Oakland's 2008 Resolution 81310, which credits migrants for neighborhood revitalization (111), deferring to neoliberal logic in defending migrants from ICE raids near school campuses. Oakland's 2007 Resolution, which celebrates cosmopolitanism, masks police racism against the African American community (120). Similarly, Watsonville, California's Resolution 98-07 construes immigrants as economically productive, contributors to diversity, and even peaceful neighbors (112). Analyzing the 2011 Ordinance

11-0-73 in Cook County, Illinois, which works to foster trust and cooperation with the police and opposes ICE detainers (which encourage racial profiling and harassment) (114), Houston and Lawrence-Weilmann find as well a neoliberal logic of protecting "useful workers" (115) rather than a focus on human rights. Economically useful model migrants appear also as an asset in Baltimore's City Council Bill 11-0298R (115). Tacoma Park Ordinance 2007-58 and Evanston I Resolution 11-R-08 acknowledge migrant discrimination and put an emphasis on human rights violations and economic deprivation in migrant countries but ultimately represent examples of neoliberal multiculturalism using the language of cultural and racial diversity (117–18) as a "commodifiable asset[s]" (119). This article by Houston and Lawrence-Weilmann thus shows the limits of sovereignty in reproducing neoliberal economic or cultural ideology by seeing immigrants as commodities even as they diversify community; where supported by political and community participation, ordinances appear more robust, including the language of antidiscrimination, human rights violations, and antiharassment. The subject of the rhetoric of ordinances and the actual sanctuary conditions is discussed in greater detail in the case of New York in chapter 4, but perhaps the examples of Philadelphia and Santa Ana are also instructive here.

As Diane Garbow (2017) explains, despite the global city boosterism policies, Philadelphia has instituted among the most progressive policies regarding the protection of undocumented immigrants. Local government, public-private partnerships, professionals, and activists promoted policies to provide social services and protect the rights of immigrants, including language access programs, job training, job placement, and naturalization programs, and the city banned its public employees from making inquiries regarding immigration status. As a result of grassroots activism, Philadelphia PD could not detain immigrants without a federal warrant; "unlike other cities that had similar policies but allowed immigrants with felony convictions to be detained, Philadelphia required judicial warrants before ICE could continue their detainers and was unique in that it applied to both police and prison departments" (Garbow 2017, 2). Former mayor Nutter, however, reversed the policy of noncollaboration with ICE in the final weeks of his second term in office; subsequent mayor Kenney "signed an executive order that declared once again city police and prisons would not honor ICE detainer requests for nonviolent criminals on his first day in office" (2). Lai and Lasch (2018, 604) report that community organizers in Philadelphia rejected policies that played up criminal histories and called for investment in education and reentry programs and "for changes that would address 'deep root causes of inequity and disparity,' and that encompassed both immigration and criminal justice reform."

And advocates in Santa Ana, California, were able to defeat a proposal to create a sanctuary ordinance that would have excluded individuals with felony convictions, outstanding warrants, or pending felony charges (Lai and Lasch 2018, 541). An ordinance without such exclusions was subsequently passed. Criminal justice policies were discussed in greater detail in chapter 2.

Except in the case of mass protests, rebel sanctuary cities do not answer Harvey's radical and revolutionary call discussed in the beginning of this section. Rebel cities, it is true, have stood up to a hostile sovereign by contesting defunding in court (San Francisco) and by trying to forge global networks of mayors (Global Parliament of Mayors). Yet while lofty mayoral rhetoric (e.g., in New York, Boston, and Seattle) during the first Trump administration signaled inclusivity (as a form of right to difference), sanctuary policies in practice fell short. With the exception of Philadelphia, municipal ordinances and resolutions failed to involve immigrants in the sanctuary process, tended to highlight only immigrants' economic contributions, and more often than not had a weak record of shielding immigrants from abuses of due process. Rather, it is the support of immigrants by social movements and local political activism that has been key to creating participatory sanctuaries, as has been discussed in chapter 2.

Rebel Governance

While the previous section considered sanctuary ordinances as examples of rebel cities, this section will briefly address the related concerns of rebel governance. Studies of rebel governance are similar to the literature on rebel cities as both point to the inadequacy of state-centric approaches to the study of governance (Arjona, Kasfir, and Mampilly 2015, 286). Rebel governance obtains particular relevance in the cases of state violence that victimizes the local population or that has failed to attend to the basic needs of the population (7).

The rebels' activities clash "with the dominant perception of rebel groups, especially those in the developing world, which, since the end of the Cold War, have been caricatured as little more than war lords" (Mampilly 2011, 3); they have also been referred to as "bandits, militias, rebels, guerillas, warlords, insurgents, even freedom fighters and terrorists" (8). However, "in order to ensure their visibility insurgent leaders cannot only be concerned with the establishment of a coercive apparatus (domination) but must also gain a degree of consent from the civilian population (hegemony)" (8). Rebels have thus shown a capacity to meet the needs of the local population, to collect taxes, to engage in active public work projects such as building roads and infrastructure, to provide services to the civilian population, to respond to health care and educational needs of the population, to provide shelter to civilians, to ensure food provision, and to respond to social problems such as theft, drug use, and prostitution (4).

Rebels can further encourage civilian participation in popular assemblies, provide administrative services, and organize and regulate commercial production
activities (Arjona, Kasfir, and Mampilly 2015, 287). Mampilly cites Ernesto "Che"
Guevara, who influenced rebels around the world and whose guerrilla warfare
"underlined the importance of demonstrating concern for social welfare of local
residents through the provision of public goods" (Mampilly 2011, 12). Moreover,
"provision of public goods could have an ameliorating effect on the insurgency's
ingrained need to use the violence in pursuit of a political agenda" (13). There
are, of course, different types of insurgencies; "communist insurgencies are more
likely to engage in governance involving greater social administration and other
interventions than groups espousing conservative social beliefs" (Arjona, Kasfir,
and Mampilly 2015, 292).

Variations in rebel governance are attributed by Mampilly to "the initial preferences of leadership and their interaction with a wide variety of local and international social and political actors" (2011, 3). Rebel governance is also dependent
upon the preconflict relationship between state and society (see also Arjona, Kasfir, and Mampilly 2015, 289); the (weak) state capacity before the civil war, in particular state abuse or alienation of civilians (Wickham-Crowley cited in Arjona,
Kasfir, and Mampilly 2015, 7, 290); and the "ethnic composition and the ultimate
strategic objective of the group" (Mampilly 2011, 16). Government structures
are constantly transformed during warfare and are influenced by military capacity and political economy of warfare (see Arjona, Kasfir, and Mampilly 2015,
291). Furthermore, rebels' own views, which can be strategically formulated, are
"malleable, not fixed" and change in response to the conflict and the demands of
insurgency (290).

Rebel governance is also significant for postconflict peace efforts, and insurgent government practices should, according to Mampilly, be seen as a precondi-
tion for recognition in the international law arena (Mampilly 2011, 7, 24). Rebels
also engage in strategies of internationalization and in active diplomacy, which
is driven by a political logic and the rebels' need to demonstrate that they can
"behave like states" (Huang 2016, 124). Huang finds that "secessionist groups,
for whom international recognition is essential for attaining independent statehood, and groups that organize domestically by investing in social service provision or creating legal political bodies, are more likely to become wartime diplo-
mats" (124).

"Like governments of traditional states, rebel leaders must negotiate with
civilians in exchange for their loyalty" (Mampilly 2011, 9). Mampilly sees governance as an "interactive process" involving a "surprising institutional interplay"
(15, 22) between insurgent organizations and the incumbent government and

finds that rebel leadership is far more constrained in their actions than is commonly assumed. Finally, one of the important aspects of the way rebels challenge state sovereignty is the appropriation of aspects of state sovereignty—Mampilly terms this "counter state sovereignty" (21). Rebel cities are thus similar to rebel governance in that they both seek to obtain legitimacy that the state has failed to provide.

Devolution Revolution?

"The city of God, city on a hill, the relationship between city and citizenship— the city as an object of utopian desire, as a distinctive place of belonging within a perpetually shifting socio-temporal order—all give it a political meaning that mobilizes a crucial political imaginary" (Harvey 2013, xvii). Yet the urban political imaginary is, importantly, legally bound. Current legal rules, instituted by the states, limit cities in pursuing their independent paths. To the extent that we can even discuss city power, it is important to emphasize that cities "only have power to the extent that they are given it by statues and constitutional provisions adopted by state governments" (Frug and Barron 2008, 231). Thus, in addition to the challenges of basic municipal service provision and of addressing critical urban problems, "bureaucratic inefficiencies, dysfunctional agencies, regional fragmentation, and democratic deficits" (231) are also influenced by legal structures. "Both the national government and the states," as Barber has noted, "insist on denying cities the right of action on issues critical to their citizens, whether or not the cities being preempted are better positioned to take action" (Barber 2017, 117).

Cities are locations where citizens should be enabled to have a voice in altering their polity. Beyond the public places that are the sites of assembly, there are "multiple practices within the urban that themselves are full to overflowing with alternative possibilities" (Harvey 2013, xvii)—protests can take place at the airports too (see also Paik 2020, 138), as has been seen in the United States, and claim them as public sites. Uncovering these practices is a part of the "political task, Lefebvre suggests, to imagine and reconstitute a totally different kind of city out of the disgusting mess of a globalizing, urbanizing capital run amok" (Harvey 2013, xvi).

This reclaiming is already taking place through a "successful revolution in urban empowerment" (Barber 2017, 37), which would represent "a powerful rebuke to national political parties wedded to neoliberal strategies of privatization and marketization as political cure-alls" (39) were the cities themselves not the sites of rampant privatization. Katz and Bradley have termed this *metropolitan revolution.* "The United States is on the verge of a historic re-sorting, in which responsibilities once reserved for higher levels of government are being fully shared with, even shifted to, cities, metropolitan areas, and the networks of leaders who govern them. . . . The federal government and the states will be motivated to do more with less by giving cities and metropolitan areas greater flexibility to design and allocate what are likely to be shrinking levels of resources" (Katz and Bardley 2013, 11, 12). The authors endorse urban pragmatism but uncritically defer to the global economic changes and their impact on metropolitan regions.

"Local democratic governments, both in the central cities and the suburbs, have been overwhelmed by the impact of the decisions made by other governments over which they have no control" (Frug and Barron 2008, 233). One of the challenges has been to influence the state government to give a greater role to the city and its citizens. As Frug and Barron note, cities should develop a clear list of priorities and present them to the state government (2008, 232); the arguments for pressuring the states to become more redistributive should not be abandoned. For the legal system to embrace a vision of the city, one must be clearly articulated by the mayor, the city council, city agencies, and, most importantly, an actively engaged local polity—if the aim of devolution is "enhance public goods and strengthen democracy" and thus oppose privatization (Barber 2017, 39). Comprehensive, participatory, sustainable citywide and regional plans are one means of engaging cities to articulate a vision of urban space that should then be supported by the institutions and not become a mere guideline to be circumvented by private development interests. Fainstein argues that the maximization of the values of equity, diversity, and democracy should direct urban planning and policy toward a just city, noting further that this can be done in an incremental manner within the current system by "constantly pushing for a more just distribution," assuming that the "reform [is] backed by political mobilization" (Fainstein 2010, 166, 170, 176).

One of the challenges in realizing a more equitable city is the fragmentation of urban governance "created by assigning specific issues to uncoordinated government institutions" (Frug and Barron 2008, 233). Regional cooperation represents a solution to this problem. Even though regional proposals are being made without regional agencies implementing them, metropolitan solutions represent the key. As Katz and Bradley have argued, cities and metropolitan regions are inextricably linked (2013, vii). "Our nation's top 100 metropolitan areas sit on only 12 percent of the nation's land mass but are home to two-thirds of our population and generate 75 percent of our national GDP" (1).

"Mired in partisan division and rancor, the federal government appears incapable of taking bold action to restructure our economy and grapple with chang-

ing demography and rising inequality" (Katz and Bradley 2013, 3). Legal structures are not sufficiently responsive to urban conditions, and most states have
not changed their city structures in a substantive way for decades (Frug and Barron 2008, 6). But even though current legal rules limit cities' exercise of control,
they also empower cities to pursue global city and tourist city policies, both of
which defer to private development interests, have resulted in increases of social
inequality, and have diminished the public purpose of planning. Thus, even the
legal rules that empower cities can be seen as limiting equitable development. As
Richard Briffault has argued, even though cities may possess formal authority,
"their economic and political power in practice is shaped by private investment
decisions" (cited in Frug and Barron 2008, 33, 34).

Reformers in the late nineteenth century envisioned home rule as a way for
cities "to become significant actors in the promotion of whatever underlying substantive vision of government the urban reformers favored" (Frug and Barron
2008, 36). The reformers, promoting a vision of good government, did not simply
seek to increase the powers of the cities but included a mixture of decreased and
increased powers depending on the city and the state in question (36). Some
reformers pursued limited government on the local level while others sought to
create an efficient bureaucratic form of local government (37).

Local control can have a dual role—"in the U.S. local governments' formal fiscal and land-use authority has often exacerbated inequality by permitting wealth-
ier local governments to shut out poorer citizens. But local authority can also
be used to ameliorate inequality" (Schragger 2016, 254). Not only are the large
cities diverse in terms of income, ethnicity, and race but they are also important
in promoting civic participation. "The geographically confined nature of local
institutions also provides an opportunity to build the kind of civic capacity that
political scientists increasingly see as necessary to sustain efforts to implement
proposed solutions to seemingly intractable public problems" (Frug and Barron
2008, 50). The response is, however, not to abandon the role of the states that can
significantly influence urban issues.

As Fainstein notes, "The purpose of inclusion in decision making should be to
have interests fairly represented, not to value participation in and of itself" (2010,
175). Citing Mansbridge, Fainstein thus favors "better representation rather than
broader participation," noting that "in the selection model, the representative's
accountability to the constituent will typically take the form of narrative and
even deliberative accountability rather than accountability based on monitoring
and sanctions" (Mansbridge cited in Fainstein 2010, 178). Nevertheless, Fainstein
states that "without a mobilized constituency and supportive officials, no prescription for justice will be implemented" (2010, 181) and emphasizes that "the

role of protest movements is crucial to a more equitable policy" (182)—a conclusion particularly relevant for the context of sanctuary activism.

The Limits of "City Power"

Richard Schragger's *City Power* reflects precisely the crucial tension between what cities should do and what cities can do—a tension that is not sufficiently elaborated on in the study, which is mostly concerned with the latter question. The author argues that the city should be liberated to "pursue ends directed towards the health and welfare of its current citizens"—"the limited connection between governance and growth, the possibility of leveraging immobile capital, and the reality of municipal redistribution suggest that cities can pursue a fairer and more equal distribution of public goods" (Schragger 2016, 248). As Benjamin Barber has argued,[4] however, Schragger's account of city power lacks a normative, prescriptive, rights-based argument. Given the bordered nation-states' inability to deliver, a space for normative power of borderless cities opens up; Barber argues that networks of cities are the key—an account that is neglected in Schragger's study.

Schragger claims that "the city's policy options are both less constrained and less determinative" (2016, 247), emphasizing that cities can govern if they are allowed to. The author notes that cities should focus more on social welfare spending, for example. "Cities should do less of what they cannot do—include economic growth through competitive labor industrial policies—and more of what they can do—provide quality basic services to their residents" (248).

But cities may be more constrained than Schragger's thesis suggests. Schragger's argument requires deeper theoretical development regarding what cities should do. Furthermore, it is not clear how far cities can go in accomplishing their goals. It is not apparent, moreover, whether there are policies that state and federal authorities cannot enact or be responsible for or whether they should devolve more power to localities. Schragger does not say anything regarding cases when federal powers have defaulted on their responsibilities, yet he notes "the significant cutbacks in federal and state support for urban initiatives" (Schragger 2016, 160). The author notes further that "since the 1980s and the pullback in federal funds, urban infrastructure has been a thoroughly private-public enterprise; there simply is not sufficient government will or money to fund even traditional municipal infrastructure—like housing, schools, roads, or parks—absent private investment. In this environment, the traditional public routes for influencing local infrastructure development are diminished" (160).

Schragger discusses urban policies that are limited in their impact or that have only heightened inequalities and discriminatory practices such as the rebuilding of downtown areas and attempts to attract the "right kind" of people (Schragger 2016, 249). He further points out that struggling cities such as Detroit, Camden, Buffalo, and Baltimore will not receive the economic development aid that they need. These cities face further challenges given the lack of federal policies. Schragger notes the need for "redistribution at the national level" but also adds that "many of these policies have either failed or not made much of a difference" (250). The author, however, acknowledges that "the current extreme degree of income inequality in the United States is not something that cities can combat on their own" (251, 252). The study does not elaborate on the role of national urban policy, leaving the significance of federal funding of cities not fully specified or, in the author's terms, a "mystery." Inequality is said to be something that the city creates and something that the city can solve (252), but the author does not sufficiently discuss either of the two.

Examples of economic development that Schragger gives are further suggestive of the ways the city has been shaped to suit the interests of global capital. When the author discusses affordable housing, he positions the discussion in the past ("forty-year span in the middle of the twentieth century" [Schragger 2016, 253]) and does not consider present efforts (and indeed obstacles) to construct affordable housing. Furthermore, Schragger discusses regionalism (2016, 251) but does not elaborate on concepts such as tax sharing. The author also completely ignores the role of planning, especially citywide and regional plans that contain sustainable development policies. The author does not discuss the case of the regional growth boundary in Portland.

Schragger's redistributive arguments are weak and include, as has been noted, only one example of city power (minimum wage, which is also an example of state power, it could be argued). The author admittedly wanted to focus on the fact that cities have to be business friendly and to implement policies that would keep businesses within the city limits, thus emphasizing only the policies that are related to the economic role of cities. Schragger thus neglects the social, cultural, political roles of the urban environment. Furthermore, the author concludes that equality should be a parameter—he falls short of arguing that it should be the chief parameter—in evaluating the power of localities. "If the formal grant of power to local governments results in massive inequality in the provision of basic municipal goods and services, it should be avoided. If the formal grant of power to local governments enhances the provision of quality goods and services to citizens, however, it should be favoured" (Schragger 2016, 254). But it is not clear who would arbitrate and how localities that exacerbate inequalities would be punished.

Schragger further cites "claims on the city" that would "reclaim democracy" (Soja cited in Schragger 2016, 254), but his account offers surprisingly little on community power and social movements or other forces that would be reclaiming democracy. While cities have, in the author's view, "a significant role to play in producing public goods and ameliorating economic inequality" (Schragger 2016, 255), it is not clear where the resources to do so are going to come from, especially in resource-constrained cities. This proposal runs the risk of creating two tiers of cities—those resource-rich ones that may engage in amelioration of inequalities and those resource-poor ones that will be abandoned by all levels of government and where inequalities will grow. This leaves Schragger in the domain of case studies of what cities have actually been doing, which is an indication of both the city's power (minimum wage ordinances) and powerlessness (community benefits agreements [CBAs], which may be summarized as deferring to developers after they have bought off the opposition to their projects).

The author's account of redistribution raises the question of agency—who represents the city in the account of city power? Is it the mayor, the city council, select institutions, or the community that can mobilize and protest? Similarly, rather than the city having power, it could be that there are more select groups in the city that are powerful, with others powerless. Schragger's account is significant, nevertheless, in that it argues for an "enlarged realm of urban governance" (Schragger 2016, 136), yet it is unclear whether this means that select projects may have a redistributive component rather than an overall redistribution strategy. When the author mentions "justice and efficacy of particular city expenditures and who benefits and loses from them" (138), he needs a more developed theory of the city's ends.

Furthermore, the relationship between the city and the state is undertheorized and is treated in case-by-case examples by Schragger. Would the city rely on the state to support its own redistributive goals, or are we entering the arena of rebel cities? Also, how can citywide activism be transformed into a statewide campaign? This leaves us again with the question of how the author theorizes power. Is it a factor of mobilization, or is he favoring a strong mayor model of urban governance?

The author does not discuss sanctuary cities or recent struggles to provide protection to immigrants, minority groups, and Muslims. Debates on legislation, litigation, and circumvention as the ways to counter exclusionary federal policies are further relevant, as are the current progressive efforts by both states and cities.

Discussion of city power can, furthermore, be framed by the protests against the first Trump administration that took place in cities across America and internationally. But Schragger does not focus on city-based movements, and the study is silent on the role of community-based mobilization or progressive engagement in cities. Likewise, the question of the new responsibilities of cities cannot be fully answered by the arguments in the study. This is all the more urgent given the federal retrenchment of resources for housing, policing, and clean air. But to the extent that cities will be impacted by recently proposed renegotiation of contracts on trade and on migration, the study does not offer any pointers.

Implicit in Schragger's argument is the significance of mayors; again, the study leaves the reader to wonder whether the author is advocating for a strong mayor type of governance. Urban political moment in which cities challenge the exclusionary state opens space for mayoral leadership on national and international levels, making Schragger's account even more relevant. Schragger emphasizes that political power is the key and leaves it up to the mayors to negotiate with the state and the federal government. The author makes a further distinction between local power and city power, arguing that local power can be discriminating, exclusionary, and NIMBY, noting the role as well for cities in advancing labor rights, environmental rights, minimum wage laws, and affordable housing. Neglected in this account are the ways in which cities can also be sites of exclusion, discrimination, and NIMBYism.

As Nestor Davidson has argued,[5] the key question is that of urban capacity including pragmatic capacity of urban institutions; these are neglected in the author's account, which is characterized by an ambiguity regarding institutions and technocracy. Davidson further points out that the conflict between cities and the federal government is suggestive of the inevitability of clashes and preemption; legal scholarship thus necessitates new theories of authority and autonomy. Alaina Harkness of the Brookings Institution, on the other hand, noted the highly variable capacities of cities to implement policy and stressed that Schragger's study leaves vague the critical question of the resources that cities would need to govern.[6]

Schragger does not focus on the role of US states in improving conditions in cities and is even dismissive of their role given that they have not, in the author's view, taken their responsibilities seriously. While the author emphasizes the question of urban justice, in particular in education and the provision of basic municipal services, this notion is not sufficiently elaborated on in the study. This is even more critical given the question of how to leverage resources in an environment where federal policies are hostile to cities, although Schragger argued that federal policies of the past, such as the urban renewal policy, have been previously characterized by hostility toward the city and its minority residents. Schragger leaves it to political contestation to fight for resources for the city, acknowledging that poorer cities just may not have the resources to implement policy.

Wendell Pritchett emphasized[7] the role of legal structures that determine the scope of urban governance, expanding Schragger's questions—Should cities govern? Can cities govern?—to include: What should cities govern? And how should cities govern? Pritchett proposes the partnering of successful cities and struggling cities to address the inequity between the resource-rich and the resource-poor cities. Pritchett argues further that cities should have abilities to tax revenue, create inclusionary housing, and institute rent controls and should pass other laws protecting employees, not just minimum-wage laws.

In conclusion, the account of city power is problematic in its undertheorized role of national urban policy on the one hand and community-based mobilization on the other. While the account of municipalities' legal powers is significant in that it opens "political space" (Schragger 2016, 154), it is less clear whether political power can be used to substantively address inequalities.

Limits of the Urban Commons

The recent debate on the commons is essential for cities and has the potential to enhance an understanding of the limits of urban sovereignty and of the participatory aspects of sanctuary organizing. David Harvey (2013, 80) has argued that urbanization perpetually produces urban commons and, along with it, shadow forms of publics spaces and public goods, but also perpetually appropriates and destroys the commons by private interests. The urban commons encompasses the living environment that we share, the languages through which we communicate, the social practices that we create, and modes of sociability that shape our relationships (Hardt and Negri cited in Harvey 2013, 72). But these aspects of the social environment of the city can be subject to "enclosure, social control, and appropriation by both private and public/state interests" (Harvey 2013, 72).

The commons is produced through a social practice of *commoning*, which captures an unsteady social relation between a specific social group and aspects of the living social and physical environment essential to that group's existence (Harvey 2013, 73). Furthermore, Harvey emphasizes that commoning in essence includes "the principle that the relation between the social group and that aspect of the environment being treated as a common shall be both collective and non-commodified—off-limits to the logic of market exchange and market valuations" (73). The commons in this view is thus defined by its use value and should not be rendered as subjected to exchange value.

Co-Cities by Foster and Iaione (2022) represents a pivotal contribution to the study of the commons, which also develops an understanding of urban inequality in relationship to the commons. Yet Foster and Iaione could further expand on how cities are chief sites of inequality, especially in the policy arenas that they do control, such as development. Following Schragger (2016), it could be argued that cities are politically and legally empowered to engage in development, but the resources that cities command have gone to upscale development projects that have benefited higher income groups and have reduced the number of public spaces, contributing to the further privatization of public spaces, while cities have withdrawn from city-wide or regional planning that might begin to address inequalities.

Foster and Iaione (2022) envision the commons as inclusive, shared, and resilient; cities, however, are also sites of conflict and social exclusion and contain ghettoes and slums. If commoning is a new way of claiming resources, as the authors imply, what role will redistribution of resources play in the commons as it is understood as an inclusive polity? A specific asset of the co-cities approach is the presence of the legal infrastructure, which introduces "reinvestment clauses on urban infrastructure thereby guaranteeing that part of the value produced is captured by locals and residents" (Foster and Iaione 2022, 236). Foster and Iaione (2022) conclude that the aim of the co-city project platform is to further racial and social justice benefiting structurally disadvantaged neighborhoods which requires a disruption of dominant economic and social ideologies (234).

Discussing the co-city principles in Rome, Italy, Foster and Iaione (2022) find that while the city neglected to ameliorate select neighborhoods, residents and the activists mobilized to reclaim local heritage (230). The co-city process enabled the creation of codesign laboratories, community gardens and placemaking activities, and helped to form a legal association to support residents' care of the park spaces (230). In turn, in Baton Rouge, Louisiana, a codesign project attempted to address systemic urban racism by investing in a community-driven process to revitalize Plank Road in the historically Black portion of the city (223–26). But what accounts of "best practices" such as these generally lack is the significance of institutional reforms at multiple levels, neglecting institutional processes, mayoral regimes, fiscal reforms, decentralization strategies, and so forth. This is important because it demarcates the limits to policy transferability (Montero and Baiocchi 2022).

Another asset, and also shortcoming, of the co-cities framework is the emphasis on "participatory, deliberative, associative, and collective democracy processes" (238) and approaches to community-building. When Foster and Iaione turn to the subject of citizen participation, even if substantive, these efforts fall short of levels of citizen power and more resemble examples of tokenism. In their discussion of community boards (164–66), Foster and Iaione (2022) might have included the role of participatory community-based plans such as 197-a plans as a possible achievement of several community boards in New York. But the authors still might note the fact that community boards are appointed rather than elected bodies, that they have historically contained entrenched local elites who would block more robust citizen participation, and that they were sites of the local patronage of city council representatives. Community boards have engaged in reactive participation, stopping or limiting development projects. The theory might thus benefit from reemphasizing that in the community-building process of co-cities not all actors are of equal order, not all have the same powers, possibilities, or influence over or access to decision-making capacities. For example, the sharing economy and the new policy experimentation projects are perhaps more suitable for business-friendly innovations; this can leave too much space for market forces to exert their influence. Another aspect of the collective democracy aspect is the issue of access. To what extent could the "smart city" devices be available in low-income neighborhoods that, unlike Harlem, New York, do not have active neighborhood groups or cannot benefit from participatory structures and how could immigrant, minority, and poor residents in these areas have access to them? More broadly, the authors include a critique of decentralization (Foster and Iaione 2022, 58) but needed to address other aspects of social inequality and cultural and political factors which prevent the flourishing of co-cities (see also Harvey 2013, 83). Although the authors mention exclusionary practices, they do not discuss gated communities, exclusionary zoning, and a lack of comprehensive planning, especially in the suburbs.

Similarly, there are implications for not only the democratic process but also the equitable outcomes of the co-cities' framework. In terms of outcomes, to the extent that sharing can refer to a joint use of resources and can be relevant for sustainability, it appears that the examples cited are mostly suggestive of piecemeal efforts at sustainability rather than of comprehensive policy change. Sustainability examples fall short of comprehensive (citywide) policy initiatives and are in effect more focused on certain exemplary (neighborhood) projects. The authors could further highlight the role of networked cities in climate change (see, for example, Barber 2017; Goh 2021), expanding the focus on the rights to housing or the decline in public investment in housing and discussing resources that the cities need to deal with natural disasters as well as the resources and commitment needed for sustainability.

It is important to situate the framing on the urban commons in the context of the debate on privatization, spatial control, and surveillance of urban space (Harvey 2013, 67). The discussion of the commons as a shared resource does not sufficiently address the question of how city policies can be altered when cities have engaged in the privatization of public resources.

Thus, a major critique of the concept of urban commons is that it leaves too much space for private actors who can be perceived as equal to public actors. What is exactly the role of private actors? Could they take over the commons? How does the commons ensure its publicness? If we can conclude based on Foster and Iaione's (2022) account that private and public actors can jointly codesign and coproduce the commons, the commons becomes neither public nor private but located somewhere in between the state and the market. This, again, leaves too much room for market actors whose influence in cities has already been too strong. The danger is that the commons thus becomes "regulated, policed, and even privately managed" and denies open access (Harvey 2013, 71).

What would it take for the specific urban commons to be classified as chiefly public, especially given that the mixture of public and private resources has meant skewing toward the market and diminishing the role of public spaces in the city? The market either excludes or does little to include, and factors that contribute to social exclusion ought to come to the foreground of the discussion of the commons.

Perhaps a way to address this question is to further tie the idea of the commons to the concept of a right to the city, as Foster and Iaione did in an earlier article, in which they argue that the city possesses "shared resources that belong to all inhabitants" and is aligned with "the right to be a part of the creation of the city, the right to be a part of the decision-making processes shaping the lives of the city inhabitants, and the power of inhabitants to shape decisions about the collective resources in which we all have a stake" (Foster and Iaione 2016, 288). The final points are suggestive of the fact that the commons can become a manner of improving or enhancing collaborative devices in cities, but this point could benefit from more development, as some of the examples included are more indicative of tokenism than of true participation. If, for example, cities can establish mechanisms to mediate conflicts, we need to acknowledge that conflicts may be more deeply rooted but that sometimes exposure of conflicts can be beneficial and can promote urban social change.

In sum, the research could have been framed around challenges in achieving urban commons, or the difficulty of urban commons, or problems with the concept of urban commons rather than an endorsement of case studies that are, as the authors acknowledge, unable to address the deeper inequalities that limit the building of co-cities as a progressive concept. While Foster and Iaione conclude by emphasizing how the concept of co-cities may indeed address urban inequalities, their examples could be bolder and include the fight for a minimum-wage increase, job training and job creation initiatives, pre-K for all programs, the right to housing and affordable housing, stronger fair-share programs, regional tax sharing, citywide and neighborhood comprehensive plans, regional sustainable development programs, and other programs that stress redistribution of resources and public sector responsibilities.

Harvey's solution to the problems of urban commons is social mobilization. In his view, the commons is not public until it is made so by "political action on the part of citizens and the people to appropriate [the commons]" and make them into public spaces (Harvey 2013, 73). The commons is thus dependent on democracy. Harvey points out that the struggle for the creation of the commons is constant. "[The commons] is not, therefore, something that existed once upon a time that has since been lost, but something that is continuously being produced. The problem is that it is just as continuously being enclosed and appropriated by capital in its commodified and monetized form, even as it is being continuously produced by collective labor" (77). Politics "is the sphere of activity of a common that can only ever be contentious" (Jacques Rancière, cited in Harvey 2013, 71).

Harvey emphasizes the corruption of the commons rooted in an urban politics that channels investments in the creation of a fake commons, resembling seemingly the actual commons, but in effect promoting private asset values for the property owners (Harvey 2013, 79). The key legal task would be to prevent the corruption of the commons. Thus, one example of the commons that is marred by the encroachment of upscale housing—the High Line in Manhattan—would become a site that would also include affordable housing rather than becoming a commons most easily accessible by rich residents. An opposing example includes labor activism to benefit low-income workers in Baltimore that resulted in the declaration of the "human rights zone" (providing a living wage for workers) in the Inner Harbor (Harvey 2013, 79).

Foster and Iaione (2022, 61–68) develop further Elinor Ostrom's notion of polycentric governance but Harvey proposes as well, following Murray Bookchin, confederal assemblies to administer and govern municipal assemblies with the delegates who would be recallable and answerable to them both (Harvey 2013, 85, 87). While Foster and Iaione's model is limited in addressing structural economic inequality and social conflict, Harvey's is limited in that he insists that the politics of the commons can solely be accomplished if it is a part of anticapitalist struggle, although many of his examples suggest that important achievements can be undertaken even within the current system.

Urban Constraints

Cities are the key proving grounds for the new arrangements of governance (Swyngedouw 2005, 1992, 1993); Erik Swyngedouw, following Harvey, accurately identifies "a desire to construct politically the market as the preferred social institution of resource mobilisation and allocation, a critique of the 'excess' of state associated with Keynesian welfarism, and a bio-political engineering of the social in the direction of greater individualised responsibility" (1998). The new innovative governance-beyond-the-state, in all its new institutional forms (which include private market and civil society) are, as Stoker notes, characterized by permeable boundaries between the private and public sectors (cited in Swyngedouw 2005, 1992, 1994) and "exhibit a series of contradictory tendencies" (1992). Swyngedouw argues that governance-beyond-the-state reveals an "undemocratic and authoritarian character" that only supposedly "offer[s] the promise of greater democracy and grassroots empowerment" (2005, 1992). Swyngedouw presents an excellent critique in terms of legitimacy, representation, and exclusion tied to the limited and problematic concept of stakeholder (or "holder") and points out that many groups rejected or opted out of participation and political action; the author errs, however, in foreclosing opportunities for civil society, which he sees merely as "the Trojan Horse that diffuses and consolidates the 'market' as the principal institutional form" (2003). Egalitarian spaces and spaces of political insurgency are limited in what Swyngedow sees as "a post-political and post-democratic city" (cited in MacLeod 2011, 2648) characterized by the foreclosure of dissent. While the prospects of resistance arising from the poorest urban populations should not be overstated, the above-discussed sanctuary city movement has suggested that cities are sites of a crucial political struggle. (This is discussed in the following chapters as well.)

Brenner has similarly argued that the pluralized and variegated formation of sovereignties within cities and regional jurisdictions has, following Ong, formed "spaces of exception" (Brenner 2011, 172), emphasizing that the new rescaled configurations of state sovereignty have "generated new forms of socio-spatial inequality and political conflict that limit the choices available to progressive forces throughout Europe" (172). Brenner falls short of arguing, however, that increases of urban sovereignty, assuming they can include a serious attempt to address urban inequalities, could contest the rise of far-right mobilization and challenge state exclusions and "neo-liberal geographies of uneven spatial development" (173)—an argument advanced in this chapter. Cities have the potential to become agents of global change but face tremendous challenges, especially as they are increasingly discharging the responsibilities of the sovereigns. While cities can be seen as incubators of democracy and sites of bottom-up citizenship, civil society, and voluntary community, there are also simultaneous worrisome trends that are a result of concrete urban policies influenced by the processes of globalization and urban restructuring and increased security concerns.

(1) Surveillance and Control of Urban Space

In his book on war and cities, Ashworth cautions that the period of 1945–89 was a "brief, curious and unique interlude in world history" (1991, 202), a precarious era of unsteady avoidance of worldwide warfare, not forgetting, of course, post-colonial struggles. Writing in 1991, the author points out that the notion that we live in an unsafe world was not evident to generations born after 1945. Ashworth writes defensively regarding the study of cities in the context of military analysis, which for most scholars occasions discussions of medieval fortifications. It has become evident, however, that defense strategies were among the crucial variables in contemporary urban development and planning (196). Historical examples are still significant, however, not only because of the heritage of fortified cities but given that scrutiny offers plentiful evidence of the influence of military technologies and military geopolitics on urban form, the morphologies of cities, and their very locations, even if the term *militarization* of urban space may not be appropriate and should be used with caution.

While new technologies and political and institutional alliances made urban intervention possible, what is significant here is the capacity to employ the resources of the state and its military and political priorities to render urban contexts of the past irrelevant and a new urban future (one of the controlled, surveilled city) not simply inevitable but necessary. This is one example where the *militarization* of space has broader implications in that it can be used to justify a specific future space of the city. This may have a significant impact on limiting the urban spaces of democracy (see also Sennett 1998). In another example, in the case of Athens, Greece, Koutrolikou has documented how a politics of fear as "a spatial manifestation of urban crisis" (constructed as a state of emergency) may evolve into a moral panic that can feature a new construction of the public and "its enemies" and can be used to impose a new definition of (il)legality (Koutrolikou 2015, 174, 175).

Stephen Graham has argued that the provision of "security" in the present political ideology has begun to overwhelm in importance the other functions of national states such as social welfare, education, health, and infrastructure development: "Security" has become the sole criterion of political legitimization (Graham 2004). One of the chief problems in cities is fear and insecurity, facilitating the increased surveillance of the city's public spaces. The militarization of urban life takes several dimensions and is evident in many spheres such as "the design of buildings, the managements of traffic, the physical planning of cities, migration policies, or the design of social policies for ethnically diverse cities and neighborhoods"—all of these are brought together under the umbrella of "national security" (11). Urban environments are saturated by surveillance systems, checkpoints, and defensive urban design. In additional examples of the militarization of space, "Tanks protect airports. Troops guard rail stations. Surface-to-air missiles sit around office blocks housing meetings of international leaders. Combat air patrols buzz around Manhattan and London. New York street police now carry pocketsize radiation detectors in hope that they might detect any nuclear 'dirty bombs' smuggled into metropolitan areas. US postal sorting depots have automatic anthrax sniffers. New York's Grand Central Station now has automatic bio-weapons detectors" (Graham 2004, 12). Some commentators have even argued that central cities should be actively decentralized to protect themselves from terrorism (12). The militarization of urban space is adding to the vicious cycle of fear and insecurity in places already affected by crime, social violence, racism, and xenophobia (Graham 2004).

One of the responses to urban surveillance and control is offered by spaces of commemoration and reflection—memorials (of the Holocaust, the Vietnam War, 9/11, etc.) as public spaces in which reckoning of the victims can take place and that might also allow for challenges to dominant narratives of victimhood rather than merely serving the interest of the nation-state.

(2) Privatization of Public Spaces

Sharon Zukin (1995) has argued that culture is a powerful means of controlling cities. Culture can convey images and memories that symbolize "who belongs" in specific places (1). Culture is furthermore a part of the economic development strategies, fueling the city's symbolic economy (one example is tourism, which "bolsters the city's image as a center of cultural innovation" [2]; another concrete example is Sony Plaza in Manhattan, which intertwines cultural symbols and entrepreneurial capital in creating a new symbolic economy in which retail dominates a public plaza). Zukin relates culture to urban fear and contestation over social difference, arguing that this has further contributed to the growth of private police forces, gated and barred communities, and a design of public spaces for maximum surveillance. Private interests have stepped into the vacuum created by the government. "Handing such [public]spaces over to corporate executive and private investors means giving them carte blanche to remake public culture. It marks the erosion of public space in terms of two basic principles: public stewardship and open access" (32). One of the characteristics of the new public spaces is thus the "withdrawal of the public sector and its replacement with the private sector" (24, 25)—private security guards patrol space, public and private sanitation workers clean it up—for example, in the case of Bryant Park, which during the 1970s was associated with crime, disrepair, and the presence of low-income and poor minorities. Homelessness increased during the 1970s—a time of deinstitutionalization, when many mental health patients were placed on the street without sufficient support of community facilities. The Bryant Park Restoration Corporation has redesigned Bryant Park, which now includes cultural events, features kiosks and food services, and is patrolled by private security guards. The park features a fashion design show during which a portion of the park is closed. The park has also adopted the social design principles of William H. Whyte ("movable chairs"). His additional idea is to bring "normal users" to the park so that there would be less space "for vagrants and criminals to maneuver" (28).

An example of participatory community-based planning in New York, 197-a plans can be seen as one of the challenges to the privatization of urban space— many plans originated in opposition to development projects that were stopped by community protests, but in their creation of waterfront access, of public open spaces on neglected, fenced-off waterfront areas, they represent an example of proactive, rather than reactive, planning.

(3) The Rise of the Luxury City, Large-Scale Developments, Megaprojects

Peter Marcuse has argued that the city is quartered, divided according to the lines "of race, of class, of occupation, of ethnicity" (2002, 94); its quarters are sometimes congruent, sometimes not; they vary by different times of the day; and they reflect the "spatial arrangements of residential life" and "the spatial arrangement of business activities" (94). Marcuse identifies the rise of the luxury areas of the city—the locations of the "power and profit" characterized by high-rise condominiums with their own security. "The new architecture of shopping malls, skywalks, and policed pedestrian malls is a striking physical mirror of the social separation" (95). The homeless and the poor are removed from sight in these areas. According to MacLeod, following Peterson and Florida, "Deluxe landscapes coupled with a spirited branding of a city's image will purportedly attract globally mobile investors alongside a creative class of professional and revenue-generating tourists" (MacLeod 2011, 2630); in these sites, MacLeod argues, citing Purcell, the "premium [is placed] on exchange value of space, perhaps ahead of any use value acquired by people inhabiting it" (Macleod 2011, 2646).

Current policies are characterized by a "single-minded focus on encouraging growth through the vehicle of public-private partnerships" (Fainstein 2010, 170). "Within the United States, national subsidies for urban programs have shifted decisively toward supporting private initiatives" (176). Even though affordable housing is the most pressing need in the three cities that Fainstein studied—New York, London, and Amsterdam—the three cities "have been instead engaged in promoting megaprojects that provide only limited amounts of low-income housing" (173). These projects are often criticized by neighborhood groups as they typically feature aggressive government intervention in collaboration with private interests—the taking of property commonly in decaying areas (waterfronts, manufacturing zones, transport infrastructures, historic district renovation). These regeneration projects revitalize the center city and clear the inner-city space of the poor, heightening the contrast with many other areas of the cities experiencing severe deprivation. Fainstein suggests that megaprojects be "subject to higher scrutiny, be required to provide direct benefits to low-income people in the form of employment provisions, public amenities, and a living wage, and, if public subsidy is involved, should include public participation in the profits. If at all possible, they should be developed incrementally and with multiple developers" (173).

Urban policies are shaping cities around the world in a similar manner, and this goes beyond the discussion of cultural homogenization countered by localism. Increasing standardization is evident in the similarity of central business districts. Sennett noted that such standardization is necessary to enable the purchasing of square footage of office space in New York from Singapore (Sennett 2002, 44, 45). Megaprojects, especially those that cater to the global markets (sports events, expositions, residential areas for the global economic elite), feature similar characteristics as they include designer buildings and forms of spectacle in the city. While they might display awareness of environmental concerns and an appreciation of urbanity (Orueta and Fainstein 2008), they represent in a manner attempts to depoliticize their developments.

Market-driven housing and commercial development are among the most critical factors of socio-spatial segregation. Many developments around the world contribute to the centralization of higher income groups and the peripheralization of poverty in cities. This further contributes to the spatial segregation of upper-income highly educated groups. This is combined with a lack of investment in low-income areas, which experience lack of services, poor infrastructure, crime, and vandalism. The poor are unable to benefit from economic growth that does not reach the periphery of cities. While there are new peripheral locations for the middle classes, there is also the emergence of gated communities for the upper classes who live outside of traditional enclaves.

Fainstein suggests that as a challenge to the current policies, the example of the Minneapolis Neighborhood Revitalization Program could be examined—the program successfully diverted funds from "downtown development to community betterment" (Fainstein 2010, 182). Fainstein further calls for the reversal of national policies that subsidize private interests, citing European examples, in particular those in the Netherlands, where government regulation and ownership are significant.

(4) Homelessness

As Matthew Desmond (2016) demonstrated in his study of Milwaukee, many poor families, especially those of single mothers living in rented homes, who had spent more than fifty percent of income in rent, were at continued risk of eviction. The National Law Center on Homelessness & Poverty estimated in 2017

that at least 2.5 to 3.5 million Americans slept in "shelters, transitional housing, and public places not meant for human habitation." An additional 7.4 million, however, lost their homes and were doubling up with others (National Law
Center on Homelessness & Poverty 2017). As has been noted, 147,518 people,
including 48,298 children, slept in the main shelter system in New York City in
April 2024; in April 2017, 61,277 people slept in homeless shelters in New York
City, and this was an increase from 36,960 in June 2010, according to the Coalition for the Homeless. Moreover, "homeless people remain a visible presence in
public spaces: on the streets, in the parks, on plazas in front of expensive apartment houses, in office building atrium lobbies, in subway cars and stations, in
railroad terminals, under bridge and highway entrances" (Zukin 1995, 27). Given
recent increases in homelessness, there is a worrisome trend of relying on business improvement districts (BIDs) to clear the homeless from public spaces. BIDs
are thus a new model for "controlling" homelessness; they allow businesses and
property owners to tax themselves in exchange for maintenance and control over
public areas. According to the NYU Furman Center newsletter of October 18,
2016, "In Denver, CO, Berkeley, CA, and Portland, OR, for example, BIDs have
campaigned to prohibit people from sitting or lying in public rights of way, and
even sued to reverse policies that encouraged tent cities and homeless camps"
(O'Regan 2016). BIDs "nurture a visible social stratification" (Zukin 1995, 36)
with large, high-income area BIDs ensuring the prosperity of their areas if the
city cannot fund improvements that make the prosperous BIDs stand in contrast to the impoverished city. BIDs' "'clean and safe' initiative increasingly render
downtowns as 'interdictory spaces', designed to exclude those adjudged to be
'out of place' and whose class and cultural habitus may diverge from developers
and their target consumers" (Flusty, cited in MacLeod 2011, 2646). The BIDs
reclaim public spaces to make them safe for suburban shoppers and those who
would have abandoned the city because of fears regarding safety. One response
to the BIDs has been a legal challenge. The Coalition for the Homeless sued a
powerful BID—the Grand Central Partnership (GCP)—for hiring the homeless
as workfare workers below minimum wage and failing to give them job training.
According to MacLeod, GCP's expulsions of the homeless "eventually [led] to
revanchist beatings of homeless people" (2011, 2646).

   As the example of New York City shows, the provision of affordable housing, which represents one response to the homelessness crisis, has been inadequate, insufficient, and certainly not supported by health services, social services, or educational and job training programs. Proposed policies, such as those
sought by Fainstein, that argue for housing construction for "households with
the incomes below the median . . . with the goal of providing a decent home
and suitable living environment for everyone" would "require a considerable

increase in government involvement through regulation and some increase in public ownership. Thus, development of affordable housing could occur via the governmental, for-profit, and non-profit sectors, but would depend on generous public subsidy and intervention" (Fainstein 2010, 172, 175). Fainstein cites the examples of Amsterdam and London, cities in which the national governments take a more significant role in affordable housing development financing and where "planning and allocative authorities are much more decentralized than New York's, have considerable power and have the potential to bring nonelite interests to bear on the planning process" (182).

According to David Harvey, "State powers are invariably obsessed with maintaining order and erasing difference when both disorder and difference are fundamental to the creativity of urban life. . . . In many a city, the homeless find that struggle to be at the very core of their everyday lives. To them, the injustice is palpable while, to the rest of society, they are simply categorized as a public nuisance and administered their just deserts accordingly" (2006, 95). Through everyday life, acts, and practices, the homeless try to assert their right to the city and to public space in spite of urban surveillance, the privatization of urban spaces, and the rise of the luxury city.

* * *

All four constraints outlined here are indicative of the decline of social planning and limited redistributive programs for the poor. All are further suggestive of the increase in the gentrified and the luxury city and of the reshaping of the city for the safety of the affluent. All four constraints further indicate the rise of the walls and barriers and the increase in the creation of citadels (see Marcuse 2002), further affirming Sassen's (2001) thesis that global cities are divided between financial elites and low-paid service sector workers, but they also represent a strategic site for disempowered and discriminated minorities (Sassen 2013). It is nevertheless important to emphasize that even though cities have recently developed programs to advance racial equity exemplified in job training and the Government Alliance on Race and Equity national network initiatives, they have historically been complicit in producing racial inequalities and still remain sites of institutionalized racism and racial segregation (Tracey and Treuhaft 2017; Denton and Massey 1993). Urban policies that would challenge the four constraints outlined above can further be enhanced by expanding the notion of the right to the city—which, according to Lefebvre, is the right to alter the urban environment and which is actualized not only via social mobilization and political struggle but also through daily actions and practices that encompass a greater range of creative urban experiences and allow for the claims on the city and its public places on the part of the excluded, the disenfranchised, and, in particular for the context of this argument, the undocumented, asylum seekers, and refugees.

Barber recommends "reanimating democracy by devolving power to cities" (Barber 2017, 62) and finding ways to "globalize democracy or to democratize globalization" (65). A similar proposal by Harvey—"alternative democratic vehicles (other than the existing democracy of money power) such as popular assemblies need to be constructed if urban life is to be revitalized and reconstructed outside of dominant class relations" (Harvey 2013, 137). Social movements against mass incarceration and political struggles for immigrant rights in the United States have demonstrated possibilities for a new democratized urban polity. But what is further critical is the use of legal resources, capacities, and institutions as cities claim increasing sovereignty and the development of regional collaboration as cities become more engaged in sustainable policies.

"The sovereigns cannot govern, but they can still ensure a paucity of municipal resources and jurisdictional competence that makes it impossible for cities to act aggressively and collectively" (Barber 2017, 114). The starting point for cities is to prepare institutional and legal infrastructures and capacities to govern, especially given the rise of urban inequalities and declining federal resources. Indeed, in the concluding sections of his book on Philadelphia sanctuaries, Vitiello emphasizes that activists there "argued that American cities could not be true sanctuaries without affordable housing, good schools, safety, and decent wages for all" (2022, 223). A similar point is made by Maira (2019) regarding how sanctuary struggles ought to be seen as a component of broader anti-capitalist activist strategies and how the right to housing in gentrifying cities should be seen as one aspect of this struggle (153).

Cities must defend their sovereignty when the parochial state denies the universal rights guaranteed by international law with which urban rights are in accord (Barber 2017, 117). Harvey's proposal goes further in asking for a fundamental restructuring of the state: "The right to the city has to be construed not as a right to that which exists, but as a right to rebuild and recreate the city as a socialist body politic in a completely different image—one that eradicates poverty and social inequality, and one that heals the wounds of disastrous environmental degradation" (2013, 138).

This chapter has probed the scope for an increase in de facto already claimed city sovereignty, especially in the face of a hostile sovereign, as has been the case in the United States, where cities such as San Francisco have become rebel cities suing the federal government to prevent defunding due to their sanctuary status. Current legal literature on "urban commons" and "city power" needs a stronger normative lens and better conceptualization of urban inequality, redistribution, and publicness. Legal rules in the United States limit cities' resources and exercise of control and are insufficiently responsive to urban conditions; Democratic cities in Republican states also face threats of defunding and preemption. While the cities may not possess sufficient resources and cannot replace the roles and powers of nation-states, the chapter has argued that cities are not utilizing the powers and resources that they increasingly do possess to sufficiently and substantively address urban inequalities and to expand urban citizenship into a fundamentally inclusive category. Rebel cities' sanctuary policies represent one arena in which cities have begun to address substantive problems of social inequality. Sanctuary cities (within limits discussed above) show effective resistance to the hostile state and are suggestive of an inclusionary polity that would expand the scope of urban citizenship to encompass provision of a range of services, issuing of municipal IDs, and, to an extent, expansion of right to the city claims on the part of the undocumented, refugees, and asylum seekers. Sanctuary cities may aim to represent "sovereignty from below," but this sovereignty is limited by serious constraints that cities face, ranging from surveillance and the privatization of public spaces to the rise of the luxury city and an increase in homelessness. Rebel cities are similar to rebel governance in that they both seek to obtain the legitimacy that the state has failed to provide. This chapter has outlined the current conditions under which the legal, political, and symbolic sovereignty of cities stands a chance of advancing the prospects of some of the poorest and the most disenfranchised populations, showing the conditions under which resistance and protests on the part of sanctuary cities may thus be the weapons of the weakest.

In summary, the notion of sovereignty discussed in this chapter aligned with Darling's (2019, 244) conceptualization of the city as a "strategically important conduit for political change." Yet there are limitations of this vision as it relies as well on existing social infrastructure that supports the environment that makes sanctuary practices possible. Under President Trump, in January 2025 the Department of Homeland Security issued "Directives Expanding Law Enforcement and Ending the Abuse of Humanitarian Parole" to abolish the thwarting of ICE enforcement in or near "sensitive" locations such as schools and churches: This may break some of the bonds that hold the sanctuaries together. The executive action may be able to instill fear among migrants and their advocates but simply cannot abolish an expanded "strong democracy" (Barber 1984/2003) of grassroots sanctuary practices of dissent, empathy, neighborliness, mutual talk, and mutual listening for the purpose of creating common good, common claims, and common ends.

4

THE POLITICAL SPACES OF
SANCTUARY CITIES

As the previous chapter argued, sanctuary cities oppose a hostile state. This chapter, informed by fieldwork research in New York, will further analyze the character of cities as sanctuaries, focusing on grassroots sanctuary practices, in contrast to sanctuary ordinances discussed in the previous chapter.

An international comparative perspective can significantly contribute to understanding the nature and functioning of this opposition. This chapter engages first in a conversation with Bagelman's (2016) analysis of sanctuary cities in the United Kingdom to deepen our understanding of sanctuary and how it is used in the United States. Bagelman (2016) relies on the single case of Glasgow to delve into the meaning of sanctuary. Without contrasting evidence, her analysis tends to overemphasize the degree to which sanctuary cities only replicate state exclusions and fail to develop solidarities with undocumented people, asylum seekers, and refugees.

Bagelman's research nevertheless usefully highlights the ways in which sanctuary practices can be limited. Bagelman challenges the notion that sanctuary cities in the UK "offer a hospitable, even sacred, remedy" to "hostile, top-down explicitly punitive politics" (Bagelman 2016, 7). On the contrary, the author argues that sanctuary cities extend the unbearable wait asylum seekers endure—what she calls the "suspended state" (5). The suspended state highlights the experience of having to wait within the charitable zone of sanctuary. Immigrants are embroiled in a process akin to pseudo-incorporation into the margins of society that "too often means integrating into destitution or chronic dependency on charity" (5). Those who have had their refugee status rejected find themselves cast to the peripheries with no access to critical rights, benefits, and services.

The sanctuary movement in the UK has emerged from a grassroots group of faith-based communities; neither a government policy nor the nonprofit sector supported the movement. In neglecting that sanctuary practices have involved a wider range of supporters, Bagelman (2016) offers a limited vision of sanctuary. While the formal sanctuary *city* might not represent a challenge to the state, disruptive everyday *practices* of sanctuary (see Darling and Squire 2013) point to the presence and the actions of migrants and constitute a real sanctuary.

This chapter evaluates how far the argument can be taken that in fact sanctuary *practices* offer secular and religious responses antithetical to the hostile state. Secular and religious currents of the movement work in synergy but also show signs of tension. On the one hand, the movement has grown, diversified, and secularized while on the other, immigrants who require physical sanctuaries are still dependent on churches for support (fieldwork notes, July 2017–June 2018). Naturally, this response is fueled by local legal and political reactions (including, controversially, to abolish ICE) and the *solidarity* of pro-immigrant social movements with the undocumented, asylum seekers, and refugees.[1] Sanctuary practices shape an inclusive polity and foster resistance to state power in the United States.

This approach contrasts with the UK, where sanctuary cities "reproduce some dominant discourses that sanctuary practices overtly seek to counter" (Lippert and Rehaag 2013, 4). It is thus crucial to emphasize the distinction between the formal empty rhetoric of sanctuary and the sanctuary *practices* of political struggle. In the context of this research, this reflects the political activism of the sanctuary movement and the ways in which it attempts to involve citizens of New York in protecting the undocumented; during fieldwork, the New Sanctuary Coalition participants consistently emphasized the role of community mobilization of both citizens and the undocumented in preventing deportations.

I draw from participant-observation fieldwork in New York with the New Sanctuary Coalition (conducted between July 2017 and June 2018) to analyze the implications of creating and pursuing sanctuary practices. The NSC works to prevent deportations and, as noted, includes one thousand volunteers who accompany immigrants to court and ICE check-in appointments and provide accompaniments, bond funds, and a weekly community meeting referred to as the Assembly (fieldwork notes, August 10, 2017). One of the key activities of the NSC that demonstrates the scope of the organization's activities is the legal clinic. As one volunteer described, "In the legal clinic, we help people who have someone in detention, negotiate legal fees and reveal unfair legal practices, we assist family reunification, help victims of crimes. We can stop or slow down the deportation process. We don't just support the undocumented; we keep the system accountable. The judges know us, ICE knows us. They fear us. They have

blocked us [from accompaniments], but we will keep going. We show up to doc-
tors' appointments, to family court, to lawyers' appointments, to Varick Street"
(fieldwork notes, August 10, 2017).

Fieldwork results show the effectiveness of the NSC accompaniment program
strategy. Numerous observed cases resulted in the slowing down of the deportation process. The presence of the mostly native-born and overwhelmingly white,
female, and middle-age to senior New York residents was critical for the success
of cases. They strongly supported undocumented Friends through their, at times,
silent presence at ICE check-ins and case hearings and at times vocal advocacy at
the Assembly, vigils, and Jericho walks.

I built on this fieldwork to expand the definition of sanctuary practices. As
Nyers (2006, 37) points out, "Noncitizens are performing some of the most
vibrant and 'authentic' citizenship practices." The practice of Sanctuary Hood,
in particular, illustrates how noncitizens participate in the creation of political
spaces and the shaping of local politics. It is a space that confronts the norms of
the United States and its responsibility to address poverty and suffering (Cunningham, 1995, 210). This is *political space* in which the undocumented, refugees, and asylum seekers can claim the right to the city (Lefebvre 1996) and
where local government, in contrast to the state government, can exercise "city
power" (Schragger 2016) to achieve social equality and to institute more equitable criminal justice policies. Thus, while the sanctuary movement can be seen
as a set of actions against the repressive state, it might also serve as an impetus
for the improvement of local governance.

The rest of the chapter articulates the nature of sanctuary practices in relation to political space. I begin by locating the NSC in relation to the notion of
sanctuary cities. The criminalization of sanctuaries has created a need for protection that also affords a voice for those seeking protection. I argue that this voice
comes through a combination of factors that give rise to political spaces. Sanctuary Hood provides *publicness*, which, when combined with *legality*, *visibility*,
and *secularization*, provides the basis for advocating with the undocumented,
refugees, and asylum seekers. I examine legality and visibility as two aspects that
put the efforts of the NSC in relief. Finally, the foregoing discussion forms the
basis for my synthesis of political space in the context of sanctuary practices.

Criminalizing the Sanctuary

I join the call to "reimagine community and solidarity anew beginning from the
experience of displacement, statelessness and illegalization" (Vrasti and Dayal
2016, 1001). I examine the ways in which the experiences of displacement and

illegalization inform the sanctuary practices of the citizens and the undocumented with the NSC. According to Bauder (2016b, 252), "'illegalized' migrants exemplify marginal populations that are denied equal participation in urban life." However, social movements, political protests, and sanctuary cities are "mobilizing a layer of possibility of belonging" to at least an urban, if not national, polity (253).

The focus on cities as sites of political contestation offers a lens through which to understand the disjunction between the label, as applied to a city in the abstract, and practices. A true sanctuary city is a site of sanctuary *practices* and crucial networks of the undocumented, asylum seekers, and refugees. This chapter refers to all three categories of immigrants who have become victims of the policies of criminalization since the rise of the crimmigration enforcement regime (see Lasch 2016, 159–60).

Distancing the NSC in New York from the official New York City administration sanctuary proclamations, a volunteer with the NSC noted that the label of sanctuary means nothing; it is merely a brand. The city claims it will not detain refugees (based on their status), but by the very criminalization of the simplest infraction (such as jumping turnstiles; see also Dowling and Inda 2013, 13), the city has tools to target individuals for deportation based on their race, ethnicity, or linguistic skill on the grounds that they broke the law (fieldwork notes, July 12, 2017).[2] According to activists, this creates a contradiction between the meaning of sanctuary city and the grassroots practice that renders the label "sanctuary city" largely vacuous.

Following the formation of Immigration and Customs Enforcement (ICE), which replaced the Immigration and Naturalization Service (INS), "immigrants are legally constructed as more than outsiders: they are potentially dangerous criminals or terrorists threatening the US" (Yukich 2013b, 112). A contrasting example of a "model" immigrant is Amanda Morales Guerra, the Guatemalan mother who sought physical sanctuary in an episcopal church in Washington Heights, as discussed in chapter 2. A community organizer with the NSC not only argued that Guerra was a victim of *el sistema migratorio* (the immigration system) but also referred to the mother as *la victima del sistema legal* (a victim of the legal system) (fieldwork notes, August 17, 2017). This further conflicts with the evidence in Yukich (2013b), who points out, "Critics of victimhood language have argued, framing immigrants as victims also unintentionally depicts them as helpless, dependent people in need of charity; for this reason, over time, New Sanctuary activists increasingly avoided the language of victimhood" (312). Furthermore, these systems are deeply biased. Many forms of gender- and racial-based injustices are embedded in the United States legal system (Lasch 2016, 188–89).

A volunteer with the NSC corroborated these observations following a press conference in support of a physical sanctuary for Amanda Morales Guerra: "The

ICE does not go after the Irish in Woodlawn or the Eastern Europeans in Brighton Beach. They go after Latin American and African immigrants. They are sending people back into the countries where they are going to be murdered" (fieldwork notes, August 17, 2017).

The NSC's scrutiny of and resistance to the criminalizing technologies of the state demonstrate another facet of the criminalization of sanctuary seeking. For example, not only is the use of ankle bracelets demeaning to the wearer but it also enriches GPS-device companies such as Libre by Nexus (Miller 2017). At a community meeting of members, one of the Friends recounted how she had to wear ankle bracelets in detention. She did not understand why she had to wear them. The ankle bracelets caused pain, sleeplessness, stress, anxiety, trauma, and problems walking, she said. It was as if the "bracelets were in her head, as when she was not wearing them she would wake up and think about the bracelets. Bracaletos en la miente [bracelets on the mind] . . . una injusticia que hace la inmigración [an injustice that the Immigration does]" (fieldwork notes, July 6, 2017).

Even in the absence of infractions, the state implements strategies to track immigrants who have had any contact with law enforcement. A member of the NSC noted at a meeting, "Even though there are declarations of sanctuary city, [the state] gets around that by fingerprinting and sharing the prints across federal databases" (fieldwork notes, September 6, 2017), suggesting the limits of resistance of sanctuary practices.

Creating Sanctuaries

An NSC organizer explained that there are three levels of sanctuary: "(1) the public declaration that we stand in solidarity with the immigrants, (2) channeling some of the resources towards sanctuary (participation in accompaniments, uses of church space for the events), and (3) physical sanctuary. We need every single level. We are never harboring or concealing people—this is a public campaign. We are giving visibility to the plight of the people—there are no mechanisms in the immigration [system] for the justice that we need" (fieldwork notes, September 6, 2017).

Physical sanctuary is a complex system that includes security, food, childcare, social activities, legal aid, building preparation, medical and social services, strategies and outreach, and the press (fieldwork notes, August 31, 2017). The NSC wants at once to emphasize the publicness and visibility of their campaign and stress the sanctuary practices that go beyond the provision of mere physical sanctuary, which is commonly the focus of the media. Detailing the case of Liliana, who was granted deferred action and eventually green-card status after claiming sanctuary for three years, Houston and Morse (2017) emphasize that her visibility followed a prescribed script (40). Even as Houston and Morse (2017) detail the downplaying of sanctuary claimants' examples—Arturo Armando Hernández García's felony charge, which resulted in a not guilty verdict; Rosa Robles Loreto's minor traffic violation; or Jose Juan Federico Moreno's aggravated DUI—and place the emphasis on the heterosexual, married, parent, and so on, and status or membership in the community and the church, these examples are not the ones that fill the media, as Lasch (2016) discusses.

Furthermore, the NSC has created a project called the Sanctuary Hood (*el barrio sanctuario*). According to a lawyer who works for the coalition, Sanctuary Hood is coming from people who live in the community. "It is about explicitly claiming public space and letting ICE know that it is not welcome. ICE uses military equipment—many are former soldiers from Iraq and Afghanistan. We want to let them know that no one wants to talk to them—no one wants to help them. This is inverting the panopticon—letting them know that they too are being watched" (fieldwork notes, interview, August 4, 2017). This contrasts with the practice of immigration panopticism "which eliminates zones in society where immigration status is invisible and irrelevant and puts large numbers of public and private actors—including law enforcement and criminal justice officials . . . in the position of monitoring and determining immigration status, identifying potential immigration law violators, collecting personal information from those individuals, and informing federal authorities" (Kalhan, cited in Cházaro 2016, 646).

The NSC was further developing a rapid response system (a hotline) in case of a possible ICE raid that would work on three levels:

1. Protecting immigrants in their houses / their workplaces / the street.
2. Partnering with Sanctuary Hoods to alert a local priest to open the church building in case of the need for an immediate physical sanctuary.
3. Informing the faith-based leaders to whom the immigrant granted a privacy waiver to accompany them to the processing center on Varick Street.

An immigrant facing an ICE raid has numerous options. These include appointing a guardian for their children, connecting with organizers to mobilize the community, working with a religious leader, and engaging a recorder to document and investigate ICE. The NSC advises these immigrants on best practices—for example, remaining silent, refraining from signing documents such as the I-407 form for rapid deportation, not opening the door, and not lying if asked any questions. The New Sanctuary Coalition distributes flyers entitled "Beyond Your Rights" to businesses and houses of worship. NSC volunteers make it clear that the Sanctuary Hood works only if the community gets involved. The involvement of United States citizens is the key.

There are different levels of sanctuary. One example is to offer a safe physical space for the person when confronted by ICE. A person can say, "I know I can go in and be accepted. It could be an LGBTQ community member or a person of color. If a business becomes a sanctuary space, if ICE tries to detain them, the business can close the door and ask for a warrant" (fieldwork notes, July 12, 2017).

This can be compared to sanctuary practices in other cities. In one case, sanctuary activists were able to drive ICE agents away during an attempted raid (Vitiello 2022, 222) in Philadelphia. Also, in South Philadelphia, Juntos, an immigrant rights organization, blocked ICE vans from exiting local offices and protested plans to detain undocumented migrant children (Vitiello 2022, 222).

Anton Flores-Maisonet, whose Casa Alterna, a hospitality house, offers sanctuary and accompaniment in Lumpkin, Georgia, sees sanctuary as "a place where a person can live free from the fear of government intrusion and forced removal," although he notes that Casa Alterna cannot in fact fully achieve that goal (Lambelet 2019, 163). Flores-Maisonet describes how Casa Alterna, along with the National Immigration Law Center and the Southern Center for Human Rights, brought a lawsuit against the city of LaGrange, Georgia, for requiring Social Security numbers for access to water, heat, and electricity, which disproportionately impacted Latino neighborhoods, resulting in a relocation of Latino immigrants to substandard housing with exploitative landlords. The lawsuit did not result in abolishing the policy but did press the city to unofficially change the practice and stop denying services if a neighbor refuses to provide a Social Security number and instituted instead a fine of $500 (164–65).

One of the youth volunteers, a member of Democratic Socialists of America (DSA), organized a sanctuary area in Bushwick and Ridgewood, diverse immigrant neighborhoods of Brooklyn, New York, that are increasingly gentrifying. "We set up a table, talked to businesses, and walked through the neighborhood distributing 'Beyond Your Rights' flyers. We made alliances with other organizations such as The Base, an anarchist group, Make the Road, and [others]. . . . We organized a church sanctuary within a local episcopal church. We contacted about 60–70 businesses and signed up for about 40. We were letting people know about the sanctuary space and what their rights are" (fieldwork notes, July 20, 2017).

As an organizer emphasized, "Sanctuary Hood should be in every spot, in every corner—that would make New York really a sanctuary city which at the moment it is not" (fieldwork notes, August 10, 2017). Another organizer noted, "Our goal is to extend sanctuary beyond churches, which are critical as sacred spaces. But we want bodegas, delis, places where people go, beauty salons, barber shops, to know what they can do to protect people" (fieldwork notes, August 30, 2017). One reason why business owners may be inclined toward sanctuary is demonstrated by Freeland's (2010, 500) evidence in the case of the LA sanctuary movement: "Los Angeles also illustrates why business owners and employers are increasingly involved in the pro-immigrant rights struggle, because undocumented immigrants in 2004 in Los Angeles represented more than a quarter of all workers in production, construction and service occupations" (500). As Villazor and Gulasekaram (2018) argue, "'sanctuary workplaces' seem to focus more on preventing hostile work environments in which employees get targeted, at times wrongly, by co-workers or customers because of their perceived undocumented status" (558).

According to the Sanctuary Hood flyers distributed at meetings, a local business could become a sanctuary hub by displaying the symbol of safety, having helpful resources, including "Beyond Your Rights" cards, and being able to close doors in case of an ICE raid and demanding a warrant. While fieldwork results are suggestive of the broadening of the movement to include the Sanctuary Hood effort, this effort would require resources that the NSC at the time of fieldwork did not have, including an active civic base in a variety of neighborhoods. Only five people participated in Sanctuary Hood in Corona, Queens (fieldwork notes, August 5, 2017), yet dozens of participants showed for the monthly Assembly at Judson Memorial Church in Greenwich Village (fieldwork notes, 2017–18), which, as Yukich (2013c) aptly describes, is characterized by "white, middle-class membership, and an anti-authoritarian tradition" (154). Decision-making is largely consensus based although also influenced by a pastor (Yukich 2013c, 154); the church has been active in LGBT rights and organized needle exchange programs, for example (Yukich 2013c, 39).

The symbolic power of the Sanctuary Hood is nevertheless significant. Sanctuary Hood suggests that sanctuary cities are not simplistic positive acts of protection against oppressive forms of state power. In contrast to Bagelman's (2016) assertions, they are legal and political sites of resistance against restrictive, parochial national policies. They are not only against the "deportation, detainment, and dispersal" regime of asylum (Bagelman 2016, 7) but also against an even more restrictive national government in the United States that, during the first Trump administration, entirely closed doors to refugees.

This argument relies on a new conceptualization of the city—a site of citizenship and rights claiming (Isin 2008). The city is a space of complexity and diversity in which noncitizen immigrants and citizens are both urban subjects shaping their new subjectivity and identity (Sassen 2013). Cities act as a "strategic frontier zone" (67) for marginalized people, for residents whose positions do not afford them entitlement to power and even robs them of power.

Urban spaces open the possibility to create new fronts of political contestation where those who traditionally lack power can carve out places within the city and make room for new political actors. Such actors could also petition the legal system to become more inclusive and equitable and could try to influence policymakers and local and state political representatives to offer support for sanctuary practices.

This is especially true in global cities where politics are necessarily transnational. This logic is captured in the chants of a crowd gathered to support Amanda Morales Guerra at a press conference: "!Aquí estamos y no nos vamos, y si hos echan, nos regresamos! [Here we are and we are not leaving, and if they make us leave, we will return!]" (fieldwork notes, August 17, 2017). And it is significant that "although the representative families profiled in the early days of the NSM had national origins from all over the world . . . , the people living in sanctuary since 2014 have predominantly identified as Latino/a" (Houston and Morse 2017, 38).

A community leader of the NSC asserted that sanctuary practices raise awareness and "change the way people feel," giving them a sense of a possibility that they will not be deported (fieldwork notes, August 30, 2017). This shapes the urban political subjectivity of sanctuary practice participants, most of whom appeared (and in some cases explicitly claimed to be) empowered by these efforts, despite the legal obstacles they may have faced. While the movement places an emphasis on individual immigrants' lives and their own sense of empowerment even in face of possible deportation, it also construes the undocumented, asylum seekers, and refugees who participate in sanctuary practices as more politically active, better organized groups.

The Sanctuary Hood effort suggests that the undocumented, asylum seekers, and refugees can become political actors and urban denizens claiming rights to the city. The claiming of *political spaces* of sanctuary could be seen as following four trajectories: (1) the movement toward *legality* (by challenging the government in court and by claiming "rights"); (2) *publicness* (through practices such as Sanctuary Hood); (3) *visibility* (by "coming out as undocumented" and increasing media exposure in seeking immigration policy reform—for example, the Dream Act or public reemphasis by Democratic mayors on maintaining sanctuary city policies); and (4) *secularization* (by the broadening of sanctuary sites beyond houses of worship and of the coalition itself to include increasingly secular support, as in the Sanctuary Hood effort; this thus goes beyond Houston and Lawrence-Weilmann's (2016) emphasis on the secularization of sanctuary related to the municipal legislations claiming sanctuary cities as a part of the political practices of sanctuary [102]). And these findings also contrast with Yukich's (2013c, 121) evidence citing a Protestant minister involved in the sanctuary movement calling for the language of the movement to remain religious and to "insert ourselves above politics, morally." Yukich (2013c) in fact finds that political activism has been seen as a form of religious practice and even religious duty by faith-based leaders (125, 127), citing the intertwining of religion and politics by Rev. Donna Sharper of New York's Judson Memorial Church and noting justice as an expression of Judaism by a rabbi affiliated with the NSM (126–27). Fieldwork findings here instead point to the secularization and diversification of the movement, as already anticipated by Yukich's (2013c) conclusions, which note the transformation of the national NSM from a religious and political movement into "a loose network of local coalitions with primarily political targets" (207) with the coalition becoming even more political by 2011 (209). The findings here attribute the NSC's capacity to attract participation of the crucial group of actors—"immigrants themselves" (Yukich 2013c, 141)—precisely to the increasing politicization of the movement.

But these four trajectories also expose the limitations of the movement. On the one hand, the emphasis on legal challenges faces the obstacle of restrictive immigration law and places the emphasis on individual cases. Public efforts, such as Sanctuary Hood, must confront insufficient resources and civic infrastructure. Visibility places in the foreground the faces of the Dreamers and relies on selective media coverage, although examples of grassroots documentary filmmaking (e.g., André Daughtry's film *New Sanctuary*) represent another form of viable resistance. Secularization is, however, indicative of the increasing strength of the movement to resist pressures of religious organizations to select "worthy" cases to support—yet support of churches still appears critical in cases of physical sanctuaries, as noted in chapter 2.

Legality and Visibility of Sanctuary Practices

Sanctuary practices represent a realm of urban law and do not exist outside of it (see Czajka, 2013, 43). It should be noted that legal protections may be a weak tool to protect the undocumented. Advocates of the sanctuary movement in the United States have argued that the state has systematically acted against international and domestic laws concerning refugees.

According to Wild (2010), "The NSM also uses a textual reading of § 1324(a) to justify its legality, stating that the section only applies to those who kept silent about illegal immigrants' presence, rather than those who have reported the immigrants' presence but continue to shelter them" (998). Further, "Some have condemned the churches for being 'staging grounds for political works,' stating that their tax-exempt status forbids such action" (998). If this is proven correct, the tax-exempt status may be revoked (999). Wild (2010) advises further that the humanitarian exception be included in the 1324(a)'s harboring provisions (1013) and in provisions under CIRA 2007 that allow applications for legal residence after two years of residency.

Sanctuary providers should be seen as following their legal and moral obligations (Czajka 2013, 47). An NSC leader corroborated this view, arguing that (in the context of detainer requests) sanctuary is about maintaining the law and not opposing it (fieldwork notes, July 6, 2017). This conflicts with the view of the Immigration and Naturalization Service (INS, which preceded ICE) officials who asserted that the sanctuary movement was intentionally breaking the law (Czajka 2013).

In relation to the law, sanctuaries can be both nonconfrontational (legal representation) and disruptive—for example, physical sanctuary in particular, which could be an act of civil disobedience (although the latter was more typical of the 1980s sanctuary movement aiding the Central American refugees [see Yukich, 2013c]).

The question is how a city can become a true place of justice and solidarity with refugees and undocumented people and not become complicit in their invisibility. Discussing the case of Amanda Morales Guerra, an organizer with the NSC explained, "Amanda and those seeking refuge are not fleeing from justice—they are running toward justice. We are not harboring criminals. We are not hiding. We are defying a law that is unjust. Sanctuary is a symbol of civil disobedience—a movement of people fleeing El Salvador and Guatemala, defying a law that was sending them to certain death" (fieldwork notes, August 18, 2017).

As Houston and Morse (2017, 30) note, the US government rejected these asylum claims, and "despite the Refugee Act of 1980, which should have eliminated geographical and ideological biases in asylum acceptance, the US government classified many Central American applicants as economic migrants rather than possible refugees fleeing from a 'well founded fear' (UNHCR 2010, 14) of persecution." Houston and Morse (2017) cite the timing on March 24, 1982, of the declaration of sanctuary in Tucson and San Francisco, among other sites, as the second anniversary of the Salvadorian archbishop Oscar Romero's assassination by right-wing militia members, thus emphasizing the formation of sanctuary as a political act (30).

Offering advice via Skype to a group of Indonesians scheduled for deportation in New Hampshire, members of the NSC noted that they needed to engage in writing, which can take many forms.[3]

An organizer stated, "In 2010, one of our cofounders got detained and this was followed by waves of civil disobedience—every week a few people got arrested and in the end 150 people in total were arrested. Phones kept ringing, the fax machine jamming, they asked us to stop calling at which point we kept calling. They released the [cofounder of the coalition] from detention" (fieldwork notes, August 30, 2017); civil disobedience strategies will be discussed further in chapter 5.

Sanctuary Cities as Spaces of Politics

Sanctuary policies in the UK are complicit in the political invisibility of asylum seekers and conform more closely to historical conceptualizations of sanctuaries as spaces outside of politics, as Bagelman emphasizes. "Life inside sanctuary is conceived of as sacred, inviolable and pure not only from violence but also from movement and political agency. This spatial understanding of sanctuary as a place 'cut off' cements an image of those seeking sanctuary as similarly cut off. Accordingly, to be 'inside' a given sanctuary is also necessarily to be 'outside' the public or political realm" (Bagelman 2016, 54).

Lippert (2004) argues that there is some politics within traditional sanctuaries—extensive discussions with migrants on political tactics, for example. Nonetheless, sanctuary in the UK fosters a subtler form of politics. Sanctuary movements tend to avoid high-visibility campaigns (Squire 2011).

While the concealment and silencing of voices is present in the United States, they are not a matter of policy (at least not until the beginning of President Trump's second term in office). Disruptive sanctuary practices in the United States are more about the exposure of undocumented immigrants and their economic, cultural, and social contributions to the city. Yet in highlighting the economic contributions, it is important to note the Houston and Lawrence-Weilmann (2016) findings that criticize "the profound implications of neoliberalism in shaping and constraining the work of sanctuary legislation" (102) and argue that the values associated with neoliberal productivity shape sanctuary legislations in the United States (103). In sum, sanctuaries accentuate the *visibility* of political subjects and participants in social movements, despite the risks of visibility and possible deportation. This strategy highlights a type of sovereignty from the bottom that gives cities a critical role in democratic accountability.

Sanctuary cities in the United States are sites of contestation where protests and political activism advance claims to national belonging (see Bauder 2016b). Social movements and protests of the Trump regime displayed, for example, banners such as "great grandson of an 'illegal' immigrant" and "we are all Muslim now." It is important to note that this messaging preceded the first Trump administration and went beyond protest of his regime. For example, protesters in San Francisco in October 2015 carried banners saying, "Defend Immigrants" and "Keep SF a Sanctuary City—ICE Out!" (Preston 2016).

My fieldwork captured this dynamic well. The discontent with the federal administration's restrictive policies energized members of the NSC, more so than the inequalities that surrounded them in New York City. This is in spite of the perception that the local administration actions were incongruent with its sanctuary city proclamations.

Activists mobilize this kind of messaging to push for greater responsiveness to the needs of a population at the margins. The literature on sanctuary cities is mute on the subject of the limited resources that the cities are facing. Cities not only contend with vulnerable immigrant populations but they also have to address a rise in homelessness, as discussed in chapter 3. The question is what resources the sanctuary cities marshal in the face of limited resources and cutbacks in state and federal funding (see also Schragger 2016).

Urban resistance is more significant given the lack of resources for migrant settlement policies and the need for "a politics of distributional fairness" given that migrants experience inequality and poverty and often lack access to resources (Amin 2016, 793). Yet, it is the visibility of the struggle embedded in sanctuary practices, the activism of noncitizens, that often led to the expansion of critical social programs such as health care, state IDs, and access to education, for example (Nyers 2006; see also Bau 1994).

The vocal activism of sanctuary-based movements shows signs of rejecting what Bagelman (2016, 8) has termed, following Foucault, the "governmentalization of the state." This reflects the United States administration's desire to have a merit-based system of immigration, a "technology that incites those people 'seeking' asylum to become good aspirational citizens" (8). Bagelman (2016, 78) argues that this is precisely the case of sanctuaries in the UK.

In contrast, the sanctuary practices of the NSC, for example, do not require immigrants to better themselves and become productive citizens. The NSC's call for "open borders" summarizes their inclusive vision of immigration and citizenship (fieldwork notes, June 2, 2018; see also Paik 2020, 104). Consistent with Isin's (2017, 195) argument that the sanctuary movement is a platform where solidarity with noncitizens reshapes conceptions of citizenship and who can perform citizenship, these new acts of urban citizenship go beyond the mere symbolic acts of resistance to the exclusionary state practices.

As Sassen (2013, 69) has argued, "The challenges of incorporating the 'outsider' became the instruments for developing the civic in the best sense of the word. Responding to the claims of the excluded has had the effect of expanding the rights of the included. Conversely, restricting the rights of immigrants has led to a loss of rights of citizens." Sanctuaries, thus, according to Czajka, "not only usurp state sovereignty, but also challenge the state's definition of who and what counts as political, and who deserves or has the right to have rights" (cited in Isin 2017, 195). They become sites of performative citizenship on the part of the undocumented, asylum seekers, and refugees.

As Abou Farman (2017) has warned:

> To call sanctuary symbolic only is to minimize the lives and efforts of precisely those people—documented and undocumented—who have stood up under its banner, and had the courage and political vision to take real risks with on-the-ground activism that has had real effects for communities. . . . Sanctuary is not a symbol, it's a commitment.

Farman (2017) and Bauder (2016a) both argue that a sanctuary could be identified as a form of local sovereignty and could even be seen as a threat to national sovereignty, as discussed in chapter 3.

Sanctuary cities in the United States are more than just "'pockets' of sovereignty, where citizens assert their visions of justice and contact the state when it drifts too far from social realities" (Lippert and Rehaag 2013, 10). Lippert (2004, 547) suggests the term "sovereignty from below" to capture the capacity to create sovereign governmental spaces as means of resistance when the state fails or becomes overly distant. Sanctuary *practices* represent a response that rises up from the streets. Sanctuary *cities* themselves are suggestive of the strength of Democratic city councils and mayoral power opposing presidential executive orders, as well as of the local sanctuary movement organizing.

But this kind of sovereignty from below can in fact exist thanks to constitutional protections. Sanctuary city administrations in the United States base their policies on the Tenth and the Fourth Amendments, which protect the rights of individuals.[4] Sanctuary cities are thus examples of how the Constitution and limits on federal power can protect vulnerable minorities and noncitizens (Somin 2016). In effect, they create a space for a return to urban law (Sassen 2013, 69)— that is, laws that replace, supplement, or reinterpret the national law. Sovereignty as encapsulated in sanctuary practices and cities fit with the narrative of rebel cities that perform civil disobedience (Harvey, 2013), as discussed in chapter 3. More importantly, they attempt, at least in the United States, to evoke alternate forms of urban legality.[5]

What is new here is that the current sanctuary movement, which is accompanied by direct legal challenges to the state, is questioning the distinction between rights of the city (legal rights) and rights to the city (social rights) (cf. Isin 2008, 273). While "politicized groups of non-status migrants are enacting themselves as citizens even when the law does not recognize them as such" (Nyers 2010, 142), they are also seeking to alter the law and to establish a new urban law to recognize and protect them, as the above-noted efforts of the NSC suggest.

Discussing the case of Amanda Morales Guerra, a community leader with the New Sanctuary Coalition emphasized that she was a mother who needed food for her children. They continued, "[I hope] that we still have a country here to protect those who are suffering. Even if the doors are locked, there is still a process. . . . We believe that there are legal options. She needs to go into that *space* and fight." Amanda thanked her supporters, saying, "No lo hago solo para mis hijos pero para toda la comunidad [I don't do this for my children only but for the entire community]" (fieldwork notes, August 18, 2018).

Bagelman's (2016) critique neglects to emphasize that many cities lack resources to adequately address problems of work, housing, education, health, and social services for undocumented people, asylum seekers, and refugees. In fact, many cities play a more active role, as examples from the United States show, in refusing to comply with the statist exclusion and do not simply represent "fluid and diffuse assemblage of practices" (Bagelman 2016, 95). Sanctuaries are thus not sites "through which the state is produced" (96) but sites where the state sovereignty is contested and where exclusionary state practices are rejected.

In San Francisco, this refers to remaining within law and within the limits of municipal jurisdiction of a governmental sanctuary that protects an inclusive polity. In New York, this is evident in the legal and political strategies of the NSC. According to Isin (2017, 196), sanctuaries are an "inversion of borders: these struggles invert inside and outside in ways that make it difficult to maintain the myth of the borders of the state as a homogenous contained space."

Sanctuary cities challenge the distinction between the rights of the city and rights to the city. They represent embodiments of new rights and legal protections for undocumented people, asylum seekers, and refugees in the city. My research echoes Squire and Darling's (2013, 69) rejection and contestation of the term *refugees* as invoking victim status or subordination. While the state increasingly constitutes subjecthood as an oppressive category, the sanctuary city is a space for the political struggle for undocumented people, asylum seekers, and refugees. Yet this space is dependent on alliances with citizens and permanent residents who join in these struggles, including in the acts of civil disobedience that will be discussed in the following chapter.

This chapter explored the shared political space of grassroots sanctuary practices of citizens *and* noncitizens who contested exclusions on the part of both the state *and* the city. Central to the conceptualization of the political space of sanctuary was the key role of grassroots activism, a force of an expanded "strong democracy": Barber's (1984/2003) vision of a participatory democracy was here widened to include not just citizens but also noncitizens. The political space of sanctuary through practices such as assembly, community meetings, accompaniments, Sanctuary Hood, and so forth creates this common tapestry of sanctuary as a political practice of urban citizenship.

Part 3

RIGHTS AND JUSTICE

5

SANCTUARY, CIVIL DISOBEDIENCE, AND ACTS OF DENIZENSHIP

On July 23, 2018, Elin Ersson, a Swedish social work student and a refugee activist, boarded an Istanbul-bound plane in Gothenburg with the intentions of stopping the flight, which would have carried an Afghan man back to his home country, and preventing an impending deportation of another man, also from Afghanistan. Acting as "an individual, an activist, and a fellow human being" (Crouch 2018b), Ersson temporarily delayed the deportation process. Filming the protest, in which she stood up inside the plane until she and the Afghan man were safely removed from the flight, she stated, "I am doing what I can to save a person's life. As long as a person is standing up the pilot cannot take off. All I want to do is stop the deportation and then I will comply with the rules here. This is all perfectly legal and I have not committed a crime" (Crouch 2018a). In fact, Ersson faced up to six months in jail for violating aviation law, although she was in the end simply fined three thousand kronor.

The man whose deportation she was trying to prevent was deported several days later from Stockholm and the man who was removed from the Turkish Airlines flight along with Ersson, and who had been previously charged with assault, was eventually also deported from Sweden. Ersson wrote, "A delayed flight can offer the possibility for new information to be evaluated, a chance for family and friends to have a proper goodbye, and for the person being deported the time to prepare for a different life. One where school, hobbies and safety are replaced with possible persecution, loneliness and war" (Ersson 2018).[1] Ersson's act occurred in the aftermath of the introduction of restrictive and exclusionary policies that shattered Sweden's image of itself as an "exceptionalist" humanitarian state (Elsrud, Lundberg, and Söderman 2023, 3631). The shrinking of the Swedish welfare state from its responsibility to provide for asylum seekers, and the hostility of the legal system in Sweden, motivated a range of sanctuary actions (Elsrud, Lundberg, and Söderman 2023, 3637, 3640) such as Ersson's.

* * *

Cédric Herrou, whose olive farm lies in the Roya Valley by the French-Italian border, has been unapologetic about helping undocumented African migrants, mostly from Eritrea and Sudan, to obtain food, shelter, and aid in France. Herrou, initially facing up to five years in prison and a fine of thirty thousand Euros, told a group of about three hundred supporters in Nice that "if we have to break the law to help people, let's do it" (Agence France-Presse 2017). At one point, Herrou hosted a group of over sixty migrants and occupied a vacant property of National French Railways, facing charges of squatting on government property and aiding undocumented migrants, especially unaccompanied minors, supposedly protected by the French state but often illegally deported. "I am accused of being a smuggler from the era when there were borders, and people smuggled goods. Except they are not objects. And the prosecutor doesn't even understand that. For him I am [a] smuggler of goods." One of the men sheltered by Herrou explained,

> In Eritrea, there is always war. After grade eight, you cannot finish your education. You have to become a soldier. No university, no college. At seven years old, I went to Sudan with my mother. My father died in the War of Independence in Eritrea. After Sudan, after 11 years . . . we also had a very big problem. The police of Sudan caught the Eritrean guys and returned us to our country. After that, again in the jail. . . . No food. Some people died in the jail. No medicine. Some children also died in the jail. 417 people in the ship. The ship is very small. The motor for the ship stopped working, on the sea. Everybody says, 'Cry! Cry! To pray to God!' All the people say, 'This time we're dead.' But by the work of God. The big ship later on came and after that we all said to God, 'Thank you God! Thanks God! Thanks God!' Three days [before I was rescued] 1,400 people died in the sea. I have my friend in the sea. Before four days, this. From Ventimiglia [Italy] we came by foot. Four times [we were] caught by police. 'Return us! Return us!' The fifth time, coming by the road of the train. Almost 10 hours . . . we were very hungry. [Finally,] Cédric's friend is getting in the road of the train. (*Guardian* 2017)

According to the *Guardian*, residents of French villages near the Roya Valley (which has a history of radical activism) have sheltered hundreds of immigrants; ten residents have been arrested, and four awaited trials in 2017. After having received almost a full acquittal in 2017, receiving a suspended fine of three thousand Euros for transporting child refugees from Italy, Herrou told the supporters who gathered in front of the courthouse, "The courts . . . have confirmed the dehumanizing conditions, inflicted on people on French soil. My fellow citizens, rise up, and let us take possession of politics. A politics of the land, a politics of the people, a politics of co-citizens" (*Guardian* 2017). In June 2018, the French Constitutional Court ruled that the principle of fraternity protected Herrou from prosecution for aiding dozens of migrants (*France 24* 2018). A self-proclaimed critic of the anti-immigrant ideology of the French state, Herrou argued that he was simply denouncing the state's failings by striving to uphold human rights (cited in Boudou 2023, 3572). Here we can thus distinguish between Herrou's rhetoric of the critique of the state and a genuine concern for human rights of migrants in Herrou's actions. The latter in fact shifted from spontaneous human-itarian aid and hospitality to support involving administrative, legal, and job assistance to migrants shaping a repertoire of sanctuary actions that included fraternity, hospitality, and solidarity (Boudou 2023, 3567–568, 3575).

And in New York, the NSC engaged in a disruptive practice attempting to pre-vent the detention of the NSC community leader Ravi Ragbir. Ragbir's detention was a targeted action against an outspoken immigrant leader and an activist. His place in the public eye could not protect him against the ICE's stepped-up, aggres-sive efforts to deport him for a felony for which he had long served a sentence. The January 11, 2018, intervention in Lower Manhattan resulted in eighteen arrests including city council representatives Ydanis Rodriquez and Jumaane D. Williams (currently public advocate) (fieldwork notes, January 15, 2018; see also Hing 2018). NYPD arrested those participants because of their resistance in protecting Ragbir. The NSC organized a packed courtroom along with an additional full room and a Jericho Walk around the ICE offices at 26 Federal Plaza in Lower Manhattan. They argued that it was community power that allowed Ragbir's legal team to win a habeas corpus petition and secure his release from custody (on the basis of due process and avoidance of cruelty) (fieldwork notes, January 29, 2018). A federal appeals court ruled on April 25, 2019, that the First Amendment protected Ragbir from retaliation on the part of ICE, which targeted the activist for deportation based on the prominence of his "political speech," at the core of which are issues of "political change" (New Sanctuary Coalition 2019). As Pastor Kaji Dousa, cochair of New Sanctuary Coalition, plainly stated, "For asserting that immigrants have rights and are not disposable, ICE sought to silence Ravi and deport him" (New Sanctuary Coalition 2019). According to a New Sanctuary Coalition press release, Ragbir's political speech "[touches] upon an area in which the importance of First Amendment protections is at its zenith"; his "speech critical of the exercise of the State's power lies at the very center of the First Amendment" (New Sanctuary Coalition 2019). Moreover, according to the press release, while the district court

FIGURE 4.   Ravi Ragbir, whose T-shirt reads "migration is beautiful."
Source: Fieldwork July 20, 2017.

had denied Ragbir's earlier motion for a preliminary injunction and "dismissed the claims challenging his deportation under the First Amendment," his appeal to the Second Circuit found that the alleged retaliatory deportation by ICE was an "outrageous" act in violation of the First Amendment and that "the Constitution requires judicial review of these claims" (New Sanctuary Coalition 2019). Ragbir faced detention and possible deportation until January 19, 2025, when he received a presidential pardon; in a statement of clemency by President Biden, the White House recognized Ragbir as an award-winning immigrant community activist and the New Sanctuary Coalition (NSC) leader. It suffices to state here that political space claimed by Ragbir and the NSC expands to include critical social discourse of protection of immigrants, including a broader range of individuals who have come in contact with the criminal justice system, as discussed in chapter 2.

As Pepperman Taylor wrote in the introduction of Thoreau's *Civil Disobedience* (2016) regarding Thoreau's address to the abolitionists, the author makes an appeal to a form of heroic individualism akin to Ersson, Herrou, and Ragbir—"a demand that each of us stand up, independently, against the state" (24)—by withholding taxes, however, not through electoral politics or by petitioning the government. Thoreau argued that "we must 'transgress' unjust laws 'at once' and allow our lives to become a 'counter friction to stop the machine' of injustice" (24). What is absent in Thoreau thus is particularly relevant for the Ragbir case and the question of civil disobedience discussed in this book—the notion of petitioning the government and appealing to the courts, elected officials, and so on.

It is the downtrodden and the oppressed who feel injustice most palpably and who may have no other means of influence through the parliament, the party system, the unions, or the mass media but might resort to civil disobedience, wrote Jürgen Habermas (1985, 104). Regarding the nonviolent protest resistance to stop the installation of NATO rockets, Habermas (1985) stated, "From the statements with which I am familiar emerges more than a mere tactical commitment to nonviolence; there is, rather, a conviction that acts of protest—even if they represent calculated infringements of rules—can have only a symbolic character and may be executed solely with the intention of appealing to the capacity for reason and sense of justice of the majority in each particular case" (99). Thus, even though it's illegal, the aim of civil disobedience is to legitimize constitutional democracy—the constitutional state itself is not a finished product but "a susceptible, precarious undertaking which is constructed for the purpose of establishing or maintaining, renewing or broadening a legitimate legal order under constantly changing circumstance" (104). Civil disobedience in this sense serves as a guardian of the legitimacy of the constitutional state (105), as Herrou's and Ragbir's cases seem to suggest as well. A key notion here is also of civil disobedience not as an individual but as a collective act by what Arendt calls "organized minorities" and "masses" (Arendt, cited in Balibar 2014, 175–76) who challenge vertical authority to form a horizontal association, reenacting "the conditions of free consent to the authority of law . . . [thus not] weakening legality but reinforcing it" (Balibar 2014, 176).

John Rawls (2009) has deemed civil disobedience essentially an appeal to principles of justice. A public, moral, political action that rests on a political conviction, civil disobedience can be understood as a "a public, nonviolent, conscientious act contrary to law usually done with the intent to bring about a change in the policies or the laws of the government" (Rawls 2009, 247). As a civil act, it manifests respect for legal procedures as forms of punishment, including arrest, that following this act might be inevitable. Seeing civil disobedience as a nonviolent act, Rawls (2009) perceives it as a form of speech, an expression of conviction (248) that does not have a necessary connection to religious or pacifist principles but that these principles may nevertheless serve it as a motivation.

Rawls (2009) saw civil disobedience a "desperate act . . . undertaken as a last resort when standard democratic processes have failed" (249) in the case of not simply grave injustices with the law but refusals to correct them. Civil disobedience acts further as a stabilizing device, making the constitutional regime more just (250). Emphasizing the need for timing and tactical considerations, Rawls (2009) warns of harsh retaliation by the majority in cases where acts of civil disobedience do not resonate with the majority's sense of justice.

Rawls (2009) argues that civil disobedience is warranted in one of the three cases relevant to this discussion—that is, the case of the "violations of the equal liberties that define the common status of citizenship" (249). It is unclear what Rawls would argue in cases of struggles to avoid deportation or claim citizenship in another country on the part of refugees, asylum seekers, the undocumented, and exiles. But perhaps, according to Rawls's (2009) theory, we could interpret individual acts of civil disobedience as "rais[ing] the degree of justice throughout society" (250), addressing in this case "the denial of the other as equal" (250).

Drawing from Rawls, José Luis Rocha Gómez (2014) has called migration itself an act of civil disobedience in that migrants hope to halt the application of laws (e.g., to deport) and hope that they can regularize their status (188). Gómez (2014) terms hospitality toward the undocumented as confrontational, opposing the state rules—yet their disobedience appeals to a greater good. Hospitality toward migrants, akin to a street-level referendum, would recognize that they did not in fact disobey the law (189). Gómez (2014) does not see hospitality as a paternalistic form of tolerance (Moffette and Ridgley 2018, 152) but rather views it as political in nature (190), seeing the undocumented as appealing to the entire electorate (190), a way for the citizen community to challenge the state and forge openings of citizenship (191).

Genevieve Negrón-Gonzales (2015) describes the first known civil disobedience action on the part of undocumented youth following the signing into law of SB 1070 in Arizona: Five youth, four of them undocumented, engaged in a sit-in at Senator John McCain's Tucson office, demanding the passage of the Dream Act and the ceasing of the practices of criminalization of immigrants (Preston 2010). The action triggered arrests and deportation proceedings for the four who were undocumented. Lizbeth Mateo, one of the protesters, explained, "We wanted to take ownership of our lives and our future. We decided to do it inside his office, because outside—they would close the office, lock us out. We need to be in their space, it's a direct thing, that's the purpose of direct action. You need to be completely unafraid and face your biggest fear. Putting ourselves in front of a huge obstacle. Doing it face to face. Going to his office" (Negrón-Gonzales 2015, 97). Risking deportation yet questioning the legitimacy of political leadership and of the laws, "mobiliz[ing] from the place of disenfranchisement in order to indict the system that systematically engages in the production of their migrant 'illegality'" (98), the undocumented youth appealed in Rawls's terms to a greater sense of justice. And in Balibar's terms, following Arendt, this could be seen as a political demand to claim rights on behalf of those who do not have the "right to have rights" (Arendt, cited in Balibar 2014, 171). This political action enfranchised thus those who were excluded from the political community to demand and claim rights that they have been precisely deprived of. Similarly, based on their ten years of experience in the immigrant rights movement, Tania A. Unzueta Carrasco and Hinda Seif (2014) explain that civil disobedience actions do not amount to mere petitions to alter the immigration law and deportation policies, but are in essence about challenging the nation-state's use of fear and threats of criminalization and expulsion to control the population (296).

(During my own fieldwork, a small group of sanctuary volunteers, students, and scholars had a brief discussion with Angela Fernandez of Northern Manhattan Coalition for Immigrant Rights, who explained that "when we organize civil disobedience, we advise the undocumented and the green card holders not to participate because they face the risk of deportation. We also engage an attorney that will be there observing. The attorneys typically speak to the police department. All of this is somewhat coordinated. The police will ask you to stop doing what you are doing, they will then repeat that and then they will take you. An act of civil disobedience is powerful when it is linked to a political strategy" [fieldwork notes, August 31, 2017].)

* * *

The subject of this book concerns in part these acts of noncitizens and of citizens to protect noncitizens, with noncitizens and citizens who are *not* acting guided by presumably heroic personal individualistic principles, narrow political or religious convictions, or professional or personal ethical codes (even if these may serve as additional powerful motivators) but who are in essence deciding collectively, as Rawls (2009) has stated, "on the basis of the principles of justice that underlie and guide the interpretation of the constitution and in light of [their] sincere conviction as to how the principles should be applied in these circumstances" (252). Social and political justice is at stake in the case of asylum seekers, refugees, and the undocumented, and this book probes the extent to which it can be found in complex, diverse, and by many accounts profoundly unjust cities, where individuals arguably disturbed by a larger state injustice toward migrants have also formed groups, collectives, networks, and organizations to aid fellow denizens. *City denizens* is in fact perhaps a more appropriate term than *citizens* or *noncitizens*, as this book strives to contribute to a "conversation across borders" (Carens 2013, 5) and to the blurring of distinctions between those groups, advancing the rights to urban membership in cases where citizenship is not easily attainable. (As McNevin [2019] has pointed out, citizens versus noncitizens are categories easily manipulated to scapegoat certain groups to deflect broader structural injustice.) These struggles (to avoid deportation, to access public services, etc.) and actions of resistance (including civil disobedience) can further be seen as examples of, in Balibar's (2014) terms, "co-citizenship" as a new (grounded) cosmopolitan form of (in this case, urban but indeed also extra-urban) belonging (276).

In a normative sense, for the purposes of the questions of civic disobedience and the limits of urban citizenship examined in this chapter, sanctuary should be a practice of radical solidarity of citizens and noncitizens with the undocumented, asylum seekers, refugees, and also permanent residents who have become deportable—solidarity that ultimately blurs the distinctions between citizens and noncitizens. Sanctuary was defined in relationship to municipal ordinances in chapter 3 and in relationship to grassroots practices in chapter 4. More broadly, from a grassroots perspective, sanctuary can be seen as a practice of resistance and a means of interrupting institutionalized violence of the deportation regime—a system of protection born out of community struggle yet a part of a larger movement to protect the rights of immigrants and minorities (de Saussure et al. 2019).[2]

Lorentzen (1991, 3, 14) termed the Sanctuary Movement, in which women outnumbered men as participants, the largest North American civil disobedience movement since the 1960s (cited in Houston and Morse 2017, 31). Wild (2010) gives 1981 as the date for the movement's start, the year in which rancher Jim Corbett began clandestinely ferrying Salvadorians across the border to the church of Jim Fife, a Presbyterian minister (986). Corbett noted that despite the sanctuary city declarations, Salvadorians and Guatemalans lived in constant fear of deportation (cited in Vitiello 2022, 6). For Fife, sanctuary was a moral choice and a necessity (Yukich 2013c, 76). Along with the growing number of congregations that joined these efforts, they provided food and shelter and smuggled immigrants. As Houston and Morse (2017) detail, sanctuary activists not only helped to transport migrants across the US–Mexico border and to provide them physical sanctuary in churches, they also provided concrete material, legal, and religious assistance and spoke out against unjust US immigration policies (30). The movement's cofounders in the Southwest (Corbett and Fife in Tucson and Father Quinones in Nogales, Mexico) stressed religious rather than political activism and noted that "the religious groups respond according to refugees' needs rather than their own political alignments or usefulness" (Jim Corbett cited in Vitiello 2022, 30). By the early 1990s, Corbett saw sanctuary "as an enduring institution" (52) and an essential component of religious practice (53). In contrast, Yukich (2013c, 77) stresses that 1980s sanctuary movement activists had an explicit political agenda; Wild (2010, 986–87) notes that members of the early sanctuary movement also invoked the Underground Railroad and Jews fleeing Nazi persecution in assisting the refugees from El Salvador and Guatemala.

According to Golden and McConnell (1986, 3), more than seventy thousand US citizens broke federal immigration laws by aiding Central American refugees (cited in Freeland 2010, 488). "In 1986, eight members of the SM [Sanctuary Movement] were found guilty of 18 felonies, primarily of harboring and transporting illegal aliens, although they were subsequently acquitted, had sentences suspended, or given parole" (Freeland 2010, 494). This was accomplished by INS's covert Operation Sojourner in 1985, during which federal agents infiltrated sanctuary communities in Arizona, resulting in the Sanctuary Trials (Houston and Morse 2017, 31). None of the defendants went to prison, and none of the refugees who testified were deported, even if they did not win the right to asylum either (Vitiello 2022).

Wild (2010) finds in the origins of the movement members who supported political change as well as those whose motivations were tied to "theologically inspired humanism" (987). "They could not agree as to whether sanctuary work was a form of civil disobedience or a just cause that should not be criminalized" (987). Importantly, Wild (2010) reports that mainstream church congregations resisted the efforts of some of their more activist members to accept primarily immigrants with pressing claims of political persecution (987–88) but finds that some members of the early SM movement believed that they themselves were acting on the basis of the 1980s refugee law and were not violating federal laws by transporting immigrants to sites to apply for asylum. In *United States v. Aguilar*, the courts found these arguments unpersuasive and convicted eight out of eleven SM defendants for conspiring to smuggle Salvadorians and Guatemalans and for concealing, harboring, or transporting an "illegal" alien (990). While Freeland (2010) notes that "in 'Legal Justification for the Legal Status of Sanctuary Communities' composed by the Center for Human Rights and Constitutional Law, NSM [New Sanctuary Movement] activities are found to be safe from prosecution as long as their sanctuary actions are public," Wild argues that the publicness of NSM's efforts satisfies the "'knowing or in reckless disregard of the fact' portion of § 1324(a), which, given the Ninth Circuit's decision under the previous, harder-to-meet standard, would be grounds for conviction" (1005).

In the early 1990s, Guatemalans and El Salvadorians obtained special refugee status based on the amendments to the INA (Wild 2010, 990), but in 2005 the House of Representatives passed the Sensenbrenner-King Bill, or HR 4437, which "rendered illegal status a felony and sough to amend § 1324(a) so as to make it a felony to aid someone in 'knowing or in reckless disregard' of their illegal status" (Wild 2010, 992, 993–94; see also Yukich 2013c, 5), criminalizing "illegal" aliens and threatening to criminalize the work of churches to assist immigrants, which was prominently protested by Cardinal Roger Mahony, Catholic archbishop of Los Angeles in his letter to President Bush. Cardinal Mahony (later removed controversially from duties due to the cover-up of child abuse) "complained in a letter to President Bush that HR 4437 would 'require of all personnel of [c]hurches and of all non-profit organizations to verify the legal immigration status of every single person served through our various entities,'" which would force priests, ministers, and rabbis to become "quasi-immigration enforcement officials" (citied in Wild 2010, 994). The *New York Times* prominently endorsed Cardinal Mahony's solidarity with the undocumented and his call for civil disobedience on the grounds that private institutions such as churches should be able to assist and serve immigrants without asking questions about their status (*New York Times* 2006). Although they raised its public profile, the policies of the Sanctuary Movement had limited impact across the country, affecting mainly political outcomes in Los Angeles and parts of the West (Vitiello 2022, 6).

As Yukich (2013c, 6) notes, the sanctuary movement represented an expression of moral outrage of religious progressives. As Reverend Alexia Salvatierra, New Sanctuary Movement activist and executive director of Clergy and Laity United for Economic Justice (CLUE)—Los Angeles, stated, "as religious leaders, we respect the rule of law as a good and holy gift. However, there are those moments in history—from the Holocaust to Rosa Parks—when the only effective way to change an unjust law is to break it. We also understand that breaking the law should and does carry consequences, but the core biblical concept of sanctuary is a response to situations in which the proposed punishment is excessive" (cited in Freeland 2010, 494).

In comparing the SM to the NSM, Houston and Morse (2017) emphasize that both draw from liberation theology and share the ethos of "welcoming the stranger" and "loving thy neighbor" (28), which strengthens the commitment to both religious beliefs and the work of social justice (28–29). Houston and Morse (2017) correctly point out that paradoxically, even if these efforts advocate for the migrants, they nevertheless render them voiceless (29); they do so by portraying the Christian faith as extraordinary and migrants lives as ordinary, construing the migrants as "others" (29). Importantly, Yukich (2016c) finds that "the absence of immigrants in the New Sanctuary Movement hurt its capacity to reach its political goals, which immigrants are often more invested in and knowledgeable about, but it hurt its religious goals as well" (170).

This book has documented the change in the politicization of the movement in New York, which indeed managed to recruit immigrants and express true solidarity with diverse immigrant groups. This research also offered an alternate reading of the NSM in New York, which may contradict the findings in Yukich (2013c), albeit proceeding along the lines perhaps anticipated in the very conclusions of Yukich's research. Yukich saw the NSM as a multitarget social movement simultaneously attempting to change both political and religious institutions (3, 10) that identified in its inception "sanctuary and family values as the religious-political tools" around which the movement was organized (123); 61 percent of her informants interviewed in 2008 found politics and religion as integrated discourses (125). But in contrast to Yukich's findings that NSM was building on the legacy of faith-based social movements and was an explicitly religious response to the immigration debate (13–15) (as a pro-immigrant movement that tried to create an inclusive religious vision of a "radical utopia of love and justice" [49], to "change hearts and minds" of the members of religious communities [47], especially the dominance of the religious right [61], to create an inclusive religious culture [50])—this book located instead NSM as a politicized movement whose target is primarily the state, as discussed in chapters 2, 3, and 4.

Thus, in terms of the analysis of the NSC in New York, the fieldwork chapters (2, 4, and 6) of this book pick up exactly where the Yukich analysis left off, concluding that the NSM transitioned from a multi-target social movement into a single-target one, focused on altering state practices while still using religious framing (Yukich 2013c, 210). Yukich even gives the example of the Kansas City movement, which has been renamed the Immigrant Justice Advocacy Movement and no longer uses the label *sanctuary movement* (210). But where Yukich's work traced the examples of social movements that entailed religious and spiritual transformation, even conversion, not merely political change (see 213–14), this book focuses on the explicitly political aims, goals, strategies, and tactics of the movement and thus the transformation of sanctuary into a political movement.

Most broadly, the sanctuary movement involves a variety of private and public institutions, ranging from houses of worship to employers, universities, and community organizations, that have appeared as *political actors* presenting ethical claims and constitutional and statutory challenges, arguing on the basis of common law and so on, forming nodes in a network, and pressuring the state regarding immigration enforcement (Villazor and Gulasekaram 2018, 568, 569). This book focuses on one such set of nodes tied in particular to community and city-based activism. But where Bagelman (2016), studying the UK found replication of state exclusion, as discussed in chapter 4, this book locates new political subjectivities and sites of grassroots resistance in New York. Nonetheless, what this book shares with the work of many critics of sanctuary, including Bagelman, is a clear emphasis that municipal branding designations of city sanctuary cannot be seen as assurances of sanctuary policy. Still, municipal ordinances should not be dismissed given the significance of institutional openings that they might afford. Nevertheless, as Moffette and Ridgley (2018) rightly point out, while sanctuary policies in Canada raise awareness, they are largely symbolic, characterized by a lack of full commitment on the part of public officials and resistance by the police (150). And focusing on governance and urban policy, Humphris (2023) demonstrates how city government in Sheffield UK used the sanctuary label to reinforce and reproduce inequality and limit the radical potential of sanctuary.

Sanctuary can even be seen as an illusive, unsafe environment, "illegalizing" and criminalizing racialized people and extending the borders into the geography of the city, as in, for example, the disproportionate measures of state violence against Black people regardless of status in the Toronto Anti-Violence Intervention Strategy of policing low-income minority neighborhoods (Fakhrashrafi, Kirk, and Gilbert 2019, 85, 88). While the city is a key site of claims making, and of the unmaking of illegality, migrants in the city experience it also as a bordered environment when they attempt to access public and social services (89). But Fakhrashrafi, Kirk, and Gilbert (2019) also cite community victories such as Black Lives Matter Toronto's successful pressure to overhaul Ontario's Police Services Act in 2017 and to replace it with new legislation, the Safer Ontario Act, which allowed additional police oversight (96). And in describing the sanctuary rooted in solidarity, Moffette and Ridgley (2018) point to alliances among activists working on migrant justice, Indigenous sovereignty, anti-Black racism, and so on (152). This book shows attempts at building one such alliance in New York through the New Sanctuary Coalition's construct of an expanded sanctuary that would do away with the distinctions between deserving and undeserving immigrants and address the needs for sanctuary of the broader group of individuals affected by the criminal justice system, as discussed in chapter 2.

Wong, García, and Valdivia (2018) demonstrate that undocumented youth express higher levels of political efficacy and of, related to their argument, political participation than the literature on immigration and political incorporation predicts, engaging in online activism and participating in political rallies, demonstrations, and acts of civil disobedience. This is consistent with the findings of this book, joining the theories as well by Nyers (2006, 2010) and Sassen (2013), who view noncitizens as political actors enacting some of the most vibrant citizenship practices and perceiving global cities as strategic sites of new claims of immigrant groups, respectively.

Related to this point, consistent with the starting thoughts on civil disobedience, and perhaps in strongest contrast with the Yukich (2013c) research on New York's New Sanctuary Movement, is the subject of the risks of sanctuary. Carney et al. (2017) argue, for example, that the movement that represents a symbol and a set of practices, a form of resistance and a form of governance, ought to have remained "unnamed" (a form of "silent" sanctuary) to protect those willing to undertake the risks of sanctuary to provide refuge to migrants. These risks, as Yukich (2013c) details, pose a threat because those involved can be charged with aiding and abetting, congregations can be placed on the government watch list, members can be fined and arrested, the undocumented can be detained and deported, and so on (160–63). This researcher found instead in New York an increasing number of individuals who were willing to take the risks of sanctuary, who did not simply fear repression but calmly expected it from the first Trump regime, shaping political subjectivities of fearless "cityzens" engaging in lawful (not lawless) resistance, and claiming rights. This subject is further developed in chapter 6.

Legal Critics of Sanctuary

Kagan (2018) argues that the *sanctuary* label inadvertently hurts immigrants in Nevada, Texas, Arizona, and so on (391) and that rhetorical declarations reduce political support for pro-immigrant actions on state and local levels (392), given the Republican Party's counter mobilization (392) and given that the *sanctuary* label may contain exaggerated promises but no actual delivery, validating the rhetoric of the right (393). Instead, the focus on the stronger role of local law enforcement, local control, and immigration management might win the votes of those who oppose sanctuary and "illegal" immigration but support the rule of law and those who are concerned about demographic change in their communities (401). But as Kagan (2018) points out, the rhetoric against sanctuary cities inflates their capacities to shield supposedly dangerous immigrants (403) and includes racial and xenophobic overtones (402, 403), manipulating fears of community change. Kagan (2018) distinguishes between policies of noncooperation with federal authorities and sanctuary declarations that aim to directly challenge federal authority (396–97). He states that only individuals (not cities and states) can engage in civil disobedience (which is in fact not the case) and that older (individual) conceptions of civil disobedience have become bases for a rhetoric of municipal policies of sanctuary (398). Kagan errs, however, in not seriously taking into account the legal grounds of grassroots practices of sanctuary, which continue the traditions of civil disobedience and are distinct from, although not unrelated to, contexts of municipal sanctuaries and may involve, as is discussed in chapter 2, a range of local political actors. This leads Kagan to another error in ruling that sanctuary is a challenge to the rule of law (403), neglecting linkages between civil disobedience and constitutional democracy (per Habermas's argument, cited above, and the points regarding legality and sanctuary developed in chap. 4). But Kagan is correct in stating that polls show that the vocabulary of legality and "illegality" certainly drives voter responses to immigration polls (404). (But he also cites a Florida poll that shows support for Tampa as a sanctuary city by 61 percent to 39 percent and that opposes sanctuary city defunding [405].) And while controversial migration policies (such as caging of migrant children) lost popular support, data shows that revelation of the true impact of President Trump's immigration policies during his first term did not alter voting preferences (Wallace and Zepeda-Millán 2020).

Motomura (2018) in turn advances a pro-sanctuary argument based on five categories—(1) the anti-commandeering principle based on the Tenth Amendment and a closely related Spending Clause, used to oppose defunding of sanctuary cities and found persuasive by two federal courts of appeals and one federal district court; (2) states and localities having decision-making powers regarding resource allocation (including, for example, police powers), found persuasive by court decisions based on federalism-based arguments; (3) substantive limits on arrests and detention, based also on the Fourth Amendment; (4) principles of fairness, equity, and proportionality that "enlarge the state and local role in ways that make it less likely that intensive federal enforcement leads to removal" (451), which can be dismissed as policy disagreement; and (5) prevention of unlawful racial and ethnic discrimination addressing the history of long-standing racialized exclusion of immigrants, which in Motomura's view represents the substantive grounding of sanctuary arguments (460) and a crucial aspect of state preemption (469).

What is relevant to the discussion here is how the emphasis on discrimination safeguards the rule of law, yet these arguments also have to be expanded to include a broader range of noncitizens and citizens impacted by the criminal justice system, as discussed in chapter 2.

Undocumented immigrants, asylum seekers, refugees, and, importantly, legal permanent residents who have become deportable (Motomura 2018, 437) stand to benefit from sanctuary policies. The undocumented in particular, many of whom are immigrants of color, represent a marginalized, vulnerable, exploited population (see Motomura 2018, 546) who are legally liminal subjects. Importantly, while the term *legal liminality*, which includes "uncertainty about the scope of reprieve from banishment, a reliance on administrative grace to effectuate freedom from banishment, an obligation to pay one's way to prevent that banishment, experiences of heightened monitoring by governmental actors, and a related vulnerability to control, exclusion, and abuse by private actors," can be used to describe legally marginalized noncitizens, the term should also be expanded to include permanent residents in immigrant communities and a broader range of citizens who have come in contact with law enforcement (Chacón 2015, 709).

Legal sanctuary policies have included not just don't ask, don't police practices concerning street-level police actions and immigration status disclosure, but also policies limiting detention merely on the basis of detainers or warrants and limiting the release-date disclosure in non-public jails (Lai and Lasch 2018, 545). Lasch et al. (2018) have categorized these legal sanctuary policies regulating local-federal relationships as

> (1) barring investigations into immigration violations [e.g., 'don't police' policies]; (2) limiting compliance with ICE detainers and administrative warrants [thus often mandating judicial warrants or documentation of probable cause]; (3) limiting ICE's access to local jails [e.g.,

New York's Local Law 58 which limited ICE's access to Rikers Island in 2015]; (4) limiting disclosure of sensitive information [including citizenship and immigration status but also, according to the Santa Ana City Council, 'person's status as a victim of domestic abuse or sexual assault; status as a victim or witness to a crime generally . . . status as a recipient of public assistance; sexual orientation; biological sex or gender identity; or disability' (1748)]; and (5) declining to participate in joint operations. (Lasch et al. 2018, 1737)

Sanctuary cities' policies range from the provision of services to legal defense for immigrants in detention to police noncooperation with ICE (Kagan 2018, 393–94); legal understandings of sanctuary cities need to be distinguished from political rhetoric (395), and they are commonly based on anticommandeering arguments (395).

Importantly, sanctuary policies may or may not represent an affirmative intervention in federal enforcement but entail a form of noncooperation with ICE (Motomura 2018, 438–39), although differences between noninvolvement and affirmative intervention are significant both legally and politically. Sanctuary policies may also be focused on incorporation of ID cards, drivers' licences, resident college tuition rates, and so on (439–40). Motomura does not discuss voting in local school board elections, in which few undocumented participate, but they are nevertheless significant in increasingly segregated school systems; Motomura argues that policies focused both on integration and on noncooperation with ICE are consequential (442–43). While according to Motomura (2018), the label *sanctuary* does not offer complete insulation from federal enforcement, it does offer incomplete protection (442).

The important supposition here is aligned with conclusions regarding the municipal sanctuary ordinances—namely, an argument that they do not flout federal law (Lasch et al. 2018, 1773). What is new in this study is that this argument regarding the legality of sanctuary practices is advanced by looking precisely at grassroots practices, as Ragbir's legal case challenges suggest.

While immigration and criminal law could be seen as policing the boundaries of membership (Stumpf, cited in Lai and Lasch 2018, 571), the discussion will now turn to the subject of urban membership as a normatively expansive category.

Urban Denizenship and Solidarity

Most broadly, migration can be seen as a fundamental right to freedom of movement (Universal Declaration of the Rights of Man [1948)], cited in Balibar, 2014,

260). The role of the agency of migrants can be viewed through an aspirations-capabilities framework that, following Sen, can shape mobility rather than it merely being determined by the push-pull factors considered by either structuralist or neoclassical economic frameworks (de Hass 2021). In turn, urban citizenship, viewed as a post-national condition, needs to "contribute to overall democratic integration within and beyond nation-states" such as by extending the franchise to coresidents (including but not limited to immigrants), thus integrating mobile populations into common membership that could go beyond cities to include rural areas, small towns, and so on (Bauböck 2020). Urban citizenship would complement the national citizenship that governs institutions and creates laws (Bauböck 2020).

The limits of urban citizenship are clearer than its degree of expansion. Yet the key question is precisely how expansive urban citizenship can be for those at the margins of cities subjected to exploitation, eviction, discrimination, and everyday humiliation, and to what extent can it offer them sustenance and concrete strategies for not just mere endurance of urban life with its economics of exploitation, but also strategies that help them to be counted as political subjects with claims and substantive rights. (This movement includes obviously not merely migrants but a broader range of marginalized populations.)

Warren Magnusson's (2011) *Politics of Urbanism: Seeing Like a City* discusses globalized urbanism and the emergence of new forms of political authority and suggests that urbanism requires a way of being, of interacting with fellow urban denizens and dwellers, indeed "a way of relating to strangers" (23)—thus here, the assumption of tolerance present in canonical urban theory (Young 1990). Tolerating and overcoming differences, urban dwellers engage in the politics of deliberation, conciliation, and compromise (Magnusson 2011, 13, 16) in search of a common purpose, a socially beneficial collective action, and even "a community of some sort" (32, 26). The limitation of this theory of the shaping of a grounded urban cosmopolitan community is that it does not engage with the commodification of difference or other aspects of urban social, economic, and political inequality.

Seeing urbanism as governmentality and a system opposed to statism (Magnusson 2011, 24–25), Magnusson's political practices in the city are so expansive as to encompass "the various practices [that] work as political practices, whether or not there is an obviously political intent and whether or not there is contact with organizations that we have previously assigned to the domains of politics and government" (53). Sanctuary practices can be seen as political in this expansive sense—such as the acts of literally laying hands on the walls of the immigration court and uttering the names of deported migrants. (This will be discussed in chap. 6.)

Yet perhaps the most perceptive arguments that Magnusson makes are for an elastic sense of urban identity, challenging the notion that sovereignty would ever offer a resolution to collective and individual identity conflicts. Instead, the author echoes an idea similar to Sennett's (2023) that urban identities might move with less predictability from one identification to the other, that these identities may sometimes be at odds. In contrast, however, the dominant sovereign identities might not in fact be desirable or, for that matter, attainable to all (32). Participatory urban migrant identities as well as identities of citizens who engage in solidarity practices to benefit people on the move could be seen in this elastic, expansive sense, challenging the dominant statist conceptions of citizenship. And indeed, solidarity practices should be seen as building transformative grounded cosmopolitan identities that can be further mobilized into a political force (Bauder 2021a).

Acting on the basis of the domicile principle (rather than nationality; see Balibar,[3] cited in Nyers 2008, 138), cities would grant equal rights and participation in everyday enactments of urbanity (see Bauder 2021a, 3216). While researchers such as Magnusson and Bauder do not discuss cases of civil disobedience, the New York fieldwork discussed in this book found an increasing number of citizens willing to undertake the risks of participation in sanctuary practices against the hostile federal policies of the first Trump administration.

Yet researchers of right to the city should also expand their focus to how urban solidarity extends beyond municipal boundaries rather than seeing it solely within the context of a resistance to restrictive national policies of migration (Bauder 2021a). Harald Bauder's (2021a) call for a global solidarity network is concerned with how the experience of migrants in cities might foster solidarity across borders and how networks of solidarity connect migrants across geographical scales. In this view, grassroots solidarities reject the territorial configurations of the state that seek to control and limit migration, and this movement involves a multiplicity of identities in pursuit of common struggles. Also significant are institutional solidarities that involve strategic alliances with local government officials, municipal councilors, and administrations, as well as the infrastructures of solidarity: Mexico's Ciudades Solidarias, for example—a network of fifty cities that promotes migrant integration in collaboration with UNHCR (3216–17).

Bauder (2021b) explores further ambiguities in the concept of solidarity, stressing a range of philosophical departure points ranging from Hobbesian rational choice to serve common interest to Hume's notion of compassion (in this case driven by solidarity with migrants) to the Kantian notion of upholding social responsibility to achieve universal rights and to the Hegelian-Marxian perspective emphasizing liberation from political and economic oppression and seeing solidarity as reciprocity or "recognitive solidarity" (Bauder 2022, 64). As detailed in chapter 2, the fieldwork in New York found all the above approaches with mostly Humean compassionate solidarity, gesturing toward Kantian universal rights and, at times, toward abolitionist conceptions of sanctuary.

Importantly, this research joins the call for theorizing urban solidarity in non-Eurocentric ways (Bauder 2022, 110). Bauder thus details non-Enlightenment traditions of solidarity, which he divides into two categories—Solidarity as Loyalty among groups sharing common histories, collective memories, and political experiences and Indigenous Solidarities based on encounters with colonialization, which may involve struggles for decolonization and Indigenous rights (see Nail, Kamal, and Hussan 2010, cited in Bauder 2022, 97).

In an account that proposes the building of sanctuary city Vancouver from below, Harsha Walia (2014) similarly takes a position that a solidarity city must engage in social justice relations with Indigenous nations (see also Walia 2013, 38, 130) and draws from a historical example of the Musqueam, who harbored Chinese residents during the early twentieth-century race riots. Walia further describes sanctuary as a holistic bottom-up movement facilitating access to critical social and health care services as well as food and housing and rejecting the empty political rhetoric of sanctuary not rooted in actual practices of solidarity and mutual aid. Walia's critique of planning that caused the displacement of low-income residents, overwhelmingly Indigenous people and people of color, in the Downtown Eastside (DTES) neighborhood of Vancouver, casts doubt on the municipal declarations of sanctuary. This accords with this study's emphasis on grassroots sanctuary activism, as elaborated in chapters 2 and 4, and urban inequality and constraints of urban policy discussed in chapter 3.

Solidarities can, however, be embedded in specific national legislative frameworks, geopolitical circumstances, and migration rhetoric (Bauder 2021b) and can include the blurring of distinctions between bottom-up and top-down initiatives, often including collaboration with local government. This argument contrasts with the fieldwork evidence, which found a distinct emphasis on the grassroots as separate from the political representatives with whom the movement nevertheless also at times collaborated. But the distinction made in chapter 4 was crucial—the sanctuary city was in fact made crucially, if not solely, of grassroots practices.[4]

In his interviews with local activists and municipal officials and representatives in Freiburg, Berlin, and Zurich, Bauder found a range of meanings of solidarity including the need to build a common social foundation, a sense of compassion that motivates solidarity acts, solidarity as a crucial link to human rights, solidarity as care, and society building. Of relevance to this study is the emphasis on solidarity and political participation in democracy: As one of the informants told Bauder, this perspective refers not just to participation in political debates "who say, let's build another city and not just who gets what rights, but how we engage in politics together. So not only for whom, but also with whom." The term expands in the direction of practical solidarity to include "debates about what kind of city we want to live in" (2021b). Interestingly, the fieldwork in New York did not find aspects of this type of solidarity, which would be considered normatively close to the promise of urban sanctuary that this book hopes for. This is discussed further in the conclusion of the book. One example of how the term *sanctuary* can be politicized and turned into an instrument of policy is given in Bauder's interviews with Die Linke, whose political representative argued that the term *solidarity* framed politics: "At the last party congress, we passed a motion precisely on the concept of the city of solidarity, Berlin as Solidarity City, where we again reiterated: What does it mean for housing, which is one of the most burning problems here in the city; what does it mean for education; what does it mean for health; what does it mean for refugees, but not only; what does it mean for workers; what does it mean for single parents?" (Bauder 2021b, 882). Yet to the extent that this relies on participatory democracy in which migrants form an active part, this concept may encounter limitations. Namely, it is perhaps demanding to call for those to participate who endure excruciating and extended work hours and to stress the need for migrants to assert their claims when evidence shows that bordered spaces within cities appear precisely in the moments when migrants attempt to claim social citizenship (see Nyers 2008, 129). Indeed in Toronto, women were placed in detention after their non-status was revealed when trying to access social services (Padgham, cited in Nyers 2008, 130) or when they called 911 requesting emergency service (Nyers 2008, 130).

Bauder's contribution is nevertheless of particular importance because it finds that on the urban scale, solidarity as a concept may transcend the arena of the political left to engage with a broader political spectrum concerned with these sectoral urban policies, including the struggles to construct affordable housing, for example.

Bauder (2022) emphasizes from the outset the transformative potential of the urban approach to migrant accommodation and incorporation (ix), aligned with new municipalism and local democratization movements (12), a site of migrant political claims and articulation of struggles for social and political rights. While Bauder notes the role of institutional local state infrastructure as well, his conclusion that these infrastructures can be easily mobilized for the purpose of migrant inclusion (12) is perhaps too automatic, especially given the constraints of urban policy discussed in chapter 3. Similarly to Barber, Bauder also makes an argument for interdependence (3) and solidarity as a transformative practice (11), and posits cities as a tangible places for social interaction and engagement (3). Solidarity is the crucial force affecting political subjectivities (72), shaping working-class movement and solidarities (72), which are altered in contemporary conditions as working-class identities are divided racially, ethnically, and in terms of gender, citizenship status, and indeed politically, as they may not support progressive political parties' urban social policies. But Bauder sees solidarity as a bond between groups that recognize their differences but also interdependences (73) and need not involve symmetrical relationships but can bridge social hierarchies in a novel way so as to create new social relations and new political subjectivities (see also Nyers 2008 on solidarity with migrant groups different from one's own). Bauder sees solidarity as a "productive and transformative practice" (73), a practice with no end point, "a creative blueprint for a utopian world" (74). Solidarity arises from local interactions with migrants in specific sites, not just cities but also workplaces, camps, and rural communities (76) and shapes "place-based politics" (Featherstone 2012, 7, cited in Bauder 2022, 76).

Finally, Bauder (2022) identifies four characteristics of urban solidarity—legal (municipal legislative acts that may include official proclamations to protect migrants), discursive (narrative depicting local community as open to migrants), identity-formative (including right to the city and the city as participatory community), and scalar (domicile rule of belonging), showing how Barcelona's Refuge City initiative includes all four dimensions (100). Bauder cites the 2010 City Council's Anti-Rumour Strategy (Estratègia BCN Antirumores), which challenges migrant stereotypes, and Barcelona's Care Service Centre for Immigrants, Emigrants and Refugees (Servicio de Atención a Inmigrantes, Emigrantes y Refugiados; SAIER), which commenced in 2015 serving 11,370 people and serviced 19,001 in 2020 (100). Barcelona en Comú included a robust proposal to extend the right of migrants to participate in political life and also politicized the questions of migration, exposing, for example, unjust conditions faced by migrants in detention centers that the city was powerless to close (Hansen 2019, 5). Numerous other examples of local solidarity can be cited, including an offer of safe harbor in 2019 to a German NGO-operated ship carrying thirty-two migrants rescued off the coast of Libya by the mayors of Naples and Palermo, Italy, and cases of solidarity cities being willing to resettle refugees, as was true in Barcelona's offer to accept one hundred refugees from Athens in 2016 (Thouez 2020; Balmer 2019; on how rescue ships might be seen as sanctuaries, see Mourão Permoser and Bauböck 2023, 3553). In terms of global impact, examples range from the participation of US cities in a UN global migration conference that was boycotted by President Trump (Allen-Ebrahimian 2017), to the influence of cities on the platform language of the UN Global Compact for Safe, Orderly and Regular Migration regarding nondiscriminatory access to essential services—a clause that was initially resisted by member states, including Australia, members of the EU, and China (Thouez 2020). Identity-formative aspects were discussed extensively in chapter 2 in the context of the criminalization of migrants, and the book will return to these points in the context of right to the city participatory practices in chapter 6.

Abolitionist Strategies

This chapter cited thus far solidarity as the key framework to understand sanctuary (Bauder 2022); another approach is to see abolitionist strategies as a normative core of the sanctuary movement along with opposition to white supremacy and xenophobia (Paik 2017, 6, 18), a movement opposed to the exclusionary state, which has the potential to alter state conceptions of membership and affiliation (2, 141). Elsewhere, Paik, Ruiz, and Schreiber (2019) perceive sanctuary as an expansive archive of social movements addressing multiple subjugations (3); this is similar to the Sanctuary for All concept linking immigrant rights to a broader group of the marginalized and oppressed (Young 2019, 178).

In her critique of the state, Paik, for example, details how immigration raids create "orchestrated insecurity of vulnerable people" by instilling fear of deportation, pressing migrants to refrain from work, schools, and public spaces, disciplining migrants into "self-deportation" (Paik 2017, 13). Sanctuary policies can remedy these practices, yet the essential point to consider here is Paik's (2017) claim that sanctuary policies may on the surface appear inclusionary but truly argue that membership of migrants is provisional. Another fundamental duality in sanctuary policies is that on the one hand they challenge the neoliberal state and on the other rely on its local government structures (Paik 2020, 110–11). As Paik emphasizes, "Indeed, many of us benefit from the systems that have not only dislocated people through economic and military violence but that also criminalize and sweep away others for our supposed security. We are thus bound to the dislocated, criminalized, and discarded, and share a mutual accountability to build a different way forward" (140). This understated conceptualization of shared citizenship is crucial for the understanding of sanctuary in the urban environment, where sanctuary practices can merge with other abolitionist struggles of marginalized groups.

Paik (2017) also positions the fight against the criminalization of immigrants and the policing of immigrant communities at the core of sanctuary (14), as does this book, which discusses strategies to resist criminalization in chapter 2. By articulating human rights principles, sanctuary can rhetorically act to expand the notion of citizenship; however, while sanctuary does not have a mechanism of enforcement, it does build an argument based on "rightful presence" rather than legal status (17). This point will be further discussed in chapter 6. The key here is to connect sanctuary to struggles of oppressed groups (Paik 2020, 103), which involves parallel fronts against capitalist exploitation and forms of state violence (103).

While recognizing the limits of sanctuary, Paik (2020) calls for reliance on sanctuary as a transformative force (119) and a "critical mode of resistance that can connect an array of interlocking struggles for social justice" (112). This represents an abolitionist approach to sanctuary that fights not just against systemic oppression but for a shared liberation of oppressed groups (112) by building new institutions and creating new structures for an abolitionist democracy (W. E. B. Du Bois, cited in Paik 2020, 115) and for the dismantling the structures of oppression (Paik 2020, 116). Notwithstanding the urban policy constraints discussed in chapter 3, this book precisely evaluates the degrees to which complex urban environments hold the potential to serve as chief sites for these struggles.

The migratory aspect of sanctuary, which designates sanctuary as a planetary, mobile practice involving smaller acts of resistance and linked with broader social movements (Carney et al. 2017), could also be seen as a form of this abolitionist practice. These aspects further involve forms of concrete aid to migrants—Carney et al. (2017) cite, for example, "solidarity clinics, pharmacies, housing initiatives, food distribution networks, entrepreneurial ventures, art collectives, and job training programs" as a part of a sanctuary network. Carney at al. (2017) also propose the creation of the Global Sanctuary Collective, a social justice collaborative to promote inclusion and challenge current policies against the undocumented, refugees, minorities, and vulnerable groups.

Similarly to Paik (2017), Block (2023) sees sanctuaries as "unique and precarious types of liberated zones" that allow for the charting of "cartographies of . . . anti oppressive struggles" and cannot merely be seen as either the assertions of sovereignty against the state or governmentalized reassertions of state sovereignty (5, 21, 3–4). In Block's view, "sanctuary mobilizations entail the participation of those with, and those without, citizenship rights by actors asserting rights-claims and enacting the pre-political foundation of the right to have rights, simultaneously targeting the state while prefiguratively enacting non-statist practices" (6–7).

In developing a theory of citizenship, Block is correct in identifying the balance that sanctuary mobilizations attempt to strike between their explicit politics of citizenship and rights-claims practices and their prefigurative, post-citizenship politics. Perhaps this is more of a tension-wrought relationship than a balance consciously performed by sanctuary participants, however. Chapter 6 will take up this theme in the context of right to the city claims.

The abolitionist project asks for whom sanctuary is being granted (understanding its exclusions and the pervasive impact of state "crimmigration" on the urban) and how radical can this concept in fact be as a way of fundamentally expanding the boundaries of citizenship and tackling racial and economic inequality (Loft 2021, 200). Or is it, as Loft asks, that sanctuaries are "providing just enough rights to disenfranchised laborers to keep the economy going" (Loft 2021, 201)?

Activists are lobbying for change in response to the neoliberal, exploitative, and hazardous conditions in some sectors that depend on migrant labor, such as construction. For example, "working centers" in Austin began in the last decade to engage in empowering migrants through pressing for pro-worker legislation, addressing social services, advocating for worker safety and health training, as well as through direct action that included pushing to prevent on-site hazards, addressing wage theft, and organizing leadership and education workshops (Torres et al. 2013, 152–53). And if in turn, as economic evidence shows, immigrants are in fact incorporating at rates similar to the earlier generations (Abramitzky and Boustan 2022), the question of social integration becomes even more significant. To the extent that the sanctuary movement can expand to forge substantive solidarities with other minority justice and urban social movements, it might be more successful in socially and politically incorporating migrants as claimants of rights.

In their examination of the Underground Railroad, Haro and Coles (2019) perceive the role of sanctuary politics as a form of enfranchised democracy with a radical potential rooted in "solidaristic power" (653). The transformative potential of sanctuary as a democratic force can further critique contemporary anti-democratic tendencies, which lead to animosity toward, and the exclusion of, the undocumented, asylum seekers, and refugees, for example. These groups should not be conflated, and this point is not unproblematic, as solidarity simply cannot be assumed: Recent evidence from Chicago (Stack 2025) points to the tensions between the Venezuelan asylum seekers and the undocumented Mexicans who perceive that the former have obtained benefits not available to the latter. The theory of an expanded strong "democracy" places tensions, conflict, and contestation in the foreground. As with Barber (1984/2003, 119, 135), the approach here is to view an expanded "strong democracy" as a transformative force that can alter existing conflicts through debate, discussion, and public action. If the stakes of refuge are not merely in the responsibilities of assistance but in the quest to expose and address the root causes of exile (Hamlin, cited in Madokoro 2024, 240), abolitionist sanctuary would tackle the roots of the exclusion of noncitizens whose participation and active deliberation could add similarly excluded perspectives on foreign policies, political conflicts, and environmental and economic conditions.

6

RIGHT TO THE CITY, RIGHT TO SANCTUARY

According to the Migration Policy Institute (Monin, Batalova, and Lai 2021), in the fiscal year 2019, the United States offered asylum status to about 46,500 individuals, "the highest level in decades, due in part to increased asylum applications and the accelerating pace of adjudications" (Monin, Batalova, and Lai 2021). However, during the fiscal year 2020, the United States resettled less than 12,000 refugees, in comparison to 70,000 to 80,000 resettled annually several years earlier and the 207,000 resettled in 1980, the year that marks the formal beginning of the US resettlement program (Monin, Batalova, and Lai 2021).

In fact, despite the change from a Trump to a Biden administration, conditions at the southern border of the United States continued to illustrate a lack of coherent and humane immigration policies and persistent inequalities faced by immigrants (see Sandoval, Romero, and Jordan 2021). Certainly, as Betts and Collier (2017) have convincingly argued, migrants deserve better than a broken refugee system, as has been discussed in chapter 2. However, they also deserve better than to be the subject of migration studies that have tended to treat them as objects of analysis rather than foregrounding the political subjectivities of migrants, as this chapter does with respect to sanctuary cities.

This chapter, then, evaluates again the evidence that sanctuary cities represent, which is, as Bagelman has argued, a suspended state, a type of governmentalizing process that traps asylum seekers into an "endless cycle of waiting and deferral" (Bagelman 2016, 39; see also Bagelman 2013) conferred by the state's "apparatus of control" (Bagelman 2016, 42) and regimes of abeyance. Even where migrants resist suspension, they are faced with punitive measures that reinforce delays and inactivity, rendering the city still a space of suspension—a place of deficient, incomplete, compromised application of refuge (Georgiou, Hall, and Dajani 2020) that perpetuates an unjust regime of exploited workers without legal status (Vitiello 2022, 10)—and migrants themselves apolitical and invisible presences (Laman, cited in Kuge 2019). Thus, researchers have questioned the extent to which immigrants in sanctuary cities realize appropriations of space and stake claims for the Lefebvrian right to the city (De Genova 2016, cited in Bagelman 2016) and have suggested the need for an alternate legal system rooted in the rightful presence (Vrasti and Dayal 2016; see also Darling and Squire 2013) that would expose the uneven relationship between the "host" and the "guest" (Squire and Darling 2013; see also Young 2010).

Drawing from Kafui Attoh (2011), this chapter applies the research lessons of the right to the city to sanctuary contexts. Attoh argues that the right to the city represents a critique of urban policy as well as a critique of the broader conception of citizenship and that it encompasses all three generations of rights in Jeremy Waldron's scheme: citizenship rights, socioeconomic entitlements, and minority rights. Particularly relevant for this research is the political conception of the right to the city. Following Dikeç (2001), Attoh (2011) argues that the right to the city is "coterminous with the rights of national citizenship" and that it is both a rebuke to restrictive conceptions of national citizenship and a form of active participation in political life, of lived civil society in the city. This theory envisions the right to the city as not a mere participatory right but, more significantly, an enabling right forged through political struggle. Hence, Attoh argues that the key right is not merely a right to urban space but rather to a politics of space that reconstitutes the city as "a space of politics." This chapter focuses also on a similar conception of political rights to the city in the case of the undocumented, asylum seekers, and refugees, who carve political spaces through active mechanisms of sanctuary practice detailed below. These forms of immigrant activism and resistance can further be seen as strides toward insurgent citizenship: challenging existing laws, policies, and institutions, shaping alternate forms of membership, and claiming rights (Holston and Appadurai 1999, cited in Leitner and Strunk 2014).

This research is based on fieldwork conducted over the period from July 2017 to June 2018 with the New Sanctuary Coalition (NSC) in New York—an interfaith coalition of congregations, organizations, and individuals engaged in a solidarity project assisting families and communities faced with detention and deportation. The primary purpose of the evidence presented here—to the contrary of the noted arguments on the suspended state of the city of refuge—is to suggest the emancipatory potential of sanctuary practices in the urban environment, in spite of the fact that in many aspects of their lives, the undocumented must remain in the shadows. Nevertheless, rejecting the binary either/or construct that would refute the literature that doubts the potential of the sanctuary, this research should instead be seen in dialogue with Bagelman's (2016) book *Sanctuary City: A Suspended State*, which provided the inspiration for this study, and which has been discussed extensively in the previous chapters.

Following Tilly (1998, cited in Castañeda 2017), this research emphasizes relational understandings of inequality that root socioeconomic status and life prospects in structural arrangements at the group level. Here we can offer only three illustrative examples. First, Castañeda (2017) documents the stigmatization of undocumented day laborers in Long Island, New York: these begin by becoming victims of wage theft and end by internalizing their roles as outsiders in their community. Second, Palmer (2017) argues that "Black immigrants live in the crosshairs of American-bred anti-Black racism and anti-immigrant sentiments" (120). Palmer calls for transformational solidarity within the Black Lives Matter and immigrant rights movements to address the inequalities of treatment (by the criminal justice system in particular) of Black undocumented immigrants. Finally, Hung's (2019) study of Eritrean squatters and their struggles for the right to public housing in Rome, Italy demonstrates how "sanctuary squats act as shelters for the persecuted from which to contest repressive governmental policies" (122).

These examples have in common the need to conceptualize active political subjectivities of migrants and their acts of citizenship that represent the instances in which subjects can contest inequalities and redefine marginality by rearticulating themselves as claimants (Maestri 2017, 6). As Zolberg and Woon (1999, cited in Castañeda 2017, 13) explain,

> immigrants do not only passively react to host decisions about structures of most relevance to them, but their views of how boundaries should be drawn, crossed, shifted, or blurred are part of the negotiations about boundaries. Though their voice might be muted as a function of their marginal position, the reinforcement of the rights of persons in liberal democracies, both as the result of internal political struggles and the spread of universal human rights, bolsters the legitimacy of the aspirations of immigrant newcomers; consequently, their views on issues involving their welfare carry greater weight in negotiations. (Zolberg and Woon 1999, cited in Castañeda 2017, 13)

This research documents how the NSC afforded an opportunity to the undocumented, asylum seekers, and refugees (as well as citizens working to support them), to express their voice regarding their marginalized position, a symptom of deeper structures of inequality, and to attempt to claim, through sanctuary practices, the right to a politics of urban space.

New York Policies and Sanctuary Practices of the NSC

Sanctuary cities were defined in chapter 3 as places where a local government or police department has passed a resolution, a city ordinance, an executive order, or a departmental policy expressly forbidding city or law enforcement officials from inquiring into immigration status and/or cooperation with the Department of Homeland Security's Immigration and Customs Enforcement Agency (ICE).[1] Cities might issue municipal identification cards or accept foreign identification documents that allow denizens to access services (see Bauder 2016a). Kuge (2019) stresses the distinction between the de facto and de jure population that represents a challenge for municipal service delivery but also an opportunity to develop urban capabilities. Rescaling of political power to cities opens opportunities for best practices for communal governing but also runs the risk of counter mobilization against cities and migrants (Kuge 2019). Regardless of status, sanctuary cities might pledge noncooperation with federal authorities and grant "access without fear" to municipal services (e.g., No One Is Illegal—Toronto, an interlinked and multilayered social movement and, in Walia's words [2013], a prefigurative humanist, anticapitalist movement working to undo border imperialism [15, 98]) (Vrasti and Dayal 2016, 996), yet these policies can be undermined by local authorities and law enforcement through the governance of security that has "speedily traversed legislative, jurisdictional and constitutional boundaries" (Hudson 2019, 96). In contrast, substantive and strategic sanctuary policies can view city ordinances as forming the city's identity and its liberal legacy, shaping places such as San Francisco that have "stood for protection of civil rights and . . . not been afraid to do the right thing even in the face of a legal challenge" (Villazor 2010, 597). These policies confer recognition and entail forms of inclusion of denizens as local citizens (Villazor 2010) and are motivated by local conceptions of justice rather than international human rights or cosmopolitan ideals (Varsanyi 2006 cited in Laman 2015). In this view, sanctuary cities can be seen as loci of local citizenship for undocumented immigrants, encouraging their participation in political life, their economic, social, and cultural contributions to the local community, their eligibility for services such as health care, education, social and mental health services, and police protection, and other privileges despite their status (see Villazor 2010). Importantly, as Bau (1994) has argued, ordinances such as San Francisco's Sanctuary City do not interfere with the enforcement of federal immigration law, and there are no reported instances of the physical prevention of the efforts of federal immigration enforcement by local officials (Bilke 2009). As Bauder (2016a) has emphasized, immigrants in sanctuary cities "remain vulnerable to detection, detention, and deportation by US federal immigration authorities" (177). While the authorities have a legal right to enter churches to seek immigrants, they have nevertheless typically not engaged in such actions because of the special moral and public status of religious institutions (Yukich 2013b).

Cities are vital for solving the refugee crisis and represent more than "the junction boxes for international interactions at the local level" (Clark 2008 cited in Bagelman 2016, 70–71) but constitute arenas of institutional intervention framed by powerful political rhetoric, as can be seen in the case of New York City. In August 2003, New York City passed Executive Order 41, which would prohibit city employees from disclosing confidential information (including immigration status) in all cases except when the individual is wanted for nonimmigration crimes or is a known terrorist (O'Brien, Collingwood, and El-Khatib 2017). Further, a 2014 New York City Council law limited the cooperation between police and corrections departments and federal enforcement authorities ("The departments would honor a hold request only from a federal judge, and only if the subject had been convicted of a violent or serious crime" [Preston 2016]). Former mayor de Blasio prominently advertised the country's largest municipal identification program, pledged not to offer the obtained information to the federal government, and vowed to fight widespread deportations, stressing that the city's free legal services were available to the undocumented (Medina and Bidgood 2016). Melissa Mark-Viverito, then the New York City Council speaker, stated that New York adopted policies that promoted inclusion by reducing the barriers to accessing city services: "One way that we do this in New York City is by ensuring that our city agencies do not require a status unless necessary to assess eligibility for public benefits or services. We're confident that all of our laws and policies fall squarely within the law and within our city's authority, and we're deeply committed to defending them. We will uphold the rule of law, but we will defy any attack by the president to force us to violate the constitutional rights of our residents" (Reynolds 2017).

New York's Eric Schneiderman, then the state attorney general, published guidance to law enforcement in January 2017 that stated that the federal government "cannot 'compel the States to enact or administer a federal regulatory program,' or compel state employees to participate in the administration of a federally enacted regulatory scheme'" (Wall Street Journal 2017). Finally, while congressional representative Alexandria Ocasio-Cortez called for the abolishing of ICE (Bseiso 2019), the New York State attorney general Letitia James released a press statement on April 28, 2020, as her critique of President Trump's threat to limit coronavirus funding to sanctuary cities and states, noting that "New York is proud of its status as a sanctuary state that welcomes and will fight to protect its immigrant residents—many of whom are fighting on the frontlines to battle the coronavirus" (New York State Attorney General 2020).

Yet, New York City lost a constitutional challenge in *City of New York v. United States*, in which it argued that sections of the US Code violated the Tenth Amendment of the Constitution "because they directly forbid state and local government entities from controlling the use of information regarding the immigration status of individuals obtained in the course of their official [duties]" (Bilke 2009, 176–77; see also Ridgley 2013, 227). This and the above examples expose the limits of local institutional sanctuary policies and practices. Thus, just city theories (Fainstein 2010; Barber 2017) err when they express too great a faith in mayoral leadership, citing, for example, how local policies made a difference through selective recognition and redistributive programs (Fainstein 2010) or how mayors ought to deliberate across borders (Barber 2017). New York examples in fact show strong rhetoric of recognition of the rights of groups (as in the noted De Blasio, James, or Mark-Viverito declarations) but weak redistributive strategies to address urban inequalities, graphically displayed in the failed attempts to address the problems of homelessness and public housing during the De Blasio administration. (Vitiello's [2022, 101] Philadelphia research similarly finds mayoral city declarations of sanctuary welcoming; however, "forms of sanctuary proved lacking, including protections from everyday violence and assistance in overcoming structural violence of persistent poverty and inequality.") Thus, the scale of urban inequalities and of lacking redistributive programs trumps the rhetoric on sanctuary cities amid the need to rebel against the hostile, dysfunctional sovereign that has defaulted on its responsibilities. The limits of city sovereignty are made apparent by the scale of inequalities heightened by federal disinvestment in poor neighborhoods and the lack of local investment in (given the pressing need for) supportive affordable housing and homeless services while increasing investment in megaprojects, luxury developments, and privatization of public spaces, as discussed in chapter 3.

It is not merely disobedient would-be sovereign cities that challenge the federal government, as it might appear from the political rhetoric by local leadership in the media, cited above; rather, this research argues that grassroots sanctuary practices constitute the real domain of sanctuary and not merely cities branded as sanctuaries.

It is thus necessary to redefine sanctuary from the grassroots right to the city perspective. The narrow definition of city sanctuary policy stated above appears insufficient when contrasted with a more expansive notion of sanctuary practice that the New Sanctuary Coalition (NSC) uses and that reflects responses to the regimes of violence and fear. First, the NSC details three scenarios under which an immigrant might seek sanctuary:

1. When ICE has told an immigrant who has a final order of deportation to report for deportation ("bag and baggage order") on a specified date, or
2. When ICE conducts a raid in a neighborhood, looking for a particular immigrant—one who has a final order of deportation, but has not been picked up because either ICE cannot find that person, or the person's family will not open the door to let ICE in to seize the person, or
3. When ICE is conducting raids in a particular neighborhood and an immigrant is afraid that he or she is, or could become, a target that ICE would detain. Many immigrants fear that they will be grabbed during a raid even if they are not a named target and may need a Sanctuary for a short time to calm down, to get accurate and up-to-date information, and to make plans (New Sanctuary Coalition 2016).

Furthermore, according to participants in an observed NSC community meeting, the notion of sanctuary extends even beyond this and encompasses the "values that the Sanctuary Hood community [intends to bring]," which include, among others:

> Do not harm, dignity, non-violence, self-determination, safety for one—safety for all, reciprocity, respeto a los derechos humanos [respect for human rights], ways of fighting fear, love and protect each other, liberation and autonomy, mutual empowerment, sovereignty [when this "value" was mentioned the community leader interrupted, saying, "We do not want sovereignty because of Arizona"[2]] . . . building blocks that are an end in and of itself, community space, practical things (clothing, washing), immigration is not a separate issue—policing, incarceration, gentrification, sanctuary is not a little box. (Fieldwork notes, August 23, 2017)

While several aspects of this expanded understanding of sanctuary might be useful here, this chapter will emphasize only the notions of "reciprocity, liberty, autonomy, and mutual empowerment" and their linkage with the emancipatory potential of sanctuary. In defining this potential, this research follows Mustafa Dikeç (2001) in arguing that spatial justice, right to the city, and right to difference come together to form a part of emancipatory politics. Thus, perhaps moments in which the sanctuary allows for at least a temporary semblance of the suppression of discrimination, domination, or repression could be seen as "moments of emancipation" (1794). Understood by NSC participants, sanctuary gestures precisely toward these moments, however fragile or uncertain they may appear at first glance—yet they are perhaps as tangible as "community space or practical things" (fieldwork notes, August 23, 2017). It could thus be argued that the right to the city in this context is less of a legal and more of a symbolic sociopolitical designation that might be claimed by noncitizens and social movements.[3]

The Right to Sanctuary City

Bauder (2016b) roots the right to the city in the notion of rightful presence (rather than property ownership, for example) and in the domicile principle of belonging to a territorial polity (Bauder 2016b). This enables the recognition of local citizen-subjecthood to be disabled on the national scale, requiring scale switching, which ensures local expressions of belonging (Allon 2013 cited in Bauder 2016b). Bagelman (2016) describes pro-sanctuary arguments citing transformative powers of the sanctuary as a set of "fluid, open-textured" (safe) welcoming practices (14) that offer a direct challenge to (violent) state practices. Disruptive everyday acts of the sanctuary (Lippert and Rehaag 2013) can shape a culture of hospitality, challenging restrictive immigration and asylum policies (Bagelman 2016). Millner (2013) has argued that the actions and claims of the sans-papiers, the success of demonstrations in Paris in February 1997, and the calls for a campaign of civil disobedience against the new Debré Law offer evidence for the "audibility of citizens' voices" in contrast to the notions of "an apparently silent migrant population" (67). Through claiming rights to the city via spatial practices, the struggles of sans-papiers further suggest that they can challenge predominant conceptions of their own identities (McNevin cited in Isin 2008). These struggles allow us to link migrant and urban justice movements (Vrasti and Dayal 2016) as sanctuary policies to render futile the distinctions between the citizen and noncitizen, "especially when the sovereign insistence on this distinction only serves to divide labor for the purposes of uneven accumulation across urban space" (998).

A criticism of sanctuaries based on evidence from the UK (including Bagelman's 2016 book) highlights the bland culture of hospitality that reinforces the distinctions and power relations between the "host" and "guest" and renders access to city services as insufficient and the normalization of undocumented status as avoidance of substantive immigration reform (Vrasti and Dayal 2016). The research evidence presented here instead suggests that sanctuary participants ought to be viewed as political subjectivities who claim rights that are seen as "illegitimate" or "misplaced" if viewed from a statist perspective (McNevin 2006, Nyers 2008 cited in Squire and Darling 2013). Critiquing notions of hospitality, Squire and Darling (2013) argue for an alternate conception of justice that would go beyond momentary politics and present a disruption in statist politics through political activism and the social action of sanctuary that challenges the unevenness between the "host" and the "guest" (Squire and Darling 2013). Sanctuary practices could certainly go further in providing the undocumented, refugees, and asylum seekers the capacity to shape the urban commons (Vrasti and Dayal 2016), thus realizing the Lefebvrian right to the city as a right to appropriate and alter the urban environment.

In "Right to the City," moreover, Lefebvre (1996) argues that social needs have an anthropological foundation. "Opposed and complementary, they include the need for security and opening, the need for certainty and adventure, that of organization of work and play, the needs for the predictable and the unpredictable, of similarity and difference, of isolation and encounter, exchange and investments, of independence (even solitude) and communication, of immediate and long-term prospects" (147; see also Mitchell 2003). If we recall Lewis Mumford's ([1938] 1981) notions of dehumanizing aspects of urban work, which make a human act similar to a machine, and if we can find in the postindustrial global cities of today forms of oppressive work environments and conditions for those on the bottom of the socioeconomic ladder—for example, the lowest-paid workers, many of whom are undocumented—the question of their social needs becomes even more significant. Cities should be planned in such a manner to satisfy a full range of social needs, especially those "not satisfied by those commercial and cultural infrastructures" (Lefebvre 1996, 147). Lefebvre concludes regarding the potential of the city, which is arguably shared with the undocumented, refugees, and asylum seekers:

> One only has to open one's eyes to understand the daily life of the one who runs from his dwelling to the station, near or far away, to the packed underground train, the office or the factory, to return the same way in the evening and come home to recuperate enough to start again the next day. The picture of this generalized misery would not go without a picture of "satisfaction" which hides it and becomes the means to elude it and break free from it. (Lefebvre 1996, 159)

Thus, the means to elude oppression and to struggle toward a just distribution might include, as Mitchell emphasizes, social action (protest) but also legal actions and forms of appropriation of space (Mitchell 2003). The right to the city, more broadly, according to Lefebvre, is dependent on a "renewed right to urban life" (Lefebvre 1996, 158), and it constitutes the urban as the "place of encounter, priority of use value" as, for Lefebvre, cities are importantly sites where dominant capitalist strategies and ideologies ought to be defeated (see also Coggin 2018; Marcuse 2012). Lefebvre (1996) sees the working class as the key agent for this social realization, and this is especially significant given that the working classes also comprise the undocumented (but also problematic given the rise in populist anti-immigrant movements). Yet, this solidarity project is insufficient and hinges upon Attoh's (2011) timely call to redefine democracy in substantive terms. Attoh argues that "within the radical openness of the right to the city concept, the right to the city can equally be a right to collective power and a right against unjust collective decisions" (677). Moreover, the concept should allow "for solidarity across political struggles, while at the same time focusing attention on the most basic condition of survivability" (678). The right to the sanctuary city is a struggle for the expansion of social citizenship for immigrants in the urban environment, the essential component of which is the attempt to expand social rights to encompass class and racial solidarity with minority groups.

Dikeç (2001) develops valuable notions of spatial dialectics of injustice (which also include, but do not overvalorize, just distribution) and uses the term égaliberté (equality-freedom), drawn from Étienne Balibar, in an attempt to seek linkage with emancipatory movements and to overcome perceived limitations of Iris Marion Young's notion of difference (1990). This is significant because the right to the city should be seen as active participation in political life—that is, an enabling process right forged through political struggle that constitutes the city as a space of politics (Dikeç 2001). While pointing to the global dynamics that affect migration, the key point here is that sanctuary cities shape the urban environment as the battleground for claiming group rights (Isin 1999 cited in Dikeç 2001) by articulating alternate ideas of membership based on urban residence rather than citizenship status (e.g., Varsanyi's [2006] idea of grounded citizenship, Holston and Appadurai's [1999] insurgent citizenship [cited in Leitner and Strunk 2014], Purcell's [2003] call for citizenship based on inhabitance [cited in Ridgley 2008], and substantive urban citizenship based on democratic participation [Brown and Kristiansen 2009]). Notably, Maestri's (2017) study of Roma migrants' claim-making struggles in Italy sees neither fully restrictive nor fully emancipatory enactments of citizenship within a campsite as "a political space where political subjectivities are also shaped from below, and that of an assemblage space, which emphasises the role of a plethora of state and non-state agencies" (14).

Urban sanctuaries can be viewed as sets of practices rather than fixed sites, yet they include concrete spaces that can at least temporarily attempt to provide safety within these territorially confined locations. Sanctuaries thus grant more fluid forms of hospitality (Bagelman 2016) based instead on "mobile solidarities," "which refers to the creation of collective political subjects through mobilisations that promote the physical movements of people as well as the multiple diversities that such movements bring about (social and economic as well as cultural and legal)" (Squire 2011, 292). In his case study of Sheffield, UK, Darling (cited in

Bagelman 2016) shows how place-based and fluid relational practices are inter-connected, expanding the prospect of the sanctuary. Darling draws on Jacobs' notion of "proximate diversity" to illuminate how sanctuary cities work through networks to create openness to diverse experiences, enabling a more open rela-tionality. Urban acts of sanctuary also allow for greater emphases on "heteroge-neity, multiplicity, fluidity, and indeterminateness" (Czajka 2013, 48) as immi-grants claim their right to the city and appropriate urban spaces. In this context, everyday routines can be laden with Lefebvrian potential, especially given Lefe-bvre's emphasis on use value and the sociopolitical potential of urbanity (see Darling and Squire 2013, 192, 201). The argument here is that the right to the city might allow immigrants who have lost their rights and, in Hannah Arendt's words (1951), "the right to have rights" (cited in Czajka 2013) to reclaim those rights in the urban environment. As noted above, this includes, for example, in the United States, rights to municipal IDs, rights to access services and education, rights to appropriate urban space, and rights to assembly and participation. This contests the view of migrants and asylum seekers as passive subjects (Bagelman 2016; see also Czajka 2013). Through acts of urban citizenship, sanctuary acts can challenge the monopoly of the state on sovereignty. It is in the city that the refugee can become "a rights bearing subject against the discourse of the state that deprives her of the right to have rights and be political" (Czajka 2013, 51); sanctuary practices within the urban environment can redefine the state monop-oly on the political.

The focus on sanctuary cities allows for further development of the concept of urban inequality in relation to the urban commons. Cities such as San Fran-cisco have proven that they are both legally and politically most powerful in the context of redevelopment and the shaping of the city as a place of lived experi-ence (Schragger 2016), as well as in cases of sanctuary policies, as discussed in chapter 1. Following Sassen's critique of the commodification and privatization of urban space (cited in Foster and Iaione 2022, 38) and pressing for intentional and deep engagement and empowerment of the most vulnerable groups in the cogovernance model (31), Foster and Iaione (2022) champion stewardship over resources, which can create a constructed, generative commons with different degrees of capacity. Foster and Iaione (2022) emphasize "that the built environ-ment constitutes a variety of potentially shareable and stewarded urban goods that can generate resources for urban residents lacking those resources" (41). When we take into consideration that cities are also sites of conflict and social exclusion (as discussed in chap. 3), we could argue for a new way of constructing the commons by taking into account the social, economic, cultural, and political contributions of the undocumented, refugees, and asylum seekers, contesting an exclusionary state.

If a critique of the concept of urban commons is related to the fact that it leaves too much space for private actors, seeing them as equal to public actors, as noted in chapter 3, the undocumented, refugees, and asylum seekers should contribute to making the urban commons public in a manner that would address the problems of social exclusion. This can be accomplished through a variety of collaborative projects that would involve the undocumented, refugees, and asylum seekers such as working centers, volunteering projects, right to housing alliances and neighborhood grassroots efforts, educational initiatives, minimum-wage-increase activist groups, community gardens, digital collaboratives, and art projects, in addition to protests and demonstrations. What is further crucial here is the capacity of local government to not, in fact, police the undocumented but to implement resettlement policies, increase wages and ameliorate working conditions, offer access to health care and social services, and promote social integration, among other practices (Mitnik and Halpern-Finnerty 2010). Local governments have mandated employment standards, regulated domestic worker activities (including by indicating employee rights and employer obligations), supported worker centers for day laborers, provided uninsured immigrants' access to health care, accepted matrículas consulares as valid forms of ID, offered municipal IDs, allowed noncitizen voting in local elections, and so on (see Mitnik and Halpern-Finnerty 2010). These could all be seen as examples of enfranchised "city power," the concept developed by Schragger (2016, discussed in chap. 3) in contrast to the notion of "local power," laden with NIMBYism—for example, the local land-use ordinances that prevent behaviors in public spaces and that have been used to police, even expel, immigrants from certain communities, as in the arrest of laborers playing soccer in Brewster, New York (Varsanyi 2010). Housing, trespassing, and antisolicitation ordinances can be used to constrain the undocumented person's right to the city (e.g., the right to claim public spaces) and the right to work and reside in a community.

The benefits of sanctuaries hinge upon seeing cities as sites of solidarity with strangers who shape new senses of urban belonging (see also Bagelman 2016). Although the notion of the stranger is itself problematic (according to Jacques Derrida, "If one determines the other as stranger, one is already introducing the circles of conditionality that are family, nation, state, and citizenship" [cited in Young 2010, 541]), the origins of the conceptualization of strangers can be found in the Bible (see Michels and Blaikie 2013), which aligns with faith-based sanctuaries. The conceptualization of strangers here follows Ash Amin's emphasis on negotiations of difference, as shared collaborative new identities, in the everyday life of multiethnic and multicultural cities (Amin 2013). Cities can be understood as sites of engagement and collaboration (Sennett 2012, cited in Amin 2013) with the stranger in everyday life. Sanctuary sites, especially faith-based sanctuaries, are associated with "hospitality towards strangers," as argued in the book of Leviticus in the third book of the Torah: "If a stranger sojourn with thee in your land, ye shall not vex him. But the stranger that dwelleth with you shall be unto you as one born among you, and thou shalt love him as thyself; for ye were strangers in the land of Egypt" (cited in Bagelman 2016, 79). Squire and Darling (2013) caution that the notion of hospitality risks reinforcing the distinction between established notions and relations of the "host" and the "guest"; cities can instead be seen as sites of struggle and claims, making for a space of refuge that is constantly being negotiated and contested (Young 2010). However, sanctuaries in this view could also carry transformative potential (Deleuze and Guattari, cited in Bagelman 2016). Bagelman (2016) notes the tremendous creativity of asylum seekers by citing the community café network and radio show and subsequently the Mapping Project—"these artistic interventions problematize the asylum seeker as both subject and supplicant, and challenge the ways in which asylum seekers are rendered emblems of victimhood" (17, 99). The argument here thus draws again from Bagelman's work while emphasizing caution regarding the conclusion that sanctuary cities are implicated in the production of state power by pacifying the asylum seeker and "de-fang[ing], smooth[ing] out and [easing] the seriousness of the problem" (38; see also De Genova, cited in Bagelman 2016). Bagelman's argument is, for the most part, limited to the condition of asylum seekers in the UK (although the author also includes Canadian examples), where the thesis appears more to reflect conditions in asylum intake centers, which at times resemble camplike oppression and imprisonment. This argument should be further evaluated in light of the "evidence of the exclusion of asylum seekers and irregular migrants from the remit of integration and cohesion" that "overlooks enactments of solidarity" (Squire 2011, 290, 292). The city-based movement in the UK is, however, more recent, and a distinction can be made between the more formal enactments of sanctuary and the disruptive everyday practices of sanctuaries (Darling and Squire 2013)—this distinction can be made based on the practices observed in the United States as well (e.g., the New York City fieldwork of July 2017–January 2018 with the New Sanctuary Coalition [NSC], discussed below). What is essential here is that sanctuaries are reinforced by "the proliferation of fear" (Bagelman 2016, 38) and indeed are a response to the state regimes of fear. However, the benefits of sanctuaries can outweigh their pacifying roles (see also Rotter's 2010 examples of Scotland, cited in Bagelman 2016, 38). While the "reprieve from marginalization" offered by sanctuary practices can, however, be merely "temporary," sanctuary practices can nevertheless represent important "acts of citizenship" (Vrasti and Dayal 2016, 1008, 1009), which can entail making rights claims and speaking out against abuses of power (see also Isin 2017) from the standpoint of a refugee, an undocumented immigrant, or an asylum seeker as an international citizen.

Legal traditions of sanctuaries can be traced to religious roots as far back as ancient Greece. In 392 CE, Theodosius enshrined sanctuaries into law, defining sanctuaries under specific church authority (Bagelman 2016). Moreover, in highlighting the linkages between religion and the city, Fustel (1864) has identified the city as a site of both civitas, a religious and political community, and urbs, a place of assembly, and especially a space of sanctuary (cited in Isin 2008). Thus, sanctuaries were originally seen as contained, enclosed, territorially fixed social practices. Sanctuary means a holy, sacred place—thus opposed to the profane and the secular (Bagelman 2016), but sanctuary can also be seen as a "safe haven, a protected space" whose boundaries are always policed (Dehaene 2008 cited in Bagelman 2016, 23). Rather than "a spatial form of protection, which implies 'escape to a location beyond the boundaries of society'" (Bagelman 2016, 24), contemporary sanctuary practices, which also involve unions such as the Teamsters and the AFL-CIO, which see unskilled labor as "prime organizing fodder" (Horowitz 2018), can be seen as sites of new political working-class subjectivities that can potentially expand the boundaries of citizenship.

While Bauder (2016a) has argued that sanctuary cities in the UK do not radically alter the city as a space of belonging and may be more concerned with the semblance of cosmopolitanism and inclusion while promoting urban neoliberal politics, there is also evidence that sanctuary cities intervene in the exclusionary discourse production of the notion of asylum seeker present in the media and in national politics, alter the meanings associated with the city and its capacity to shelter asylum seekers, and offer asylum seekers opportunities to become active participants in the urban community. In the United States, sanctuary cities have been incorporated into local government institutions, as noted above, moving away from their roots in faith-based organizing (Ridgley 2013). However, sanctuaries have also attempted to exert moral authority in cases where, in their view, the federal government failed (see also Cunningham 1995). In emphasizing the failures of the state to protect vulnerable populations or claiming that the state or the police have acted in an inhumane manner with refugees or the undocumented, communities and churches have "stepped into this role and, in doing so, claimed higher moral ground" (Michels and Blaikie 2013, 30).

This research suggests that sanctuary cities might be able to provide an emancipatory space of resilience where the undocumented, asylum seekers, and refugees can claim rights to the city and challenge spaces of exclusion. Projects such as Mapping the City can also demonstrate that only specific spaces in the city can be claimed as refuges (Young 2010, 536). Another example is Caleb Duarte's

Casitas voladoras, a sculptural performance project performed in 2008 in El Pital, Honduras, as well as New Temporary Sanctuary Movement, a public intervention art project performed in San Francisco, California, in the same year (see McIntire and Duarte 2019). Other examples of immigrant-inspired and human rights–inspired art include the Alto Arizona Art campaign (artists Ernesto Yerena, César Maxit, Melanie Cervantes, and Chandra L. Narcia) and political "border artists" (Marcos Ramirez, Ana Teresa Fernández, Ricardo Dominguez) (cited in Carney et al. 2017). Moreover, the "possibilities of refuge are struggled over not only through the formal, bureaucratic channels of the immigration system or the social services sector, but also through the intimate, lived practices of all residents of the city" (Young 2010, 557).

The sanctuary movement is "place-based" but not "place-bound" (Bagelman 2016, 48), a dense network moving toward welcoming policies and a political culture of solidarity (see also Bagelman 2016, 47). Following Doreen Massey (2005, 2007), "solidarity emerges through everyday grounded and imminent relations of the urban, which is less a physical place than a protean way of life" (Massey 2005, 2007 cited in Bagelman 2016, 47). The key point here is that cities have the potential to offer an inclusionary space for the undocumented, asylum seekers, and refugees via coalitions such as the NSC in New York, which assume social and political responsibility for this population through concrete sanctuary city practices. This opening up of urban space is in contrast to a sense of containment that these groups experience in their lives given the statist regime's proliferation of fear that governs their lives.

Fieldwork with the New Sanctuary Coalition: Results

I conducted participant observation fieldwork in New York with the New Sanctuary Coalition (NSC), selected because of its significance, prominence, and diligence with sanctuary work, from July 2017 to June 2018, to test whether the sanctuary movement represented urban resistance to exclusionary statist regimes and to examine the ways in which it might possibly contribute to the struggles for the right to the city. As discussed in chapter 2, during this period, I attended weekly community meetings known as the Assembly, vigils at the Varick Immigration Court, and Jericho Walks in front of 26 Federal Plaza and conducted dozens of unstructured interviews and discussions with the participants of the sanctuary movement (selected on the basis of the snowball sample). Observation included active participation as a volunteer assisting with meetings, sharing my own immigration story, helping the efforts of the coalition, participating in vigils and Jericho Walks, and sharing my previous research with the coalition. All meetings were conducted in English and in Spanish.

Immigrant Solidarity and Urban Residence

Fieldwork in New York showed disrupted distinctions between the host and the guest—between, that is, volunteers and Friends. Fieldwork findings further posed strong challenges to statist politics by placing an emphasis on the immigrant experience and immigrant solidarity and on the rejection of nationalism, of the first Trump political regime in the United States, and even of borders themselves.

When a Friend asked volunteers to explain their motivations for helping the NSC, one volunteer noted, "I left Iran in the 1980s, we crossed illegally. We were involved with the immigrant solidarity work, helping other Iranians, Kurds, then worked closely with Salvadorians in Washington. We are not obsessed with being an ideal American immigrant. When you eliminate nationalism, you have other values that take place such as solidarity. Borders become nonsensical. Sanctuary is something very familiar—a place where we can create a community beyond the bureaucratic norms [governing] what an immigrant should be doing" (fieldwork notes, July 20, 2017).

Another volunteer explained, "I grew up with the ideal of living in a US that is inclusive and equal, and if you were not hurting anyone you would not be punished for what you cannot control. Most of my ancestors were Jews and when I hear the way Donald Trump talks about immigrants, it reminds me of how dictators talked about us. I have a lot of immigrant Friends and I have come here to stop unfair treatment and deportations" (fieldwork notes, July 20, 2017).

The same linkage with immigrant history, and further with US and transnational civil rights movements, was claimed by Ydanis Rodriguez, City Council District 10 (Washington Heights, Inwood, Marble Hill) representative, and Congressmen Adriano Espaillat (New York's 13th congressional district) when discussing a physical sanctuary offered to Amanda Morales Guerra in Holyrood Church in Washington Heights. Rodriguez notes, "Northern Manhattan is giving permanent residence to Amanda. We have been built by immigrants—Jews, Irish, Italians, Germans, Dominicans, a real melting pot. We are a progressive community that stands for the values of America. Amanda came from Guatemala, the land of Rigoberta Menchu. We are all Guatemalan now" (fieldwork notes, August 18, 2017).

Espaillat claims, "Amanda is a common resident in this neighborhood. History has been stopped by the actions of common residents. Rosa Parks was just a common woman. Caesar Chavez was just a common Mexican. The actions we take today will be historic tomorrow. This is a city of dreams and aspirations of immigrants. . . . Germans, Jews, Dominicans, African Americans, Mexicans, Irish, all settled in Washington Heights. What better place than this one to shelter Amanda?" (fieldwork notes, August 18, 2017).

Fieldwork findings correspond to previous research that shows incorporation into the urban environment and new claims on the city as the key to migrant empowerment (see Yukich 2013b). The testimonies of the undocumented increasingly stress life in the receiving country and not political conditions in the country of origin (which was not the case with the Central American Sanctuary Movement) (see Caminero-Santangelo 2013).

Refuge as a Human Right

Another aspect of this rightful presence can be rooted in the idea of respect for all human beings. When an organizer with the NSC asked community members to engage in role-play to identify a problem and a solution and to act out a situation, one of the members of the community responded:

> The problem is that Latinos are not united. We don't care about each other. No hay respeto para el lugar, hay que respetar a todas las personas—respect for all of us, for the place where we are now, respect for what we do—para el lugar donde estamos ahora—respeto por lo que hago. Estoy parada acá. Necesito demostrar respeto para este sitio. . . . I am standing here. I need to show respect for this place. . . . Hablar con personas con palabras destructivas para dismenuirnos y hacer nos menos. Hablar usando palabras destructivas nos minimizan. [Talking with destructive words diminishes us.] No importa el color de la piel, si uno es indocumentado o no. [The color of the skin doesn't matter, whether one is undocumented or not.] Uno debe mostrar interés en la gente. [One has to show interest in the people.] ¿Como representamos un santuario? [How do we represent a sanctuary?] Respecto a la gente cuando nos acercamos a ellos [Respect for people when we approach them]. (Fieldwork notes, July 6, 2017)

Another Friend felt empowered by community participation: "It has made me stronger. I have become a community leader. It is also about meeting people who care about those who have no voice" (fieldwork notes, August 3, 2017).

The space that the NSC provides is, moreover, not just a physical space but a spiritual support space. The NSC held a meeting in which cartas de aliento, or support letters, were sent to a Friend's twenty-two-year-old son in detention in Texas.

He was imprisoned when crossing the border illegally. He refused to join a gang in Honduras, and the gang is after him. He signed his own deportation papers—he was manipulated into signing as he thought that he was signing a political asylum application (fieldwork notes, August 3, 2017).

One Friend explained the significance of cartas de aliento for people in detention: "Cuando recibí la carta de aliento [apoyo], supe que le importaba a alguien. [When I received a letter of support, I knew that I mattered to someone.] Me dio la fuerza para superar—una fuerza divina [It gave me force to overcome—a divine force]. . . . Alguien estaba pelando por mi (llorando) [Someone was fighting for me (crying)]. Fue un mensaje de mucha esperanza [It was a message of great hope]. Un mensaje también que este movimiento está creciendo [A message as well that this movement was growing]" (fieldwork notes, August 3, 2017).

A volunteer translated and explained further, "She thought that she had no value. She had lost her hope, has given up and then . . . like in a Gospel but it was real to her—somebody made her seem that she was important" (fieldwork notes, August 3, 2017).

As Rotter argues, sanctuaries rely on religious frameworks that are "drawn upon to make sense of the predicaments; activities were undertaken to shift attention away from the strain of waiting; and hope, which oriented them to the positive modality of waiting, was carefully fostered through social interaction" (Rotter cited in Bagelman 2016, 36). Bagelman argues that sanctuary cities in the UK in this manner "perhaps risk providing a sort of false hope, without affecting change" (2016, 36). This may, however, apply to sanctuaries that remain tied solely to religious organizations.

The Ethics of Sanctuary and Social Justice

Lippert (2004) notes a progressive secularization of the sanctuary city movement since the 1980s, as it has increasingly moved from churches toward secular institutions such as universities and entire cities. During my fieldwork in New York, I found that interfaith efforts dominated the New Sanctuary Coalition but also that secularization was acknowledged by the movement.

Fieldwork on July 13, 2017 involved a walk outside 26 Federal Plaza in which about fifty people participated and which included a number of faith-based leaders and members of the NSC. One of the members told the protesters, "I can't tell you how powerful the prayer is. I don't do this [only] for justice but because God was a political exile [and] because of the . . . persecution that people are facing around the world" (fieldwork notes, July 13, 2017).

A Lutheran priest participating in the Jericho Walk on August 3, 2017 (in which about ten people participated) outside of 26 Federal Plaza emphasized that it was not a "protest but a prayer—a beautiful spiritual [event]" (fieldwork notes, August 3, 2017); the priest emphasized that it was an interfaith effort (fieldwork notes, August 10, 2017). An Episcopal priest who participated in the accompaniment on July 13, 2017 noted, however, that the sanctuary movement was both faith-based and secular. She noted a number of middle-aged Jewish women as participants in the coalition.

"People do sanctuary work because it is an ethical thing to do" (fieldwork notes, July 13, 2017). Her church wanted to offer assistance to immigrants who came from Long Island who were farm workers, who paid $150 for a taxi ride to come to an ICE check-in at four a.m. "The church hopes to provide shelter" (fieldwork notes, July 13, 2017).

> At a meeting dedicated to the support of the Deferred Action for Childhood Arrivals (DACA) program, people held stretched out hands around the Dreamer (see fig. 5) and the organizer asked to rebuild our . . . society along the truths of justice, equality for all—we stand in solidarity with the Dreamers and their families. That they may feel those hands that care for them—in every step that we take, may we say that we owe them as we owe to our parents and grandparents, that we may be able to give our love to our new generation, that they know our care, our generosity. (Fieldwork notes, September 5–6, 2017)

The organizer completed the support words by saying, "May whoever God is to you [give you support]." At the next meeting it was emphasized that "we don't really care about faith. We care about justice" (fieldwork notes, September 5–6, 2017).

Interfaith leadership placed emphasis on social justice in other meetings as well. Following a local rabbi who offered support to Amanda Morales Guerra, a priest offering sanctuary to the mother stated at a press conference on August 17, 2017, "This is a people's movement. They lied to us when they said that the big division was going to be between people who believe in God and people who do not. The big division is and continues to be between those who practice justice and those who do not practice justice" (fieldwork notes, August 17, 2017).

Urban Enactments of Sanctuary, Inequality, and the Right to the City

A vigil in front of the Varick Immigration Court organized by NSC included the following protest. Protesters pressed their hands against the wall of the building and uttered the names of their Friends facing deportation (see figs. 6–8). Then, they walked twice around the building guarded by police, who observed the protesters with disinterest. The organizer described the case of a twenty-one-

FIGURE 5.   Support for a DACA recipient, New Sanctuary Coalition, New York. Source: Fieldwork, September 5, 2017.

year-old father who faced possible deportation due to two old tickets for dirt bike riding and one for failure to appear in court. The organizer described the fear people feel in the immigration court and argued that the new rules "normalize" the separation of families and the breaking of communities (fieldwork notes, July 6, 2017).

Back in the Judson Memorial Church room in Greenwich Village with about twenty adults and several children present, the organizer performed a role-play where participants representing "la migra" (ICE) and "el pueblo" (the people) took turns standing up and changing seats. When the organizer said "la redada" (raid), everyone stood up and ran around the room looking for a seat. Members congratulated a Friend for having been released from detention after six months. The organizer used wordplay on breaking a community and breaking ICE, emphasizing that this was a community effort: "¿Como vamos a romper el poder que la migra tiene de nostros [How can we break the power that ICE has over us]? El pueblo se puede unir y levantarse [The people can unite and rise up]. . . . This is what we do as we gather as a community. We are dismantling the

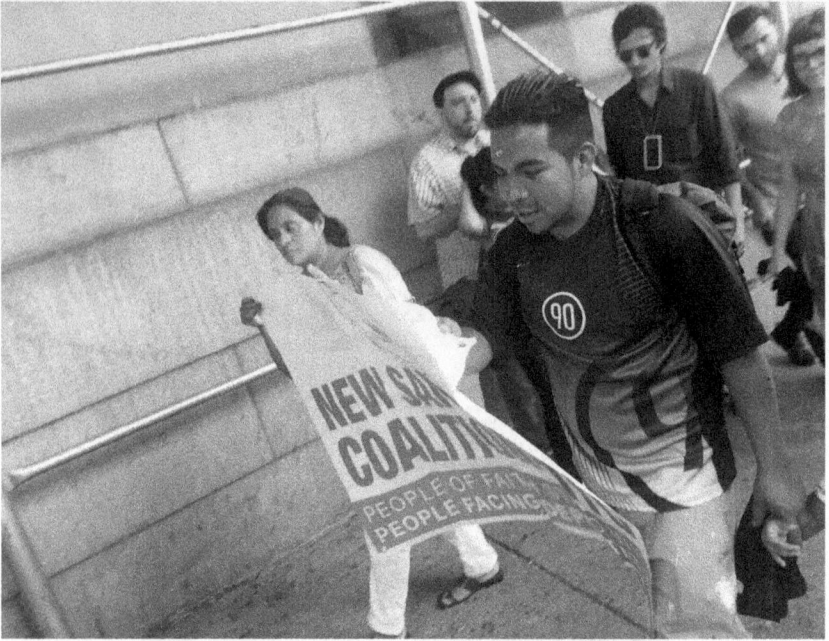

FIGURE 6. Participants in a vigil in front of the Varick Immigration Court, New York, walk two times around the building with a banner that reads "New Sanctuary Coalition—NYC: People of Faith Stand with People Facing Deportation." Source: Fieldwork, August 10, 2017.

power of ICE. It is about being strong enough not to let ICE break us" (fieldwork notes, July 6, 2017).

The organizer emphasized community solidarity and the building of strong communities in which US citizens would support the undocumented (fieldwork notes, July 6, 2017; fieldwork notes, August 10, 2017). At another vigil in front of Varick Immigration Court, one organizer referred to the building as "a symbol of oppression, racism, injustice, and intolerance" while another emphasized the visibility and publicness of the effort, contrasted with the silence of those who could not participate (fieldwork notes, August 10, 2017). The emphasis on visibility was further underscored by an NSC volunteer who discussed the collaboration with the Proof: Media for Social Justice organization. To raise awareness regarding immigrants' plight, the volunteer asked the immigrants who brought their children to the assembly to participate in sharing a story with photographs about immigrant children who crossed the border illegally (fieldwork notes, August 10, 2017).

FIGURE 7. Participants in a vigil place their hands on the wall of the Varick Immigration Court, New York, uttering the names of Friends facing deportation. Source: Fieldwork, August 10, 2017.

Reflecting on Amanda Morales Guerra's case and on the DACA program, a community organizer with the NSC noted the precariousness of the migrant condition:

> There is this sense of mourning. Our nation is mourning. We wake up with a dreadful feeling in our spirit, and I hope that we don't wake up from that as that can cause us to look for decent human ways to build and engage with one another. We are in solidarity with many Amandas and many Dreamers. We are in solidarity with—and this is a violent image—with those at the edge of a guillotine. If we can embrace that, we can embrace the opportunities that this brings—we need to mourn that so that whatever dies a new life can spring up. (Fieldwork notes, September 5, 2017)

Attoh (2011) notes that the right to the city can also be seen as a "right against police brutality, surveillance, and state overreach," a crucial domain of the right to the city in the context of sanctuary cities. Other related rights concern the

FIGURE 8. A vigil in front of the Varick Immigration Court, New York, includes an act of holding hands against the wall and uttering the first names of Friends. Source: Fieldwork, July 6, 2017.

use of public spaces, including, in Attoh's (2011) words citing related research, "a right to occupy [Mitchell 2003], design [Van Deusan 2005], and define what public space is [Gibson 2005]." Through actions such as vigils and Jericho walks, the sanctuary movement activists in New York attempt to redefine public spaces as sites in which the undocumented are demonstrating their rightful presence. These public demonstrations, protests, and civil disobedience campaigns as well as other disruptive practices of sanctuary demonstrate the right to the city in David Harvey's (2006) terms as a collective rather than an individual right. According to Attoh (2011), "The right to the city, for Harvey, 'depends on the exercise of collective power to reshape the process of urbanization'" (676)—this and other examples presented here emphasize the significance of democratic participation within the concept of the right to the city.

Socioeconomic entitlements are, however, an essential part of a liberal city sanctuary policy (e.g., access for all to municipal services), although most of the debate on sanctuary city policies has to do with the context of the criminalization of immigrants, discussed in chapter 2. The de-emphasis on socioeconomic entitlements (found as well in fieldwork in New York) and on the role of the state (see Coggin 2018, 11, 15–20) and local government limits the right to the sanctuary city as a critique of urban inequality.

Struggles for Justice and the Right to the City

While it could be argued that sanctuary cities buy social peace, they cannot be reduced to another means of controlling migration. This is Bagelman's (2016) claim, arguing that sanctuary cities in the UK "function as a form of governmentalizing process, inducing asylum seekers to commit to the rules of the game, while simultaneously trapping them in an endless cycle of waiting and deferral" (39). Bagelman perhaps expects too much of oppressed groups, and even those that meet her criteria tend to have their efforts dismissed as futile, dooming fragile acts to aid migrants. Bagelman's argument that while sanctuary "may extend a particular kind of hope, it risks sustaining a state of suspension, rendering it more durable and paralyzing," and that this "engender[s] a sense of passivity among asylum seekers and refugees" (41–42), may serve as a critique of the charitable components of sanctuaries or may apply to specific drop-in centers that serve refugees but appears unconvincing when contrasted with the evidence of the benefits of sanctuary cities.

Sanctuary practices observed during fieldwork in New York represent precisely the opposition front to the state "apparatus of control" (Bagelman 2016, 42) and regimes of abeyance. The New Sanctuary Coalition in New York provides accompaniment assistance that extends sanctuary to places where the immigrants are being targeted—for example, the Federal Plaza:

> Volunteers go with Friends to court dates and bear witness to what is happening. We do not care about the circumstances of immigration. We recognize their humanity and we defend them. The amount of anxiety that people feel who go to the courtroom without a lawyer is enormous. Additionally, you realize that this is sanctuary. You are providing a space—an internal peace to go through something that is difficult. We emotionally and physically accompany people to go through that process so that they don't have to do it alone. . . . We don't participate in the demonization of immigrants [that] dehumanizes people. (Fieldwork notes, July 12, 2017)
>
> One of the volunteers promoted Nature Walks at the NSC where Friends and volunteers would address stress levels, bond, pray, and connect with nature; the purpose of the walks would be to create this space in an extra-legal way. We would connect with people not just by providing a job or a shelter but there is something about this place, about

being in a place, making a place something we can share. (Fieldwork notes, July 20, 2017)

This is not an ironic escape from the city but rather suggestive of Lefebvre's (1996) "right to nature"—an opportunity for an immigrant family to experience an excursion that is not affordable to them even if the only cost is a regional train (buses were planned as well) (fieldwork notes, July 20, 2017). Indeed, Vitiello (2022, 29) notes as well the conception of sanctuary as a therapeutic space.

The evidence suggests that sanctuary practices of the NSC oppose state repression and regimes of abeyance. Sanctuary practices alleviate the fear that has been increasing due to changes in federal policies; as a result of that fear, the number of people seeking sanctuary has been increasing, and the number of volunteers participating in accompaniments has dramatically increased (fieldwork notes, July 12, 2017). Leaders also noted, however, that they were not seeing as many raids in the area, which they attributed to the strength of community activism in New York during the first Trump administration (fieldwork notes, July 6, 2017).

Finally, the tension that Attoh (2011) identified between the democratization of city spaces and efforts that place constraints on democracy is crucial for sanctuary research. Much of the work of the New Sanctuary Coalition in New York focuses on individual legal cases that attempt to challenge unjust laws. It is difficult to grasp from these efforts the relevance of the right to the sanctuary city as a broader collective right. This is also particularly the case as legal tools may fail to protect the undocumented; during President Trump's first regime, the state acted to limit rights to asylum and against international laws concerning refugees. On the other hand, other emancipatory collective projects, such as vigils, demonstrations, protests, and walks, discussed here, are suggestive of the democratization of the city space.

Sanctuary movements in the United States and Canada are distinct from the UK sanctuaries used to frame arguments in this chapter. However, the Bagelman (2016) UK study is perhaps the most accomplished contribution to the sanctuary literature and, along with other works, shows sanctuary as a contested space, arguing, however, against the grassroots potential of sanctuaries, which was the subject of this chapter. Yet, there is perhaps sufficient evidence within Bagelman's study as well to seek emancipatory potential within the sanctuary. Thus, cautiously expressed, conclusions made here are specific to New York's sanctuary practices of the NSC. It cannot be overstated that while the conclusions might not apply to the sanctuary movement more broadly, the focus here is on a small set of examples of sanctuary practices of the NSC's 2017–2018 grassroots activism. Indeed, the NSC's vision of sanctuary is quite different from what most of the sanctuary literature offers.

Even if sanctuary can be seen as a set of processes that gives rise to different possibilities, the NSC posits sanctuary as essentially an emancipatory space. There is, however, a disconnect between critical local policies (affordable housing, homelessness, etc.) in New York and the activities of the group, which does not seem to have as developed a coalition as other organizations focused specifically on local or neighborhood politics. The politics of the city and the right to the city are then mostly targeting the state, advancing the rights of immigrants, and using the space of the city to pressure the federal government. In turn, the literature addressing the right to the city does not focus on these types of pressures on the federal government; this study contributes to the expansion of the right to the city's political space to include claims on the state (see also Coggin 2018).

Sanctuary cities, it could be cautiously argued, have a potential to more robustly realize the appropriations of urban space of the Lefebvrian right to the city and are suggestive of alternative legality grounded in rightful presence primarily through the formation of empowered political subjectivities and the grassroots rhetoric of social justice rather than, for example, through an institutional policy that would address deep urban inequalities. Nonetheless, the NSC in New York actively dismantles the binary relations between "host" and "guest" and disrupts the state monopoly on the legal and political through its accompaniment program and through a variety of sanctuary acts and practices.

The particular concern of this chapter has been with the "political potential" of presence (Darling 2019, 256), here attributed to grassroots sanctuary activism in New York. This potential can further be seen as the embodiment of an expanded "strong democracy" that enfranchises both citizens and noncitizens who participated in sanctuary practices. Expanded "strong democracy" is, as in Barber's (1984/2003, 137) account, dependent on the "active consent of participating citizens who have imaginatively reconstructed their own values as public norms through the process of identifying and empathizing with the values of others." This empathy is forged through deliberation to which the "mutualistic act of listening" (175) is central: "I will put myself in his place. I will try to understand, I will strain to hear what makes us alike, I will listen for common rhetoric evocative of a common purpose and a common good" (175). The urban environment presents a complex arena of community building for the purpose of creating common goods, and this demands active citizens and noncitizens presenting claims on the city.

Conclusion

THE PROMISE OF SANCTUARY

The city is a site of *sanctuary practices* that, along with the policies actually implemented by local government, hold the potential to resist crimmigration policies. These practices are the loci of crucial networks of solidarity with the undocumented, asylum seekers, and refugees that are antithetical to a hostile, parochial, repressive state regime. Yet the practices also depend on municipal institutional openings that allow access to a broader range of services or protection from policies enacted by the hostile state.

One of the rabbis interviewed by Grace Yukich (2013c), describing the tradition of Sukkoth, said that "people go into tents, drink, and eat together. It's all about fragile structures, really. . . . The tent is like New Sanctuary; it's a sanctuary that is fragile, but one we can be secure in" (171); the Muslim imam she likewise consulted described sanctuary activism as actions against the system that engages in a "'war against poor people'" (171).

This book is about these fragile acts and practices by, and in solidarity with, the undocumented, refugees, and asylum seekers, yet it has argued that in contrast to the informants in Yukich's study, sanctuary practice participants are not engaged in religious conversion but are rather carving political spaces in the city. To the extent that they show signs of religiosity, these signs appear mostly instrumental, a part of politicized strategies of a movement that advocates for some of the poorest urban populations.

This research has found, however, that it is not merely disobedient, rebel cities that challenge the federal government, as it might appear from statements by US mayors in the media or from the political rhetoric more broadly; rather, it is the grassroots sanctuary practices that constitute the real domain of sanctuary and not cities simply branded as sanctuaries. Taking this argument a step further, Simon Behrman (2019) recently noted, in the context of municipal sanctuary declaration, that the movement's politics should remain grassroots, that when sanctuary moment practices are solidified in the form of official proclamations and programs, they are eroded, ossified, and bureaucratized. But this need not always be the case, as the San Francisco example discussed in chapter 1 seems to suggest; however, pressures from nonprofit organizations and social movements have helped to shape San Francisco's sanctuary ordinance and its sanctuary actions. This book cautiously uses this as an example of urban social justice, if not entirely a form of a symbolic right to the city but in the very least a striving toward it.

The just city theories examined in this book—Fainstein's (2010) and Barber's (2017) theories in particular—seem to express too great a faith in mayoral leadership, citing, for example, how local policies made a difference through selective recognition and redistributive programs (see Fainstein on Mayor Lindsey) or how mayors ought to deliberate across borders (Barber), as has been noted in chapter 6. But as the San Francisco case shows, it was former mayor Newsom who proposed policies that would criminalize migrant youth, and it was the Sanctuary City Board, in contrast, that rejected those policies. And the New York examples show strong rhetoric of recognition of the rights of groups (as in the cited speech by former mayor De Blasio) but weak redistributive strategies, graphically displayed in the failed attempts to address the problems of homelessness and public housing during the De Blasio and subsequent Adams administrations. Thus, it bears restating the points made in chapter 3 on the limits of city sovereignty—the scale of urban inequalities and of lacking redistributive programs trumps the rhetoric on sovereignty amid the need to rebel against the hostile, dysfunctional sovereign that has defaulted on its responsibilities. This book calls in the introduction for creating a federal resettlement agency (perhaps instead of a restructured, if not an abolished, ICE) that would aid immigrants, undocumented as well as temporary and permanent residents; this should not be a program created to the detriment of other programs for the poor but one that should be seen in synergy with broader urban redistributive strategies. Barber's (2017) vision should not be interpreted to abandon pressures on the sovereign no matter how irresponsible or hostile the federal entity; as Fainstein's (2010) examples demonstrate, cities have become more equitable (including through the provision of affordable housing), if not necessarily better integrated or more inclusive, where national policy has been more redistributive (e.g., in Amsterdam versus in London and New York). The lesson here is that sanctuary cities cannot be seen as apart from other urban policies if they are to go beyond mere rhetoric.

Nonetheless, rhetoric itself is important, as the federal rhetorical outbursts during the first Trump administration and during his 2024 presidential campaign have posed outright threats of defunding cities (even if only a small percentage of budgets would be affected), which were blocked in courts, and threats of expanding the scope of criminalization of immigrants (as discussed in chap. 2), which were resisted by the city administrations who refused police cooperation with ICE (although this changed at the beginning of the second Trump administration). These rhetorical outbursts against fragile grassroots efforts and administrative forms of branding have served the purpose of heightening ethnic and racial hostilities, scapegoating immigrants, otherizing communities, manufacturing emergencies, and instilling fear in migrants to refrain from the use of social and health services. Beyond this lies a more insidious agenda of urban disinvestment while increasing pressures on cities to provide jobs, shelter, and services for the poorest populations. Indeed, these findings are confirmed as well in Vitiello's (2022, 17) research that documents the arrival of new immigrants to Philadelphia—a city that became a new immigrant destination in recent decades at the same time as the city's neighborhoods and public services were experiencing disinvestment.

Chapter 2 tackled the notion of an expanded sanctuary, demonstrating struggles to resist the criminalization of immigrants by forging a broader movement against mass incarceration along with advancement of the rights of immigrants and minorities. This required the abandoning of distinctions between deserving and undeserving immigrants, arguing in essence that expanding the rights of noncitizens bears upon the rights of citizens.

The fieldwork in New York found the NSC struggling toward an expanded sanctuary; rejecting deserving/underserving immigrant characterizations; assisting immigrants regardless of their contact with the criminal justice system; seeking to aid not just immigrants but numerous other or overlapping categories of urban membership including women, LGBTQ individuals, Muslims, and people of color; and seeking to expand sanctuary beyond houses of worship to include schools, hospitals, and entire communities through efforts such as Sanctuary Hood (fieldwork notes, March 8, 2018). These efforts (expanded sanctuary, Sanctuary Hood, accompaniments, protests, civil disobedience, walks, vigils, etc.), as this argument demonstrates, claim a political space created by both noncitizens and citizens alike as they struggle for more equitable social and criminal justice policies.

With its legal clinic and accompaniment program, the NSC worked to disrupt the state monopoly on the legal and the political by resisting the criminalization of immigrants. The research here is aligned with Sharpless's (2016) critique of hyperincarceration and Cházaro's critique of deserving/underserving immigrant distinctions. The research challenges conclusions by Yukich (2013a, 2013b, 2013c) and Houston and Morse (2017) regarding the boundaries between the "host" and the "guest"—the language that efforts by NSC have rendered vacuous. Chapter 2 also responds to the moral panic created by the federal regime regarding the threat of the criminality of immigrants (Rumbaut, Dingeman, and Robles [2019]—a negative stereotype that clashes with the empirical evidence of a drop in crime rates (in categories ranging from violent to serious property crime), lower incarceration rates for immigrants, and the fact that a significant percentage of immigrants deported for criminal offenses have in fact committed only minor crimes (Sharpless 2016, 697, 705). As Sharpless (2016) points out, the criminalization of immigrants is tied to a racial critique of hyperincarceration, as convicted noncitizens are seen as foils for deserving immigrants (692), heightening inequality (702).

The immigration enforcement regime and the incarceration regime (see also Sharpless 2016, 718) are entwined and point to sanctuary efforts in New York to dismantle the deserving/undeserving immigrant or, more broadly, the deviant/respectable narrative as a racialized system of control of Blacks and marginalized groups and to shape the political subjectivities of migrants.

As a form of civil disobedience, sanctuary practices attempt, to use the words of Cédric Herrou cited in chapter 5, "to take possession of politics" or, in the words of John Rawls, to present an appeal to the principles of justice. As indeed Herrou's own example points out, cities are not the only sites where claims to justice can be made—we can think of airports, valleys, small towns, and urban peripheries, for example. But perhaps the right to the city can become more than a symbolic emancipatory claim in sites of complex urban diversity where sanctuary cities might complement other grassroots movements and work with them—from anti–mass incarceration to youth and squatter movements and urban commons. Yet none of these movements represents a strike at citizenship in the ways that the sanctuary movement and struggles for immigrant rights do by deliberately demanding that we blur the distinctions between citizens and noncitizens. On the one hand, we can agree with Sassen that these are new political actors in the city; on the other hand, one might express concern over an increase in a population without political representation. But arguments highlighting commitment to diversity and inclusion within sanctuary policies are still important given that they may offer "stronger bases to argue against provisions that treat members of the community differently based on prior criminal history" (Lasch et al. 2018, 1753). Amid the "unshackling of deportation resources" that is taking place (1773), sanctuary policies can, however, also be seen as affirmative policy choices (1772) in which local government shapes presumably inclusive and equitable forms of policymaking, including in the arena of criminal justice.

Beyond the apparent lack of resources, other limitations of the movement (discussed in chap. 4) highlight the focus on legal challenges that places an emphasis on individual cases—indeed, the sanctuary effort is disproportionately small, given the size of the undocumented population. What is left of the relevance of sanctuary does speak to the empowered subjectivities of migrants (consistent with Nyers's [2006, 2010] research on politicized noncitizens enacting themselves as citizens) who are offered more than just simple hope that they will not be deported. And they are offered by the sanctuary movement concrete assistance to achieve the goal of nondeportation, if not assistance toward resettlement (absent noted federal, state, and city investments).

Through sanctuary practices, immigrants attain empowerment, often revealing state injustice through their narratives; this does not seem linked to a prophetic narrative or to faith-based leadership grooming (contra Yukich 2013a, 313) but appears to be tied with social and political activism in the context of legal struggles. It bears restating that an NSC organizer referred to this disruption in the state monopoly on the legal as enforcing the line of rights—"we are literally standing at that line and making sure that we hold that line and enforce [immigrant] rights" (fieldwork notes, October 19, 2017). Yet this book's call for the participation of migrants in sanctuary practices can prove difficult to fulfill in a climate of heightened fear amid stepped up deportations that have the effect of 'silencing' sanctuaries, such as that present at the beginning of the second Trump administration.

It can be argued, based on this book's evidence, that sanctuary sites are not sites where the state is reproduced, as Bagelman (2016) has argued, but rather where processes and practices are enacted aimed at a rejection of the repressive state. As has been stated clearly, this does not mean cities merely branding themselves as sanctuary sites and Democratic mayors simply using the language of recognition and identity, which does not cost them anything. This entails an active grassroots movement—one that can also contribute to the improvement of local governance and change in federal policy. In this sense, sanctuary is the space of political struggle to expand not only legal rights but also social rights for immigrants and minorities more broadly. The prospects of the movement or the expanse of its political space, if you will, depend on the linkage between immigrant rights and the broader politics of racial justice, including especially those efforts tied to the social struggles to end hyperincarceration.

Finally, given that much of what amounts to municipal sanctuary in action is simply the rhetoric of sanctuary, it is important to finally reevaluate the conclusions from chapter 1 regarding the linkages between anti-urban and anti-immigrant biases. As noted in the preface, anti-urban sentiments present in social planning and urbanist discourses have a long history in American political culture and can be seen as rooted in part in anti-immigrant biases, which have resurfaced in the recent political context. Thus Bender's (2002) citation of an outraged journal editor retorting to Randolph Bourne in 1916, "You speak as if the last immigrant should have as great an effect upon determination of our history as the first band of Englishmen" echoes through the current polarized political environment in which questions of social cohesion and communal change are at stake, not merely the question of jobs, housing, education, health, and so on. As has been noted, sanctuary cities can be seen as a social justice intervention only if they are backed up by a strong grassroots social movement in support of the undocumented, refugees, and asylum seekers, yet this is not as Purcell (2016) would argue planning without the state. Chapter 1 highlights the role of planning that ought to have confronted social biases, including against immigrants, through the accomplishments of social reform movements, yet which presented a limited challenge to social problems and urban biases. Anti-urban biases are bound to return given the lack of substantive, sustained, and sustainable urban policy—only they will be less apparent in the luxury and gentrified sections from which the homeless have been expelled and more visible in the neighborhoods left for abandonment and decay where the poor, indeed many of whom are immigrants, reside. Perhaps a warning is appropriate here, however, that even if we follow Fainstein's (2010) just city prescription, the planning process (that Fainstein's theory in part undermines), including in this case planning with and for immigrants, remains pivotal.

Sovereignty from below is perhaps possible in the sanctuary movement if a more substantive set of rights can be accomplished on the basis of rightful presence in the city. Each category of migrants discussed by Carens, who advances the case for open borders, could in theory encounter a more generous implementation policy in the city in terms of more rapid access to work authorizations, municipal IDs, services, legal support, housing, education, and so on, assuming these would also be supplemented by active participatory frameworks and political representation and that this could be supported by a new federal resettlement agency.

Perhaps it is not simply, then, as Isin (2017) has argued, that sanctuaries represent an inversion of borders but that complex diverse, majority-minority cities such as New York have nevertheless become sites where borders have come crashing down, where it becomes apparent not just that justice in this view entails open borders, but that cities, unlike states, are borderless. Liberties taken away from noncitizens reverberate as limitations on broader notions of citizenship, highlighting perhaps a moment in which urban denizenship as an inclusive category of no illegality or, as NSC argues, of no deportations, would grow into a struggle for social rights of the urban marginalized poor, including immigrants, the homeless, and minority youth.

Efforts such as Sanctuary Hood are suggestive of the publicness, visibility, legality, and secularization trajectories of the movement's political space. What is perhaps interesting here in conclusion is the combination of the legal and the grassroots efforts that the sanctuary entails as can, for example, be seen in the ACLU-organized grassroots initiative People Power as resistance to SB1070 in Phoenix, Arizona. But at the same time, legal tools may be weak to protect the undocumented; the state has acted to limit the rights to asylum and against international laws concerning refugees.

Habermas's point that civil disobedience represents a form of legitimacy of constitutional democracy rings accurate in the context of the sanctuary movement, as shown as well by Herrou's and Ragbir's examples discussed in chapter 5. Disruptive practices of sanctuary make visible political subjectivities of sanctuary participants and challenge the state to assert not just their right to have rights but claims to expand the limited national categories of belonging. This represents a direct threat to President Trump's plans to limit birthright citizenship and introduce a merit-based system of admission.

Although this point is made only implicitly, the fieldwork endorsed the grounded urban cosmopolitanism of immigrants from Mexico, Honduras, Guatemala, Venezuela, Iran, China, and other countries whose ethnic belonging went so often unnamed and unuttered in the meetings, vigils, or walks. And indeed, migrants did not make claims based on the ethnic particularisms that critics of multiethnic societies feared; rather, migrants of different groups acted collectively, partaking in sanctuary practices with the citizens and permanent residents who joined them in accompaniments, legal clinics, assemblies, Jericho Walks, and Sanctuary Hood efforts. Demonstrating togetherness in struggles to fight deportations, apply for asylum, resolve legal liminality, or simply aid others, these "co-citizens" acted despite their differences amidst conditions of racialization, pressing an increasingly exclusionary state to uphold human dignity. It is not too farfetched to suppose that the sanctuary fieldwork witnessed a form of togetherness of co-citizens struggling to build a community of equality and human rights that advocates of grounded cosmopolitanism would hope for in New York City—a site, in Sassen's terms, of "unmoored" identities. The New York City of the sanctuary movement during the first Trump administration thus affords a reflection of a deeper solidarity which, to paraphrase Derrida, has indeed arrived but perhaps yet needs to be recognized. This solidarity enfranchises co-citizens by reclaiming the "right to have rights," countering the assumptions that migrants diminish a polity, weaken cohesion, and merely seek economic incorporation.

The meetings in which co-citizens shared food and participated in assemblies included more genuine sociocultural interaction and sharing than the city life usually affords. Together, sanctuary participants helped to shape a more inclusive urban citizenship in New York City, a place marked by the commodification of diversity and difference where the poor and the homeless are regulated, marginalized, and criminalized. Hence the appeal made here for sanctuary activism to join in a broader social movement to address inequalities in housing or urban commons—struggles that have yet to be realized. Challenging countermobilizations that would render them voiceless, self-deportable, or cast them to the margins of the city, however, the movement's participants called for sanctuary to expand to include a broader group of individuals affected by criminalization, as has been discussed in chapters 2 and 5. Thus, the call here is for institutions to respond to these claims on the part of newly enfranchised political subjectivities who have demonstrated their rightful presence, and for the formal polity (through linkage with political representatives, for example), to respond to those existing outside of its boundaries yet not outside of the city's borders.

In a city so relentlessly focused on upscale development, rezoning for urban growth, and policing for public safety, all the while celebrating its commodified diversity and supposed tolerance to difference that often masks indifference, New Yorkers could counter xenophobia by joining the sanctuary movement. By entering conversations with these co-citizens, urbanites stand to gain a genuinely experienced multiethnic diversity with its elastic, "unmoored" urban identities. The smallest of sanctuary efforts, Sanctuary Hood, for example, showed the city as a true locus of encounter where co-citizens shared with residents and small business owners strategies regarding how to "know your rights" (in case of an ICE raid, for example), and in this manner shaping the urban legality, visibility, and publicness of the sanctuary movement. It could be debated whether small-scale activism of this kind advances the right to the city with its grassroots critique of urban democracy; nevertheless, it strives to emancipate political subjectivities of migrants if it cannot dismantle the regimes of fear.

If the right to the city hinges primarily on undoing the capitalist appropriation of space, grassroots sanctuaries fall short. But if transformative outcomes of social movements can plant seeds of change that grow over longer periods of time, sanctuary practices represent an important, if tiny, sprout expanding and democratizing urban citizenship. The city, selected here as the chief, although not only, site of "co-citizenship," would in this theory contribute to broadening of the restrictive national categories of belonging. The conditions of super-diversity in New York City, with its kaleidoscopic microcosm of the grassroots, shaped a grounded urban cosmopolitanism more durable than the fragile, abolitionist sanctuary efforts that aimed to resist criminalization and hyperincarceration. And if the question of what cities can govern pivots around the complexity of this newly enhanced (if not always expanded) urban citizenship, then the answer to "How can cities govern?" must involve the provision of resources for this complex and conflictual governance. Given the urban constraints outlined in chapter 3, these resources will be difficult to marshal without radical restructuring of urban policy in the direction of equity. Amidst the conditions of urban inequality, public opinion easily scapegoated migrants to mask a lack of substantive urban amelioration, affordability, and inclusivity. This was accompanied as well by a striking return of early twentieth century anti-immigrant biases, discussed in chapter 1. As the state effectively mobilized such biases during the initial months of President Trump's second term in office, so too did it descend to demolish the local institutional openings that broaden, if not necessarily substantiate, sanctuary. The grassroots sanctuary efforts discussed in this book will always remain crucial under such conditions.

Perhaps we can conclude with the starting point that sanctuary practices oppose a hostile state, but now this needs to be placed in the context that during fieldwork, many sanctuary participants did not necessarily oppose an unjust city even if this remains an implicit point. Outraged at the federal regime, fearing the threat of stepped-up deportation and targeting by leadership, during fieldwork, sanctuary participants rarely aimed at expressing discontent with urban inequalities and focused instead on opposition to the federal government—a national sovereign that has defaulted on the social contract and grown tyrannical, uninformed, and savagely cruel. (This indeed stands in stark contrast to the evidence from Vitiello [2022], which finds that the sanctuary movement in Philadelphia during the pandemic in 2020 advocated for housing rights, antieviction and rent protection, and funding for parks, homeless services, and libraries [Vitiello 2022, 223].)

In the end, in evaluating the sanctuary movement, one might probe questions for future research not addressed in this study regarding citizens who assist noncitizens during accompaniments as perhaps more of the older, female middle-class population and wonder whether poor citizens competing for the same jobs as noncitizens would be equally likely to participate in sanctuary efforts, although the argument about job competition easily pits working-class citizens against immigrants (Lisa Cacho cited in Paik 2020, 126). Yet there is also hope that Sanctuary Hood would bring sanctuary to communities where such alliances might be forged.

This study unfortunately offered very little of what one immigrant referred to as "el trauma que vivimos los inmigrantes" [the trauma that immigrants experience] beyond the demeaning experience of wearing an ankle bracelet. Yet silences about traumatic experiences reflect respect for the Friends and their supporters—and that would be a subject for another perhaps very different study.

Finally, the hope of this book is for an expanded "strong democracy" (Barber 1984/2003) where neighbors who are both citizens and noncitizens engage in "common talk, common decision, and common work" (224) leading to a participatory politics of urban resistance.

Notes

INTRODUCTION

1. For example, describing how class identities shape urban cosmopolitanism in the popular press, as his neighbors lost their rent-controlled apartment on the Upper West Side of New York and were forced to move back to the Dominican Republic, Kevin Baker recounts the "exuberant diversity" of a working-class city that is being lost to upscaling, gentrification, and tourism. "Beneath me I could hear a hive of dinnertime conversations carried on in half a dozen languages, smell cooking that came from all over the world, hear someone ringing a gong and repeating a Buddhist chant" (Baker 2018).

2. For example, "Festivals might reproduce stereotypical identities, further contributing to their 'exoticisation', while promoting rather superficial encounters and potentially strengthening perceptions of 'otherness' by treating cultures as 'exotic' consumption goods" (Koutrolikou 2012, 2060).

3. Examples of emancipatory aspects of hybrid belonging, preferences for shared residence with other groups, the acceptance of urban diversity as a category of identification, and citizenship practice by the immigrant groups in Western democracies with advanced multicultural policies (e.g., Canada) suggest that second and subsequent generations of immigrants might find within contexts of urban diversity a broader range of ethnic identity, although not socioeconomic mobility, options. These examples further allow for an analysis of the extent to which state endorsements of both incorporative modes of assimilation and elements of multiculturalism would result in the blurring of boundaries and select hybridization, even if this may not in the end apply to (or be desirable for) all groups.

4. The Kerner Report (prepared in July 1967 by the National Advisory Commission of Civil Disorders appointed by President Lyndon Johnson) examined the riots that were taking place in American cities since 1964 and found that the United States was "moving toward two societies, one black, one white—separate and unequal." Following the assassination of Martin Luther King Jr. in April 1968, rioting occurred in more than one hundred cities, one month after the Kerner Report was issued. Charging that a "system of apartheid" existed in major cities, the report recommended investments in low-income areas and ghettos, the creation of jobs, job training programs, and adequate housing, which were however not adopted. Recent research on European multiethnic cities, for example, recommends policies that facilitate the process of social integration "prioritising neighborhoods that concentrate newcomers" (Pratsinakis et al. 2015 14), that increase access to labor market and welfare services, as well as measures that promote interethnic dialogue and counter racial stereotypes (Pratisnakis et al. 2015, 14).

5. In turn, empirical research shows that investment in targeted policies only strengthens the number of and the interconnectedness among immigrant organizations highlighting the significance of "local integration policies" based, in this case, on neighborhood-level organizations or groups representing the immigrant community fostering civic "multicultural democracy" (Penninx et al. 2004, 13).

6. Peterson argued forcefully that the study of local government cannot ignore the city's limits, developing further a typology of urban policies: those that enhance the city's productivity are called developmental, those that benefit communities are called redis-

tributive (which may have adverse economic impact), and those whose economic effects are more or less neutral are referred to as allocational. Peterson showed how national government shoulders the greatest responsibility for redistributive policies while local governments are predominantly focused on allocational policies. But even Peterson acknowledged that in big cities, redistribution does take place as well on the local level.

1. PLANNING INTERVENTIONS AND SOCIAL BIASES AGAINST IMMIGRANTS

1. The CCP argued for industrial decentralization and the reduction of housing density in the Lower East Side, and Benjamin Marsh advocated for comprehensive social planning. As Marcuse notes, "The Society for Decongestion of the Population and the movement for reform of the tenement house laws and the National City Planning Conference were originally substantially joint affairs; they separated out only in 1910 in a series of events that signaled the separation of the reform from the deferential technicist approaches of planning" (Marcuse 2011, 649).

2. Olmsted Jr. argued that planning should be "more hospitable to the accommodation and harmonizing of existing city-building forces than to the fundamental reshaping of the metropolis" (Peterson 1996, 53).

3. An alternate classification in Lees's study of historical and literary discourses of European and American large cities finds that in the 1880–1918 period, critical views of inner-city neighborhoods were associated with "denunciations and explanations of immorality," "the dangers of the political disorder," and "cultural aversions to the crowd." The classification in this chapter is focused on concerns specific to planning (see Lees 1985, 153–88).

4. It is impossible to understand the development of the nineteenth-century Western city and the modern twentieth-century landscape without studying the consequences of the Industrial Revolution. The different factors, conditions, and underlining processes that have had profound effects on the urban environment due to the Industrial Revolution include: (a) the dramatic increase in population since the late 1700s until early 1900, in particular the growth of urban areas (a commonly cited example: in 1760, Manchester had 12,000 inhabitants, and by the 1850s it had 400,000); (b) the increase in life expectancy and the decline in infant mortality (in particular during the second half of the 1800s); (c) economic expansion due to technological advances, in particular significant expansion in the provision of goods and services; (d) expansion of transportation and communication systems (railways, steamships, turnpikes, etc.), or, in Mumford's terms, the growth of the paleotechnic phase ("the mine, the factory, the railroad"); (e) "far-reaching transformations": increases in mobility (and, by some accounts, the beginning of the global world) (f) the acceleration of modernity and its forces of creation and destruction in both physical and social senses; and (g) the notion of land as a marketable asset and the notion that buildings, structures, and even entire communities are replaceable (see Benevolo 1980; Berman 1982; Krueckeberg 1983; Mumford 1961).

5. Differences between the American and British models are notable in the degrees of moral and social outrage over the conditions of the slums and in approaches to amelioration. Yet in both the American and the British models we can detect the articulation of the need for planning to intervene in the economy. As Mearns summarized the sentiment of the reformers: "without State interference nothing effectual can be performed upon any scale" (Hall, 1995, 19).

6. I thank a peer reviewer for this point.

7. In another article titled "6,000,000 More Here in 1930," published on March 27, 1909, in the *New York Times*, discussing an urgent need for a plan for Brooklyn, Marsh proposed the tenement house law, a reduction in density, and the introduction of zoning as the separation of uses (Marsh 1909, 3).

8. As M. Christine Boyer (1983, 67) has argued, while the United States was rapidly industrializing and its cities swelling under waves of migrants from the south and immigrants from Europe, social reformers "struggled to combat the moral disorder and physical decay that larger cities bred, problems that seemed to require some form of collective action."

9. Wilson argued moreover that in the context of "increasing specialization, rising professionalism, and burgeoning bureaucracy," the City Beautiful movement was stigmatized by the City Practical movement as "excessively concerned with monumentality, empty aesthetics, grand effects for the well-to-do and general impracticality" while the City Social proponents argued that cities ought to be planned for social benefit, remarking, "We have rushed to plan showy civic centers at gigantic cost," inspired by "civic vanity . . . when pressing hard-by, we see the almost unbelievable congestion with its hideous brood of evil; filth, disease, degeneracy, pauperism, and crime. What external adornment can make truly beautiful such a city?" (Wilson, 1989, 285, 287).

10. Although this discussion is beyond the scope of the chapter, as a process and an outcome, these planning discourses and their representational aspects were also structured by the specific interests of urban elites and institutions, albeit perhaps not simply predetermined by them. For instance, as can be seen in the case of Baron von Haussmann through the well-known large-scale urban renewal projects in the 1850s in Paris, his planning discourses promoted a vision of a "radical break" in creating a new urban realm in order to legitimize his role and render irrelevant previous forms of urban planning; for this to happen, a new "urban ideal" had to be created so he could demolish and rebuild Paris the way he did. According to Harvey, this allowed Haussmann to "engage in creative destruction on a scale hitherto unseen" (Harvey, 2003, 10).

11. In the late nineteenth and early twentieth centuries, civic groups, government institutions, chambers of commerce, charity organizations, architectural professionals, beautification movements, and business associations proposed conflicting visions for the redevelopment of American cities. The process of mediation among different interests, "a many faceted process, simultaneously speaking for contradictory capital interests . . . and divided among social and economic needs," evolved into what became known as city planning. Torn between the need to ameliorate urban conditions for the benefit the public good and to respond to the interests of the dominant economic and political constituencies, the planning profession emerged with an economic mandate, with the presumption of (for the most part false) neutrality, and as a mediating force between contradictory interests. Even though planning attempted to represent an "ideological reconciliation of these contradictory forces," however, it did not assign equal weight to the conflicting interests; rather, planning acted as "an effective instrument in the service of capital productivity" (Boyer 1983, 67–68).

12. Which might, it should be noted, in any case apply differently to New York than to other cities.

13. This has been the case in the past several decades, especially, since "the rise of the 'crimmigration' enforcement regime in the late 1980s and 1990s and the federal government's post-9/11 effort to enlist state and local law enforcement to engage in immigration enforcement activities" (Lasch 2016, 159–60).

14. "At the height of the sanctuary movement, an estimated 20,000 to 30,000 church members and more than 100 churches and synagogues participated in the sanctuary movement," which also had support from forty-seven members of Congress. The movement further "encompassed a number of religious and faith-based groups around the country, with additional support coming from university campuses, civil rights organizations, lawyers, and a host of other concerned parties." See O'Brien, Collingwood, and El-Khatib 2017, 3–40.

15. According to Bau (1994, 60), "The San Francisco ordinance was passed as a statement of local government opposition to the federal government's discriminatory treatment of Central American refugees and the city's own distrust of the INS." Bau (1994, 50) notes that "between 1983 and 1991, the INS denied 97% of Salvadoran asylum claims and denied 98% of Guatemalan asylum claims." Wild (2010, 985) finds that "from June 1983 to September 1986, Iranian applicants had a 60.4 percent approval rate, and applicants from Soviet bloc countries had approval rates ranging from 51 percent (Romania) to 31.9 percent (Hungary). Meanwhile, applicants from El Salvador and Guatemala were amongst those with the lowest approval rate, at 2.6 percent and 0.9 percent respectively."

16. In response to these political biases against Central American refugees, Ridgley argues that "what began as a group of faith-based organizations in Arizona and California that provided housing, transportation, and legal assistance to asylum seekers who were trying to escape deportation, eventually expanded its base and activities. In addition to providing basic services, many people who associated themselves with the Sanctuary Movement organized to protest U.S. foreign policy and military activity in Central America. Although church congregations and faith-based groups formed the heart of the movement, university campuses, legal, human rights, and civil liberties groups in the United States and abroad also became important sites of activity" (2008, 66).

17. Municipal IDs can be used to "open bank accounts, borrow books from public libraries, and access municipal services such as the public beach, the garbage dump, and public parking" (Bilke 2009, 186).

2. RESISTING THE CRIMINALIZATION OF IMMIGRANTS

1. See also Cházaro (2016) on compelling immigrants to disavow the "criminal" and "illegal" populations among them and to embrace respectability (651). Cházaro (2016) draws from her experience as a lawyer representing twelve hundred immigrants in detention during a fifty-six-day hunger strike in Tacoma, Washington, in 2014: "The group of hunger strikers included a mix of long-time Lawful Permanent Residents with serious criminal records, recent arrivals seeking asylum, and long-term undocumented residents whose road to detention had begun with a single DUI. They made broad-based demands, from improvements in their conditions of confinement to an end to all deportations, all without drawing distinctions between their worthiness for such changes on the basis of their respective criminal records" (662–63). See, furthermore, Yukich (2013c) on "model immigrants" (97, 99–100). See also Ngai (2004) on the discriminatory disciplining strategies that present positive immigrant stereotypes only to pit them against low-income native-born African Americans, Puerto Ricans, and other minorities (268).

2. See US Immigration and Customs Enforcement, "Secure Communities," https://www.ice.gov/secure-communities.

3. Note, on the one hand, that San Francisco sanctuary city policies focus on preventing local police from "stopping, questioning, or detaining any individual solely because of the individual's national origin, foreign appearance, inability to speak English, or immigrations status" (Mancina 2013, 215–16). But on the other hand, subfederal immigration policies have led to the opposite outcomes—for example, Arizona's SB 1070 along with similar policies in Alabama and Georgia (Mollenkopf and Pastor, 2016, 1), that allowed police to ask for proof of citizenship during routine traffic stops. Research found that SB 1070 had a negative impact, resulting in racial profiling and reducing trust between the Latino community and local officials (Waslin, cited in O'Brien, Collingwood, and El-Khatib 2017).

4. In discussing recent examples of sanctuary in the UK, Bagelman demonstrates how criminalization is often imposed on the asylum seeker; as one of the asylum seeker informants in her study stresses, he feels that he has been turned into a criminal even though

he never committed a crime—"one is governed on the basis that it is not a question of 'if' one commits a crime, but 'when'" (cited in Bagelman 2016, 40).

5. Given that during fieldwork, I have observed the NSC assisting all three groups of migrants (including as well permanent residents who have become deportable because of their interaction with the criminal justice system), I have decided to include references to all of these groups of immigrants.

6. In contrast to the findings in Yukich (2013c), where one of the chief aims of the NSM was religious conversion and religion was accordingly not a mere resource for political activism (91), this research presents a politicized landscape of sanctuary *practices* with implications for urban governance, especially given the disconnect between the official sanctuary city designation in New York, a form of branding of a sanctuary city, and the NSM with its aims of political and social reform to aid immigrants, especially those affected by the criminal justice system, as will be discussed in chapter 4.

7. Of course, this raises ethical concerns, and it should be noted that participants in sanctuary practices were for the most part aware that I was a researcher of the movement.

8. Discussion with Matt Block, September 15, 2023.

9. Collingwood and O'Brien (2019) also note that nearly all GOP presidential candidates included opposition to sanctuary cities as a part of their platforms (17, 39).

10. Cited in *USA Today*, January 24, 2018.

11. Furthermore, "while never explicitly invoking race, the use of images and rhetoric [in the media, especially Fox News] successfully conveyed the racial script, 'stoking fears that white women will be raped and murdered by racial minorities . . . like Trump, Fox News used the Steinle story to create an antisanctuary narrative of non-white violence against whites that dovetailed with broader anti-immigrant agenda'" (Lasch 2016, 180, 181).

12. More specifically, media references to crime increased from 33 percent to 48 percent, linking the policies to crime and undocumented immigrants. Human-based analysis finds "no mentions of immigrant criminality in the 1980–1989 and 1990–1999 periods. By the 2000–2009 period, criminality had begun to enter the conversation and approximately 28% of articles mentioned crime in their coverage of sanctuary cities. This would dip a little in 2010–2014, only to rise to almost 38% by the 2015–2017 period as a result of the Steinle shooting" (O'Brien et al. 2019, 768–69).

13. More broadly, sanctuary cities in the United States can be defined as a *process* (rather than a place; see Houston 2019) whereby a local government or police department has passed a resolution, a city ordinance, an executive order, or a departmental policy expressly forbidding city or law enforcement officials from inquiring into immigration status and/or cooperation with the Department of Homeland Security's Immigration and Customs Enforcement (ICE) agency, as discussed in the following chapter.

14. Ridgley ties sanctuary policies to the notion of basic entitlements and argues that these policies diminish the fear that limits social and political participation (2008, 73). Sanctuary cities in this view lead to better cooperation with the police on the part of the undocumented and better incorporation (58–59). See also Blanco 2017; Villazor 2010, 594; Wong 2017; Bilke 2009, 183. Yet, according to Cházaro (2016), there is a problem with the framing of this argument regarding "a need for restored trust" between the police and the undocumented, which "frames them as respectable (non)citizens owed the state's protection, not its sanction," given that, if we take into account the contexts of racial profiling of Blacks and Latinos and overpolicing of these groups along with the queer and gender nonconforming immigrants of color, "the call to a return to a time of healthy relationships between police and communities may ring hollow for those who are targeted by the police whether or not ICE is collaborating with them" (653).

15. The source notes further that sanctuary policies could aid incorporation and lead to lower crime rates in sanctuary jurisdictions; it states that undocumented immigrants

are more likely to be the victims, rather than perpetrators, of crime (Lyons and Kittrie as cited in O'Brien, Collingwood, and El-Khatib 2017). This aligns with research that shows on average lower crime rates for immigrants than for native-born citizens in the United States; research that notes that in comparison with cities that have fewer immigrants, cities with a higher percentage of immigrant population have lower crime rates (cited in Minkoff and Carr 2017; see also Lasch 2016, 187; Wong 2017); and research that lists the incarceration rate of native-born males as 3.3 percent in comparison to 1.6 percent for young foreign-born males (Garcia 2016; see also Lyons, Velez, and Santoro 2013).

16. As Buff points out, the 1951 Refugee Convention created the judicial figure of the refugee with right-bearing membership entitlement, contrasted with the figure with the migrant who is excluded and not entitled to the same rights (Buff 2019, 19, 23). Buff argues that the erosion of the distinction between refugees and migrants eventually allowed for the possibility of asserting the right to freedom of movement (32).

17. Discussion with Matt Block on September 15, 2023.

18. Sharpless (2016) finds that 14 percent of criminal offenses by aliens are traffic offenses, citing how immigrants are, for example, precluded from obtaining drivers' licenses by state law then persecuted for driving without a license (727–28). Note here, however, that the focus on just minor crimes may be seen as problematic in perpetuating the deserving immigrant narrative (711).

19. This space, according to Father Barrios, refers to a manner in which Amanda Morales Guerra constituted the notion of "*mi casa*" (my house) amid the church sanctuary.

20. "To be eligible for sanctuary, an undocumented immigrant must be in deportation proceedings, have a good work record, and agree to undergo training to overcome fear of public exposure in order to articulate their cases at news conferences and public gatherings. They also must not have committed any crimes, and they must have US-born children to make the case that to separate them would destroy a family" (as cited in Freeland 2010, 494).

21. The authors cite an NSM "pamphlet [that] recommends recruiting families with the following characteristics: . . . a good work record and a history of contributing to their community. It is also helpful when families can speak from the heart about their love for their children, their neighborhood, their community and this country, as well as their religious faith" (Houston and Morse 2017, 38).

22. "For instance, when a family was accompanied after ICE arrests, a group including five religious activists went down with them to the holding facility and stayed with them for five hours while ICE went through various procedures and paperwork (C. Tschirhart, 2008, personal communication). This group refused to let ICE arrest the family, and only when threatened with a press conference did ICE let them go, with the provision that they would be arrested in a week, which gave NSM activists time to work out alternatives to deportation" (Freeland 2010, 499).

23. See also Walia's account (2013, 183) of No One Is Illegal's direct support work, which addresses migrants' material conditions and holds the potential to politicize migrants and increase their participation within the movement, as well as her discussion of No One Is Illegal's ambivalences regarding collaboration with politicians (109).

24. Aligned also with Daniel Denvir's (Fair Punishment Project) proposals stated in "On the Media: Looking Beyond 'Sanctuary Cities,'" WNYC, February 24, 2017.

3. THE LIMITS OF CITY SOVEREIGNTY

1. See Howlett and Ramesh on different types of governance, including especially on "legal governance," situated at the intersection of civil society and the government.

2. Discussion with Rose Cuison-Villazor, May 5, 2017.

3. Correspondence by Sheila Foster, April 26, 2017.

4. Comments made at the Fordham Urban Law Journal event at Fordham University, "City Power: Urban Governance in a Global Age," Monday, January 23, 2017.

5. Comments made at the Fordham Urban Law Journal event at Fordham University, "City Power: Urban Governance in a Global Age," Monday, January 23, 2017.

6. Comments made at the Fordham Urban Law Journal event at Fordham University, "City Power: Urban Governance in a Global Age," Monday, January 23, 2017.

7. Comments made at the Fordham Urban Law Journal event at Fordham University, "City Power: Urban Governance in a Global Age," Monday, January 23, 2017.

4. THE POLITICAL SPACES OF SANCTUARY CITIES

1. Solidarity can be understood, following Pierre Rosevale, as "a 'community of sentiment' that is based on involvement" (cited in Squire 2011, 301). This concept can be expanded to include working-class citizens (including Indigenous peoples) and noncitizen immigrant solidarities in the urban environment—a strategic site of political struggle (Bauder 2016b, 258–63)—and across borders (Isin 2017). This is similar to the research that links sanctuaries with "a philosophy of solidarity whereby equality becomes shared by various social movements that embrace the existence of a universal community of migrants that precedes those categories that are closely tethered to the nation-state" (Lippert and Rehaag, 2013, 7).

2. Another lawyer who works for the Coalition emphasized that subways should be seen as public spaces, given that turnstile jumping can lead to deportation (fieldwork notes, interview, August 4, 2017).

3. "Letters, [planning] demonstrations, signing privacy waivers, pressuring deportation officers and their superiors, escalating pressure with each action, forming alliances with Black Lives Matter and DSA, faith and political leaders, a variety of political groups including libertarian, unions, organizing accompaniments, engaging in civil disobedience, finding points to disrupt the detention and deportation process, [and] recording events" (fieldwork notes, August 30, 2017).

4. The Tenth Amendment mandates that powers not delegated to the United States by the Constitution, nor prohibited by it to the states, are reserved to the states or to the people. The Fourth Amendment protects the individual against search and seizure without a warrant.

5. Discussions of sanctuary movements also note that sanctuary practices further "actuate higher forms of law, including international law" (Lipper and Rehaag 2103, 2) or in the case of churches emphasize natural law and the obligation of churches to assist the vulnerable population (Michels and Blaikie 2013, 31). Activists further "invoke[d] the principles of personal accountability developed in the Nuremburg tribunals" while some "referred to it as a new 'Underground Railroad,' drawing on religious and moral principles of the 19th-century US abolitionist movement, and building off of the experience of the 1960s with civil disobedience campaigns against racial segregation" (Powell 2017).

5. SANCTUARY, CIVIL DISOBEDIENCE, AND ACTS OF DENIZENSHIP

1. The International Federation of Social Workers wrote in Ersson's support, "Social work practitioners, educators and students throughout the world use their skills and knowledge to support vulnerable people in all societies and bring attention to human rights violations and the impact of unjust policies. This example highlights the capability of social work students in upholding the values of the profession, promoting human rights and supporting people through dramatic changes in their lives (such as displacement due to war)" (International Federation of Social Workers 2018).

2. Regarding Mourão Permoser and Bauböck's (2023, 3557) useful distinction among the three spheres of sanctuary—territorial (state actors enacting public polices, laws, and

regulations), social (civil society organizations engaged in social practices), and discursive (local or regional governments' but also social movements' discursive practices)—chapters 2, 4, and 6 could be seen as focusing on social sanctuary while chapters 1 and 3 discuss territorial sanctuary. This chapter considers all three spheres. But given that the participant-observation fieldwork chapters of this book document as well the discursive constructions of urban social sanctuary, the spheres could be seen as overlapping to an extent.

3. Explicating Arendt's theorem in *The Origins of Totalitarianism*, where she considers the condition of masses of stateless refugees, Balibar discusses human rights that encompass the broader community of human beings on the international level and recognize the essential dignity of people who do not belong to the same political community within the nation-state. Yet Balibar also notes that when civic rights within the nation-state are abolished, so are the human rights, because the latter in fact rest on the former (see Balibar 2014).

4. Elsewhere, Bauder notes that the distinction between a solidarity city as a site of bottom-up practices and a sanctuary city as a site of top-down practices associated with mayors and city councils is too simplistic. Rather, urban politics of migrant assistance can include both top-down and bottom-up practices (2022, 91). The commonality among these practices involves the highly contextualized urban scale that hosts a wide range of different solidarities (92).

6. RIGHT TO THE CITY, RIGHT TO SANCTUARY

1. While the sanctuary city movement is international, the definition applied in the case of this research is focused on the data from the United States, although UK and Canadian examples are included for comparison—in both literatures, however, sanctuary cities are seen as "a set of practices, including spatial practices" (Lippert and Rehaag 2013, 2; see also Bauder 2016a). Members of the sanctuary movement have voiced strong objections against immigration laws in the United States, the UK, and Canada, arguing that the laws were unjust and complaining, for example, about the lack of an appeals process in Canada (see Michels and Blaikie 2013).

2. This is a reference to Arizona's 2010 restrictive Support Our Law Enforcement and Safe Neighborhoods Act or SB 1070 bill aiming to "discourage and deter the unlawful entry and presence of aliens and economic activity by persons unlawfully present in the United States." See https://www.azleg.gov/legtext/49leg/2r/bills/sb1070s.pdf (accessed on September 30, 2020).

3. See also Teresa Irene Gonzales's emphasis on civic action and local elections in Gonzales 2016.

References

Abramitzky, Ran, and Leah Boustan. 2022. *Streets of Gold: America's Untold Story of Immigrant Success*. New York: PublicAffairs.

Abu-Lughod, Janet L. 1999. *New York, Chicago, Los Angeles: America's Global Cities*. Minneapolis: University of Minnesota Press.

Alba, Richard. 2020. "Discussion of Richard Alba's The Great Demographic Illusion." Seminar, International Migration Program at CUNY Graduate Center. New York, September 11.

Alcindor, Yamiche. 2017. "Activists for Liberal Causes Join Forces against Common Foe: Trump." *New York Times*, February 15.

Aleinikoff, Thomas Alexander, and Douglas Klusmeyer. 2001. *Citizenship Today: Global Practices*. Washington, DC: Carnegie Endowment for International Peace.

Allen-Ebrahimian, Bethany. 2017. "U.S. Cities Want to Join U.N. Migration Talks That Trump Boycotted." *Foreign Policy* 5 (December). https://foreignpolicy.com/2017/12/05/u-s-cities-want-to-join-u-n-migration-talks-that-trump-boycotted/.

Amin, Ash. 2013. "The Land of Strangers." *Identities* 20: 1–8.

Amin, Ash. 2016. "On Urban Failure." *Social Research* 83: 777–98.

Arjona, Ana, N. Nelson Kasfir, and Zachariah Mampilly. 2015. *Rebel Governance in Civil War*. Cambridge, UK: Cambridge University Press.

Ashworth, Gregory J. 1991. *War and the City*. London: Routledge.

Attoh, Kafui A. 2011. "What Kind of Right Is the Right to the City?" *Progress in Human Geography* 35 (5) (February 14): 669–85. https://journals.sagepub.com/doi/10.1177/0309132510394706.

Ayers, Ava. 2021. "Missing Immigrants in the Rhetoric of Sanctuary." *Wisconsin Law Review* 473 (May), Albany Law School Research Paper. Available at SSRN: https://ssrn.com/abstract=3844618.

Bagelman, Jennifer. 2013. "Sanctuary: A Politics of Ease?" *Alternatives: Global, Local, Political* 38: 49–62.

Bagelman, Jennifer J. 2016. *Sanctuary City: A Suspended State*. New York: Palgrave Macmillan.

Baker, Kevin. 2018. "The Death of a Once Great City." *Harper's*, July. https://harpers.org/archive/2018/07/the-death-of-new-york-city-gentrification/.

Balibar, Étienne. 2014. *Equaliberty: Political Essays*. Durham, NC: Duke University Press, 2014.

Balmer, Crispian. 2019. "Naples Mayor Offers to Welcome in Stranded NGO Migrant Boat." Reuters, January 3. https://www.reuters.com/article/world/naples-mayor-offers-to-welcome-in-stranded-ngo-migrant-boat-idUSKCN1OX158/.

Barber, Benjamin. (1984) 2003. *Strong Democracy: Participatory Politics for a New Age*. Berkeley: University of California Press.

Barber, Benjamin R. 2013. *If Mayors Ruled the World: Dysfunctional Nations, Rising Cities*. New Haven, CT: Yale University Press.

Barber, Benjamin R. 2017. *Cool Cities: Urban Sovereignty and the Fix for Global Warming*. New Haven, CT: Yale University Press.

Bau, Ignatius. 1994. "Cities of Refuge: No Federal Pre-emption of Ordinances Restricting Local Government Cooperation with the INS." *Berkeley La Raza Law Journal* 7 (1): 50–71.

Bauböck, Reiner. 2020. "Cities vs States: Should Urban Citizenship Be Emancipated from Nationality?" *Verfassungsblog*, January 20. https://verfassungsblog.de/cities-vs-states-should-urban-citizenship-be-emancipated-from-nationality/.

Bauder, Harald. 2016a. "Sanctuary Cities: Policies and Practices in International Perspective." *International Migration* 55 (2): 174–87. https://onlinelibrary.wiley.com/doi/10.1111/imig.12308.

Bauder, Harald. 2016b. "Possibilities of Urban Belonging." *Antipode* 48 (2): 252–71.

Bauder, Harald. 2021a. "Urban Migrant and Refugee Solidarity beyond City Limits." *Urban Studies* 58 (16): 3213–29. https://doi.org/10.1177/0042098020976308.

Bauder, Harald. 2021b. "Urban Solidarity: Perspectives of Migration and Refugee Accommodation and Inclusion." *Critical Sociology* 47 (6): 875–89. https://doi.org/10.1177/0896920520936332.

Bauder, Harald. 2022. *From Sovereignty to Solidarity: Rethinking Human Migration*. New York: Routledge Taylor & Francis.

Bazurli, Rafaelle, and Els de Graauw. 2023. "Explaining Variation in City Sanctuary Policies: Insights from American and European Cities." *Journal of Ethnic and Migration Studies*, 49 (14): 3649–670. https://doi.org/10.1080/1369183X.2023.2198811.

Beauregard, Robert A. 1993. *Voices of Decline: The Postwar Fate of U.S. Cities*. Oxford: Routledge.

Behrman, Simon. 2019. "Grassroots Asylum: Escaping the Statist Paradigm." Paper presented at the "Escaping Violence: New Approaches to Forced Migration." Zolberg Institute Conference, New School, New York, April 12.

Bender, Thomas. 2002. *The Unfinished City: New York and the Metropolitan Idea*. New York: New Press.

Benevolo, Leonardo. 1967. *The Origins of Modern Town Planning*. Cambridge, MA: MIT Press.

Benevolo, Leonardo. 1980. *The History of the City*. First edition. Cambridge, MA: MIT Press.

Bennett, Katy, Allan Cochrane, Giles Mohan, and Sarah Neal. 2016. "Negotiating the Educational Spaces of Urban Multiculture: Skills, Competencies and College Life." *Urban Studies* 54 (10): 1–17.

Berman, Marshall. 1982. *All That Is Solid Melts into Air: The Experience of Modernity*. New York: Simon & Schuster.

Betts, Alexander, and Paul Collier. 2017. *Refuge: Transforming a Broken Refugee System*. London: Penguin Random House.

Bilke, Corrie. 2009. "Divided We Stand, United We Fall: A Public Policy Analysis of Sanctuary Cities' Role in the 'Illegal Immigration' Debate." *Indiana Law Review* 42 (1): 165–93. https://journals.iupui.edu/index.php/inlawrev/article/view/3986/3944.

Binnie, Jon, ed. 2006. *Cosmopolitan Urbanism*. London: Routledge.

Blake, Michael. 2021. "Two Models of the Sanctuary City." *Migration and Society: Advances in Research* 4: 19–30. https://doi.org/10.3167/arms.2021.040104.

Blanco, Octavio. 2017. "Sanctuary Cities: What's at Stake?" *CNNMoney*, January 27. http://money.cnn.com/2017/01/27/news/economy/funding-sanctuary-cities/.

Block, Matthew. 2023. "Sanctuaries as Liberated Zones: From Citizenship to Border-Abolition, and Beyond Both." Unpublished manuscript shared by the author.

Bloemraad, Irene. 2006. "Becoming a Citizen in the United States and Canada: Structured Mobilization and Immigrant Political Incorporation." *Social Forces* 85 (2): 667–95.

Boudou, Benjamin. 2023. "Repertoires of Sanctuary: Building a Network of Safety at the French–Italian Border." *Journal of Ethnic and Migration Studies* 49 (14): 3566–584. https://doi.org/10.1080/1369183X.2023.2198807.

Boyer, M. Christine. 1983. *Dreaming the Rational City: The Myth of American City Planning*. Cambridge, MA: MIT Press.

Brash, Julian. 2011. *Bloomberg's New York: Class and Governance in the Luxury City*. Athens: University of Georgia Press.

Brenner, Neil. 2011. "Urban Locational Policies and the Geographies of Post-Keynesian Statehood in Western Europe." In *Cities & Sovereignty: Identity Politics in Urban Spaces*, edited by Diane E. Davis and Nora Libertun de Duren, 152–75. Bloomington: Indiana University Press.

Brown, Alison, and Annali Kristiansen. 2009. *Urban Policies and the Right to the City: Rights, Responsibilities and Citizenship*. Paris: UN-Habitat Management of Social Transformations.

Bseiso, Faris. 2019. "Ocasio-Cortez Suggests Eliminating Department of Homeland Security." CNN. Last modified July 11. https://www.cnn.com/2019/07/11/politics/alexandria-ocasio-cortez-department-of-homeland-security/index.html.

Buenker, John D. 1973. *Urban Liberalism and Progressive Reform*. New York: Scribner.

Buff, Rachel Ida. 2019. "Sanctuary Everywhere: Some Key Words, 1945–Present." *Radical History Review* 135 (October): 15–42.

Burciaga, Edelina M., and Lisa M. Martinez. 2017. "How Do Political Contexts Shape Undocumented Youth Movements? Evidence from Three Immigrant Destinations." *Mobilization: An International Quarterly* 22 (4) (December 1): 451–71. https://doi.org/10.17813/1086-671X-22-4-451.

Caminero-Santangelo, Marta. 2013. "The Voice of the Voiceless: Religious Rhetoric, Undocumented Immigrants, and the New Sanctuary Movement in the United States." In *Sanctuary Practices in International Perspectives: Migration, Citizenship and Social Movements*, edited by Randy K. Lippert and Sean Rehaag, 92–105. New York: Routledge.

Carby, Hazel V. 1992. "Policing the Black Woman's Body in an Urban Culture." *Critical Inquiry* 18 (Summer): 738–55.

Carens, Joseph. 2013. *Ethics of Immigration*. New York: Oxford University Press.

Carney, Megan, Ricardo Gomez, Katharyne Mitchell, and Sara Vannini. 2017. "Sanctuary Planet: A Global Movement for the Time of Trump." *Society and Space*, May 16. https://www.societyandspace.org/articles/sanctuary-planet-a-global-sanctuary-movement-for-the-time-of-trump.

Castañeda, Ernesto. 2017. "Understanding Inequality, Migration, Race, and Ethnicity from a Relational Perspective." In *Immigration and Categorical Inequality: Migration to the City and the Birth of Race and Ethnicity*, edited by Ernesto Castañeda, 1–25. New York: Routledge.

Castles, Stephen. 1995. "How Nation-States Respond to Immigration and Ethnic Diversity." *New Community* 21 (3) (July): 293–308.

Chabard, Pierre. 2009. "Competing Scales in Transnational Networks: The Impossible Travel of Patrick Geddes' Cities Exhibition to America." *Human Ecology* 36 (2) (August): 1911–13.

Chacón, Jennifer. 2015. "Producing Liminal Legality." *Denver University Law Review* 92 (4): 709–67.

Chapple, Karen. 2017. "Income Inequality and Urban Displacement: The New Gentrification." *New Labor Forum* 26 (1): 84–93. https://www.jstor.org/stable/26420046.

Cházaro, Angelica. 2016. "Challenging the 'Criminal Alien' paradigm." *UCLA Law Review* 63: 594–664.

"City Power: Urban Governance in a Global Age." 2017. Comments, Fordham University, Fordham Urban Law Journal Event, New York, January 23.

Coalition for the Homeless. 2024. "Facts about Homelessness." Coalition for the Homeless, New York. http://www.coalitionforthehomeless.org/the-catastrophe-of-homelessness/facts-about-homelessness.

Coggin, Thomas. 2018. "Law & the New Urban Agenda: A Role for the Right to the City?" *Fordham Urban Law Journal.* Accessed November 30, 2021. https://www.academia.edu/37274575/Law_and_the_New_Urban_Agenda_a_role_for_the_right_to_the_city.

Collingwood, Loren, and Benjamin Gonzalez O'Brien. 2019. *Sanctuary Cities: The Politics of Refuge.* Oxford: Oxford University Press.

Coutin, Susan Bibler. 2013. "Exiled by Law: Deportation and the Inviability of Life." In *Governing Immigration through Crime: A Reader,* edited by Julie A. Dowling and Jonathan Xavier Inda, 233–47. Stanford, CA: Stanford University Press.

Crouch, David. 2018a. "Swedish Student's Plane Protest Stops Afghan Man's Deportation 'To Hell.'" *Guardian,* July 26. https://www.theguardian.com/world/2018/jul/25/swedish-student-plane-protest-stops-mans-deportation-afghanistan.

Crouch, David. 2018b. "Swedish Student Who Grounded Deportation Flight Faces Prosecution." *Guardian.* Last modified October 19. https://www.theguardian.com/world/2018/oct/19/elin-ersson-swedish-student-video-grounded-deportation-flight-prosecution.

Crul, Maurice, and Frans Lelie. 2024. "Trumpism around the World: How Do We Formulate a Progressive Answer on Living Together in a Diverse World?" Immigration Seminar Series (Spring), CUNY Graduate Center Sociology Department, New York, April 18.

Cunningham, Hilary. 1995. *God and Caesar at the Rio Grande: Sanctuary and the Politics of Religion.* Minneapolis: University of Minnesota Press.

Czajka, Agnes. 2013. "The Potential of Sanctuary: Acts of Sanctuary through the Lens of Camp." In *Sanctuary Practices in International Perspectives: Migration, Citizenship, and Social Movements,* edited by Randy K. Lippert and Sean Rehaag, 43–56. New York: Routledge.

Darling, Jonathan. 2019. "Sanctuary, Presence, and the Politics of Urbanism." In *Sanctuary Cities and Urban Struggles: Rescaling Migration, Citizenship and Rights,* edited by Jonathan Darling and Harald Bauder, 242–64. Manchester UK: Manchester University Press.

Darling, Jonathan, and Harald Bauder. 2019. *Sanctuary Cities and Urban Struggles: Rescaling Migration, Citizenship, and Rights.* Manchester, UK: Manchester University Press.

Darling, Jonathan, and Vicki Squire. 2013. "Everyday Enactments of Sanctuary: The UK City of Sanctuary Movement." In *Sanctuary Practices in International Perspectives: Migration, Citizenship, and Social Movements,* edited by Randy K. Lippert and Sean Rehaag, 191–204. New York: Routledge.

David, O. 1911. "Relief of Congestion." *New York Times,* March 8.

Davis, Diane E. 2011. "Conclusions: Theoretical and Empirical Reflections on Cities, Sovereignty, Identity, and Conflict." In *Cities & Sovereignty: Identity Politics in Urban Spaces,* edited by Diane E. Davis and Nora Libertun de Duren, 226–56. Bloomington: Indiana University Press.

Davis, Diane E., and Nora Libertun de Duren, eds. 2011. *Cities & Sovereignty: Identity Politics in Urban Spaces.* Bloomington: Indiana University Press.

De Frank, John, and Emma Fitzsimmons. 2023. "Adams Visits the Border to Step Up Pressure on Biden for Migrant Funds." *New York Times,* January 15.

De Genova, Nicholas. 2013. "The Legal Production of Mexican/Migrant 'Illegality.'" In *Governing Immigration through Crime: A Reader,* edited by Julie A. Dowling and

Jonathan Xavier Inda, 41–57. Stanford, CA: Stanford Social Sciences, Stanford University Press.

De Graauw, Els. 2016. *Making Immigrant Rights Real: Nonprofits and the Politics of Integration in San Francisco*. Ithaca, NY: Cornell University Press.

De Graauw, Els. 2021. "City Government Activists and the Rights of Undocumented Immigrants: Fostering Urban Citizenship within the Confines of US Federalism." *Antipode* 53: 379–98. https://doi-org.ezproxy.cul.columbia.edu/10.1111/anti .12660

De Haldevang, Max. 2017. "America's Liberal Cities Are Readying to Battle Donald Trump on Almost Every Front." *Quartz*, January 28.

de Haas, Hein. 2021. "A Theory of Migration: The Aspirations-Capabilities Framework." *Comparative Migration Studies* 9, 8. https://doi.org/10.1186/s40878-020-00210-4.

Demirjian, Karoun. 2025. "Bill to Expand Deportations of Migrants Accused of Crimes Sails Ahead in Senate." *New York Times*, January 9.

Denton, Nancy A., and Douglas S. Massey. 1993. *American Apartheid*. Cambridge, MA: Harvard University Press.

Derrida, Jacques. 2001. *On Cosmopolitanism and Forgiveness*. London: Routledge.

De Saussure, Jade, Rev. Leo Guardado, Byron Cruz, Rev. Randy Mayer, Vanessa Suarez, and Padre Alejandro Solalinde. 2019. "Connecting Sanctuaries across North America— Grassroots Approaches." Presentation at the "Immigration in the Age of Criminality, Precarity, Resilience and Resistance," John Jay College conference, April 29.

Desmond, Matthew. 2016. *Evicted: Poverty and Profit in the American City*. New York: Crown.

Dikeç, Mustafa. 2001. "Justice and the Spatial Imagination." *Environment and Planning A: Economy and Space* 33 (10): 1785–805.

Dowling, Julie A., and Jonathan Xavier Inda. 2013. "Introduction: Governing Migrant Illegality." In *Governing Immigration through Crime: A Reader*, edited by Julie A. Dowling and Jonathan Xavier Inda, 1–36. Stanford, CA: Stanford Social Sciences, Stanford University Press.

Duneier, Mitchell. 1999. *Sidewalk*. New York: Farrar, Straus and Giroux.

Duneier, Mitchell. 2012. "Qualitative Methods." In *The Wiley-Blackwell Companion to Sociology*, edited by George Ritzer and Wendy Wiedenhoft Murphy, 73–81. Hoboken, NJ: Blackwell. https://onlinelibrary.wiley.com/doi/10.1002/9781119429333.ch4.

Ellison, Treva. 2019. "From Sanctuary to Safe Space: Gay and Lesbian Police-Reform Activism in Los Angeles." *Radical History Review* 135 (October): 95–118.

Elsrud, Torun, Anna Lundberg, and Emma Söderman. 2023. "Transversal Sanctuary Enactments in Sweden: Challenges, Opportunities and Implications. *Journal of Ethnic and Migration Studies* 49 (14): 3629–648. https://doi.org/10.1080/13691 83X.2023.2198810.

Engels, Friedrich. [1845] 1996. "The Great Towns." In *The City Reader*, edited by Richard T. LeGates and Frederic Stout, 46–55. London: Routledge.

Epstein, Reid J., Dana Rubinstein, and Zoltan Kanno-Youngs. 2023. "Democrats' Phalanx Around Biden Has an Eric Adams-Size Hole." *New York Times*, May 20.

Ersson, Elin. 2018. "I Stood Up on a Plane to Protect an Asylum Seeker. Now All of Us Must Join the Protest." *Metro*. Last modified August 1. https://metro.co.uk/2018 /08/01/i-stood-up-on-a-plane-to-protect-an-asylum-seeker-now-all-of-us-must -join-the-protest-7699670/?ito=cbshare.

Fainstein, Susan S. 2010. *The Just City*. Ithaca, NY: Cornell University Press.

Fakhrashrafi, Mitra, Jessica P. Kirk, and Emily Gilbert. 2019. "Sanctuary Interrupted: Borders, Illegalization, and Unbelonging." *Canadian Geographer* 63 (1): 84–99.

Farman, Abou. 2017. "In Defense of Sanctuary." *Baffler*. Last modified April 6. https:// thebaffler.com/latest/in-defense-of-sanctuary-farman.

"Federal Appeals Court Holds That the First Amendment Protects Immigrant Rights Activists from ICE Retaliation." 2019. Justice for Ravi Ragbir. Last modified April 25. https://istandwithravi.org/2019/04/25/press-release-federal-appeals -court-holds-that-the-first-amendment-protects-immigrant-rights-activists -from-ice-retaliation.

Foglesong, Richard E. 1986. *Planning the Capitalist City: The Colonial Era to the 1920s.* Princeton, NJ: Princeton University Press.

Foster, Sheila, and Christian Iaione. 2022. *Co-Cities: Innovative Transitions Toward Just and Self-Sustaining Communities.* Cambridge, MA: MIT Press.

Foster, Sheila R., and Christian Iaione. 2016. "The City as a Commons." *Yale Law Policy Review* 24: 281–349.

France-Presse, Agence. 2017. "French Farmer on Trial for Helping Migrants across Italian Border." *Guardian.* Last modified January 4. https://www.theguardian.com /world/2017/jan/04/french-farmer-cedric-herrou-trial-helping-migrants-italian -border.

France 24. 2018. "French Constitutional Court Sides with Farmer Who Aided Migrants." Last modified June 7. https://www.france24.com/en/20180706-france-constitu tional-court-sides-farmer-herrou-who-aided-migrants-fraternity.

Freeland, Gregory. 2010. "Negotiating Place, Space and Borders: The New Sanctuary Movement." *Latino Studies* 8 (4): 485–508. https://doi.org/10.1057/lst.2010.53.

Frug, Gerland E., and David J. Barron. 2008. *City Bound: How States Stifle Urban Innovation.* Ithaca, NY: Cornell University Press.

Fuller, Thomas. 2017. "San Francisco Sues Trump over 'Sanctuary Cities' Order." *New York Times,* January 31.

Gabaccia, Donna R. 2008. "Nations of Immigrants: Do Words Matter?" (Fall) [Academic paper, e-mailed by the author].

Garbow, Diane. 2017. "The Fragility of Sanctuary." *Anthropology News,* May 3, 1–3.

Garcia, Angela S. 2016. "The Sanctuary Cities Debate." *SSA Magazine,* Winter.

Gelinas, Nicole. 2023. "No Room at the Inn—Except in New York." *City Journal,* May 16.

Georgiou, Myria, Suzanne Hall, and Deena Dajani. 2020. "Suspension: Disabling the *City of Refuge*?" *Journal of Ethnic and Migration Studies* (July 7): 1–17. https://doi .org/10.1080/1369183X.2020.1788379.

Global Parliament of Mayors. 2017. Internal memo from Mayor Marvin Rees (Bristol, UK), Consultative Committee, to Steering Committee re: Crowd-funding Campaign to Support US Sanctuary Cities (appendix to the proposal GPM Support Fund). February 3.

Goh, Kian. 2021. *Form and Flow: The Spatial Politics of Urban Resilience and Climate Justice.* Cambridge, MA: MIT Press.

Goldberg, Michelle. 2025. "Democrats Will Regret Helping to Pass the Laken Riley Act." *New York Times,* January 13.

Golden, Renny, and Michael McConnell. 1986. *Sanctuary: the New Underground Railroad.* Maryknoll, NY: Orbis Books.

Gómez, José Luis Rocha. 2014. "Hospitality as Civil Disobedience." *Peace Review* 26 (2) (April 1): 185–91.

Gonzales, Roberto G. 2016. *Lives in Limbo: Undocumented and Coming of Age in America.* Oakland: University of California Press.

Gonzales, Teresa Irene. 2016. "Sanctuary Policies and States Rights." *Everyday Sociology Blog,* Last modified December 21. http://www.everydaysociologyblog.com/2016 /12/sanctuary-policies-and-states-rights.html.

Graham, Stephen. 2004. *Cities, War, and Terrorism: Towards an Urban Geopolitics.* Malden, MA: Blackwell.

Guardian. 2017. "The Valley Rebels: The Farmer Helping Refugees Cross to France." *Guardian*, April 28. https://www.theguardian.com/news/2017/apr/28/the-valley -rebels-the-farmer-helping-refugees-cross-to-france.

Habermas, Jürgen. 1985. "Civil Disobedience: Litmus Test for the Democratic Consti- tutional State." *Berkeley Journal of Sociology* 30: 95–116.

Hall, Peter. 1995. "The Turbulent Eight Decades: Challenges to American City Plan- ning." In *Classic Readings in Urban Planning: An Introduction*, edited by Jay M. Stein, 13–24. New York: McGraw-Hill.

Hall, Peter G. 1988. *Cities of Tomorrow: An Intellectual History of City Planning in the Twentieth Century*. Oxford: Blackwell.

Hansen, Bue Rübner. 2019. "City of Refuge and Migration: The 'Barcelona en comú' Movement: Forming European Networks of Solidarity." In *Solidarity Cities in Europe [Solidarische Städte in Europa]*, edited by Wenke Christoph and Stefanie Kron. Rosa Luxemburg Stiftung. https://www.rosalux.de/fileadmin/rls_uploads /pdfs/sonst_publikationen/Broschur_SolidarischeStaedte_engl_web.pdf.

Haro, Lia, and Romand Coles. 2019. "Reimagining Fugitive Democracy and Transfor- mative Sanctuary with Black Frontline Communities in the Underground Rail- road." *Political Theory* 47 (5), 646–73. https://www.jstor.org/stable/26785883

Harvey, David. 2003. *Paris, Capital of Modernity*. New York: Routledge.

Harvey, David. 2006. "The Right to the City." In *Divided Cities*, edited by Richard Scholar. Oxford: Oxford University Press.

Harvey, David. 2013. *Rebel Cities: From Right to the City to the Urban Revolution*. Lon- don: Verso.

Hing, Julianne. 2018. "ICE Is Going after People Who Were Once Off-Limits." *The Nation*. Last modified January 19. https://www.thenation.com/article/archive/ice -is-going-after-people-who-were-once-off-limits/.

Hirt, Sonia A. 2014. *Zoned in the USA: The Origins and Implications of American Land- Use Regulation*. Ithaca, NY: Cornell University Press.

Hoag, Alexis. 2020. Discussion of *"Unfinished Work: Black Lives Matter and Policing after the Protests."* The Center on Race, Law and Justice, Fordham University, New York, September 10.

Honig, Bonnie. 2003. *Democracy and the Foreigner*. Princeton, NJ: Princeton University Press.

Horowitz, Carl. 2018. "NYC-Area Teamster Council Is Now a 'Sanctuary Union'; Defies Immigration Law." National Legal and Policy Center. Accessed on February 2, 2019. http://nlpc.org/2018/02/20/nyc-area-teamster-council-now-sanctuary-union -defies-immigration-law.

Houston, Serin. 2019. "Conceptualizing Sanctuary as a Process in the United States." *Geographical Review* 109 (4): 562–79. https://doi.org/10.1111/gere.12338.

Houston, Serin D., and Olivia Lawrence-Weilmann. 2016. "The Model Migrant and Multiculturalism: Analyzing Neoliberal Logics in US Sanctuary Legislation." In *Migration Policy and Practice: Interventions and Solutions*, edited by Harald Bauder and Christian Matheis, 101–26. New York: Palgrave MacMillan.

Houston, Serin D., and Charlotte Morse. 2017. "The Ordinary and Extraordinary: Pro- ducing Migrant Inclusion and Exclusion in US Sanctuary Movements." *Studies in Social Justice* 11 (1): 27–47. https://doi.org/10.26522/ssj.v11i1.1081.

Howlett, M., and M. Ramesh. 2014. "Three Orders of Governance Failure: Policy Capac- ity, Problem Context and Design Mismatches." In Proceedings of the IPSA World Congress, Montréal, QC, Canada.

Huang, Reyko. 2016. "Rebel Diplomacy in Civil War." *International Security* 40: 89–126.

Hudson, Graham. 2019. "City of Hope, City of Fear: Sanctuary and Security in Toronto, Canada." In *Sanctuary Cities and Urban Struggles: Rescaling Migration, Citizenship, and Rights*, edited by Jonathan Darling and Harald Bauder, 77–104. Manchester, UK: Manchester University Press.

Humphris, Rachel. 2023. Sanctuary City as Mobilising Metaphor: How Sanctuary Articulates Urban Governance. *Journal of Ethnic and Migration Studies* 49 (14): 3585–601. https://doi.org/10.1080/1369183X.2023.2198808.

Hung, Carla. 2019. "Sanctuary Squats: The Political Contestations of Piazza Indipendenza Refugee Occupiers." *Radical History Review* 135 (October 1): 119–37.

International Federation of Social Workers. 2018. "Statement in Support of Social Work Student Elin Ersson." Last modified October 25. https://www.ifsw.org/statement-in-support-of-social-work-student-elin-ersson.

Isayev, Elena. 2018. "Hospitality: A Timeless Measure of Who We Are?" *Migration and Society* 1 (1) (December): 7–21. https://doi.org/10.3167/arms.2018.010103.

Isin, Engin F., ed. 2000. *Democracy, Citizenship, and the Global City* London: Routledge.

Isin, Engin F. 2008. "The City as the Site of the Social." In *Recasting the Social Citizenship*, edited by Engin F. Isin, 261–80. Toronto: University of Toronto Press.

Isin, Engin F. 2017. "Enacting International Citizenship." In *International Political Sociology: Transversal Lines*, edited by Tugba Basaran, Didier Bigo, Emmanuel-Pierre Guittet, and Rob B. J. Walker, 185–204. London: Routledge.

Jackson, Kenneth T. 1984. "The Capital of Capitalism: The New York Metropolitan Region." In *Metropolis 1890–1940*, edited by Anthony Sutcliffe, 319–53. London: Mansell.

Jones-Correa, Michael. 2009. "Riots as Critical Junctures in Urban Policy." In *The City in American Political Development*, edited by Richardson Dilworth, 179–99. New York: Routledge.

Judd, Dennis, and Annika M. Hinze. 2019. *City Politics: The Political Economy of Urban America*. New York: Routledge Taylor & Francis.

Kagan, Michael. 2018. "What We Talk About When We Talk About Sanctuary Cities." *UC Davis Law Review* 52: 391–406.

Katz, Bruce, and Jennifer Bradley. 2013. *The Metropolitan Revolution: How Cities and Metros Are Fixing Our Broken Politics and Fragile Economy*. Washington, DC: Brookings Institution Press.

Katznelson, Ira. 1981. *City Trenches: Urban Politics and the Patterning of Class in the United States*. New York: Pantheon.

Katznelson, Ira. 1992. *Marxism and the City*. Oxford: Oxford University Press.

Keith, Michael. 2005. "Racialization and the Public Spaces of the Multicultural City." *Racialization: Studies in Theory and Practice*, edited by Karim Murji and John Solomos, 249–70. Oxford: Oxford University Press.

King, Desmond S. 2000. *Making Americans: Immigration, Race, and the Origins of the Diverse Democracy*. Cambridge, MA: Harvard University Press.

King, R. 2017. "Liberals Matriculate at Calhoun College; in the Trump Era, Progressives Are Now Most Likely to Secede." *Wall Street Journal*, February 15. https://www.wsj.com/articles/liberals-matriculate-at-calhoun-college-1487204348.

Knight, Heather. 2005. "Can San Francisco's New Mayor Make the City Shine Again?" *New York Times*, January 7.

Koutrolikou, Penny. 2015. "Governmentalities of Urban Crisis in Inner-city Athens, Greece." *Antipode* 48: 172–92.

Koutrolikou, Penny-Panagiota. 2012. "Spatialities of Ethnocultural Relations in Multicultural East London: Discourses of Interaction and Social Mix." *Urban Studies* 49 (10) (August): 2049–66.

Krueckeberg, Donald A. 1983. *Introduction to Planning History in the United States*. New Brunswick, NJ: Center for Urban Policy Research.

Kuge, Janika. 2019. "Uncovering Sanctuary Cities: Between Policy, Practice, and Politics." In *Sanctuary Cities and Urban Struggles: Rescaling Migration, Citizenship, and Rights*, edited by Jonathan Darling and Harald Bauder, 50–76. Manchester, UK: Manchester University Press.

Lai, Annie, and Christopher N. Lasch. 2018. "Crimmigration Resistance and the Case of Sanctuary City Defunding." *Santa Clara Law Review* 57: 539–610.

Lake, Robert. 2002. "Bring Back Big Government." *International Journal of Urban and Regional Research* 26: 815–22.

Laman, John. 2015. "Revisiting the Sanctuary City: Citizenship or Abjection? Spotlighting the Case of Toronto." York University, Center for Research on Latin America and the Caribbean, Toronto (unpublished paper).

Lambelet, Kyle B. T. 2019. "Sanctuary in a Small Southern City: An Interview with Anton Flores-Maisonet." *Radical History Review* 135 (October 1): 160–69.

Lasch, Christopher N. 2016. "Sanctuary Cities and Dog-Whistle Politics." *New England Journal on Criminal and Civil Confinement* 42 (2): 159–90.

Lasch, Christopher N., R. L. Chan, Ingrid V. Eagly, Dina F. Haynes, Annie Lai, Elizabeth M. McCormick, and Juliet P. Stumpf. 2018. "Understanding 'Sanctuary Cities.'" *Boston College Law Review* 59: 1703–74.

Lees, Andrew. 1985. *Cities Perceived: Urban Society in European and American Thought, 1820–1940*. New York: Columbia University Press.

Lefebvre, Henri. 1996. *Writings on Cities*. Cambridge, MA: Blackwell.

Leitner, Helga, and Christopher Strunk. 2014. "Spaces of Immigrant Advocacy and Liberal Democratic Citizenship." In *Annals of the Association of American Geographers, Special Issue: Migration* 104 (2): 348–56.

Leyro, Shirley P., and Daniel L. Stageman. 2018. "Crimmigration, Deportability and the Social Exclusion of Noncitizen Immigrants." *Migration Letters* 15 (2): 255–65.

Light, Michael T., and Ty Miller. 2018. "Does Undocumented Immigration Increase Violent Crime?" *Criminology* 56 (2): 370–401. https://doi.org/10.1111/1745-9125.12175.

Lippert, Randy. 2004. "Sanctuary Practices, Rationalities and Sovereignties." *Alternatives* 29: 535–55.

Lippert, Randy K., and Sean Rehaag. 2013. "Introduction: Sanctuary across Countries, Institutions, and Disciplines." In *Sanctuary Practices in International Perspectives: Migration, Citizenship, and Social Movements*, edited by Randy K. Lippert and Sean Rehaag, 1–12. New York: Routledge.

Loft, Gesche. 2021. "Sanctuary for Whom? Negotiating 'Crimmigration' and Local Membership in the 'City of Immigrants.'" PhD diss., Free University, Berlin.

Lorentzen, Robin. 1991. *Women in the Sanctuary Movement*. Philadelphia: Temple University Press.

Lovrich, Nicholas P., John Pierce, and Christopher A. Simon. 2021. *Sanctuary Ordinances: The Contemporary Politics of Immigrant Assimilation in America*. Lanham, MD: Lexington.

Lubove, Roy. 1967. *The Urban Community: Housing and Planning in the Progressive Era*. Englewood Cliffs, NJ: Prentice-Hall.

Lyons, Christopher J., Maria B. Velez, and Wayne A. Santoro. 2013. "Neighborhood Immigration, Violence, and City-Level Immigrant Political Opportunities." *American Sociological Review* 78 (4): 604–32. https://doi.org/10.1177/0003122413491964.

MacLeod, Gordon. 2011. "Urban Politics Reconsidered: Growth Machine to Post-democratic City?" *Urban Studies* 48: 2629–60.

Madokoro, Laura. 2024. *Sanctuary in Pieces: Two Centuries of Flight, Fugitivity, and Resistance in A North American City*. Montreal: McGill-Queen's University Press.

Maestri, Gaja. 2017. "Struggles and Ambiguities over Political Subjectivities in the Camp: Roma Camp Dwellers between Neoliberal and Urban Citizenship in Italy." *Citizenship Studies* 21: 1–17.

Magnusson, Warren, 2011. *Politics of Urbanism: Seeing Like a City.* New York: Routledge.

Maira, Sunaina. 2019. "Freedom to Move, Freedom to Stay, Freedom to Return: A Transnational Roundtable on Sanctuary Activism" *Radical History Review* 135 (October 1): 138–59.

Mampilly, Zachariah Cherian. 2011. *Rebel Rulers: Insurgent Governance and Civilian Life During War.* Ithaca, NY: Cornell University Press.

Mancina, Peter. 2013. "The Birth of a Sanctuary-City: A History of Governmental Sanctuary in San Francisco." In *Sanctuary Practices in International Perspectives: Migration, Citizenship, and Social Movement,* edited by Randy K. Lippert and Sean Rehaag, 205–18. New York: Routledge.

Mancina, Peter. 2016. "In the Spirit of Sanctuary: Sanctuary-City Policy Advocacy and the Production of Sanctuary-Power in San Francisco, California." Unpublished PhD dissertation, Vanderbilt University.

Marcuse, Peter. 1980. "Housing Policy and City Planning: The Puzzling Split in the United States." In *Shaping an Urban World,* edited by Gordon E. Cheery, 23–58. New York: St. Martin's.

Marcuse, Peter. 2002. "The Layered City." In *The Urban Lifeworld: Formation, Perception and Representation,* edited by Peter Madsen and Richard Plunz, 94–114. London: Routledge.

Marcuse, Peter. 2011. "The Three Historic Currents of City Planning." In *The New Blackwell Companion to the City,* edited by Gary Bridge and Sophie Watson, 643–55. Oxford: Wiley-Blackwell.

Marcuse, Peter. 2012. "Whose Right(s) to What City." In *Cities for People, Not for Profit: Critical Urban Theory and the Right to the City,* edited by Neil Brenner, Peter Marcuse, and Margit Mayer, 24–41. New York: Routledge.

Marsh, Benjamin C. 1909. "6,000,000 More Here in 1930." *New York Times,* March 27.

Marsh, Benjamin C. 1911. "Plans to Relieve Congestion Menace." *New York Times,* April 23.

Martinez Jr., Ramiro, Jacob I. Stowell, and Matthew T. Lee. 2010. "Immigration and Crime in an Era of Transformation: A Longitudinal Analysis of Homicides in San Diego Neighborhoods, 1980–2000." *Criminology* 48 (3): 797–829.

Martinez-Beltrán, Sergio. 2024. "Biden's New Executive Order Denies Asylum Claims to Most Migrants Crossing the Border Unlawfully." NPR. Last modified June 4. https://www.npr.org/2024/06/04/nx-s1-4991917/biden-executive-order-asylum-migration-border.

Massey, Douglas. 2020. "Discussion of Richard Alba's The Great Demographic Illusion." Seminar, International Migration Program at CUNY Graduate Center. New York, September 11.

Mayer, Margit. 2009. "The 'Right to the City' in the Context of Shifting Mottos of Urban Social Movements." *City: Analysis of Urban Trends, Culture, Theory, Policy, Action* 13 (2–3) (June): 362–72.

Mays, Jefferey C. 2023. "Mayor Adams Criticizes Biden in Rare Public Rebuke over Migrant Crisis." *New York Times,* April 19.

McIntire, Rachel, and Caleb Duarte. 2019. "Tiny Flying Houses and Other Forms of Resistance and Survival." *Radical History Review* 135 (October 1): 181–91.

McNee, Georgina, and Dorina Pojani. 2022. "NIMBYism as a Barrier to Housing and Social Mix in San Francisco." *Journal of Housing and the Built Environment* 37: 553–73. https://doi.org/10.1007/s10901-021-09857-6.

McNevin, Anne. 2019. "Offshore Practices of Sovereignty." Paper presented at the "Escaping Violence: New Approaches to Forced Migration" Zolberg Institute Conference, New School, New York, April 12.

Medina, Jennifer, and Jess Bidgood. 2016. "Cities Vow to Fight Trump on Immigration, Even if They Lose Millions." *New York Times*, November 27.

Michels, David H., and David Blaikie. 2013. "'I Took Up the Case of the Stranger': Arguments from Faith, History and Law." In *Sanctuary Practices in International Perspectives: Migration, Citizenship, and Social Movements*, edited by Randy K. Lippert and Sean Rehaag, 28–42. New York: Routledge.

Miller, David. 2016. *Strangers in our Midst: The Political Philosophy of Immigration.* Cambridge, MA: Harvard University Press.

Miller, Michael E. 2017. "This Company Is Making Millions from America's Broken Immigration System." *Washington Post*, March 9. https://www.washingtonpost .com/local/this-company-is-making-millions-from-americas-broken-immig ration-system/2017/03/08/43abce9e-f881-11e6-be05-1a3817ac21a5_story .html?utm_term=.bb2f51916379.

Millner, Naomi. 2013. "Sanctuary sans frontièrs: Social Movements and Solidarity in Post-war Northern France." In *Sanctuary Practices in International Perspectives: Migration, Citizenship, and Social Movements*, edited by Randy K. Lippert and Sean Rehaag, 57–70. New York: Routledge.

Miroff, Nick, and Maria Sacchetti. 2024. "U.S. Deportations at Highest Level Since 2014, ICE Report Shows." *Washington Post*, December 19. https://www.washingtonpost .com/immigration/2024/12/19/immigration-enforcement-deportations-biden/.

Mitchell, Don. 2003. *The Right to the City: Social Justice and the Fight for Public Space.* New York: Guilford.

Mitnik, Pablo A., and Jessica Halpern-Finnerty. 2010. "Immigration and Local Governments: Inclusionary Local Policies in the Era of State Rescaling." In *Taking Local Control: Immigration Policy Activism in U.S. Cities and States*, edited by Monica W. Varsanyi, 51–72. Stanford, CA: Stanford University Press.

Modood, Tariq. 2009. "The State and Ethno-religious Mobilization in Britain" In *Bringing Outsiders In: Transatlantic Perspectives on Immigrant Political Incorporation*, edited by Jennifer L. Hochschild and John H. Mollenkopf, 233–49. Ithaca, NY: Cornell University Press.

Moffette, David, and Jennifer Ridgley. 2018. "Sanctuary City Organizing in Canada: From Hospitality to Solidarity." *Migration and Society: Advances in Research* 1: 147–55.

Mollenkopf, John. 2020. "Discussion of Richard Alba's The Great Demographic Illusion." Seminar, International Migration Program at CUNY Graduate Center. New York, September 11.

Mollenkopf, John, and Manuel Pastor. 2016. "The Ethnic Mosaic: Immigrant Integration at the Metropolitan Scale." In *Unsettled Americans: Metropolitan Context and Civic Leadership for Immigrant Integration*, edited by John Mollenkopf and Manuel Pastor, 1–16. Ithaca, NY: Cornell University Press.

Monin, Kira, Jeanne Batalova, and Tianjian Lai. 2021. "Refugees and Asylees in the United States." Migration Policy Institute. Last modified May 13. https://www .migrationpolicy.org/article/refugees-and-asylees-united-states-2021.

Montero, Sergio, and Gianpaolo Baiocchi. 2022. "A Posteriori Comparisons, Repeated Instances and Urban Policy Mobilities: What 'Best Practices' Leave Behind." *Urban Studies* 59 (8): 1536–555. https://doi.org/10.1177/00420980211041460.

Montgomery, Kenneth. 2020. Discussion of *"Unfinished Work: Black Lives Matter and Policing after the Protests."* The Center on Race, Law and Justice, Fordham University, September 10.

Motomura, Hiroshi. 2011. "The Discretion That Matters: Federal Immigration Enforcement, State and Local Arrests, and the Civil-Criminal Line." *UCLA Law Review* 58: 1819–58. https://www.uclalawreview.org/the-discretion-that-matters-federal -immigration-enforcement-state-and-local-arrests-and-the-civil-criminal-line.

Motomura, Hiroshi. 2018. "Arguing about Sanctuary." *UC Davis Law Review* 52: 435.

Mourão Permoser, Julia, and Rainer Bauböck. 2023. "Spheres of Sanctuary: Introduction to Special Issue." *Journal of Ethnic and Migration Studies* 49 (14), 3549–565. https://doi.org/10.1080/1369183X.2023.2198806.

Mueller, Elizabeth J., and J. Rosie Tighe, eds. 2022. *The Affordable Housing Reader*. London: Routledge.

Müller, Floris. 2011. "Urban Alchemy: Performing Urban Cosmopolitanism in London and Amsterdam." *Urban Studies* 48 (16): 3415–31.

Mumford, Lewis. [1938] 1981. *The Culture of Cities*. Westport, CT: Greenwood.

Mumford, Lewis. 1961. *The City in History: Its Origins, Its Transformations, and Its Prospects*. 1st ed. New York: Harcourt Brace & World.

National Law Center on Homelessness & Poverty. 2017. "Homelessness in America: Overview of Data and Causes." Accessed February1, 2025. https://www.scribd.com/document/465038607/Homeless-Stats-Fact-Sheet.

Negrón-Gonzales, Genevieve. 2015. "Undocumented Youth Activism as Counter-Spectacle: Civil Disobedience and Testimonio in the Battle around Immigration Reform." *Aztlán: A Journal of Chicano Studies* 40 (1): 87–112.

Newman, Peter, and Trevor Hogan. 1981. "A Review of Urban Density Models: Toward a Resolution of the Conflict between Populace and Planner." *Human Ecology* 9 (3) (September): 269–303.

New Sanctuary Coalition. 2016. "How to Be a Sanctuary Congregation." November. Memo provided by an organizer.

New Sanctuary Coalition. 2019. Press Release. April 25. Provided by an organizer.

New York City Council. 2020. "Our Homelessness Crisis: The Case for Change." New York, January.

New York State Attorney General. 2020. "Attorney General James Responds to President Trump Signaling That Sanctuary Cities and States Will Not Be Eligible for Coronavirus Funding." Press release. Last modified April 28. https://ag.ny.gov/press-release/2020/attorney-general-james-responds-president-trump-signaling-sanctuary-cities-and.

New York Times. 1908a. "Death Rate and Congestion." *New York Times*, January 12.

New York Times. 1908b. "Efforts to Remedy New York's Greatest Evil." *New York Times*, April 5.

New York Times. 1908c. "The Growing Evil of Congestion in New York." *New York Times*, February 9.

New York Times. 1914. "Immigration: Three Interesting Books on an Important Problem." *New York Times*, November 1.

New York Times. 2006. "The Gospel vs. H.R. 4437." *New York Times*, March 3. https://www.nytimes.com/2006/03/03/opinion/the-gospel-vs-hr-4437.html.

Ngai, Mae M. 2004. *Impossible Subjects: Illegal Aliens and the Making of Modern America*. Princeton, NJ: Princeton University Press.

Nowrasteh, Alex. 2019a. "Deportation Rates in Historical Perspective." Cato Institute, September 16. https://www.cato.org/blog/deportation-rates-historical-perspective.

Nowrasteh, Alex. 2019b. "Illegal Immigrants and Crime: Assessing the Evidence." Cato Institute. Last modified March 4. https://www.cato.org/blog/illegal-immigrants-crime-assessing-evidence.

Nyers, Peter. 2006. "The Accidental Citizen: Acts of Sovereignty and (Un)making Citizenship." *Economy and Society* 35 (1): 22–41.

Nyers, Peter. 2008. "Community without Status: Non-Status Migrants and Cities of Refuge." In *Renegotiating Community: Interdisciplinary Perspectives, Global Contexts*, edited by Diana Brydon and William Coleman, 123–38. Vancouver: University of British Columbia Press.

Nyers, Peter. 2010. "No One Is Illegal between City and Nation." *Studies in Social Justice* 4 (2): 127–43.

Nyers, Peter. 2017. *Irregular Citizenship: Anti/deportation and Struggles for Political Subjectivity.* Book prospectus.

O'Brien, Benjamin Gonzalez. 2018. *Handcuffs and Chain Link: Criminalizing the Undocumented in America.* Charlottesville: University of Virginia Press.

O'Brien, Benjamin Gonzalez, Loren Collingwood, and Stephen Omar El-Khatib. 2017. "The Politics of Refuge: Sanctuary Cities, Crime, and Undocumented Immigration." *Urban Affairs Review* 55 (1): 3–40. https://doi.org/10.1177/1078087417704974.

O'Brien, Benjamin Gonzalez, Elizabeth Hurst, Justin Reedy, and Loren Collingwood. 2019. "Framing Refuge: Media, Framing, and Sanctuary Cities." *Mass Communication and Society* 22 (6): 756–78.

Offenhartz, Jake. 2016. "Inside the Churches That Are Leading New York's Sanctuary Movement." *The Nation*, December 2.

"On the Media: Looking beyond 'Sanctuary Cities.'" 2017. WNYC. Last modified February 24. https://www.wnycstudios.org/podcasts/otm/segments/looking-beyond-sanctuary-cities.

O'Regan, K. 2016. "How Low Income Neighborhoods Change." Furman Center for Real Estate and Urban Policy, October 18.

Oreskes, Benjamin. 2025. "New York City Can't Allow Noncitizens to Vote, Top State Court Rules." *New York Times*, March 20.

Orueta, Fernando Diaz, and Susan S. Fainstein. 2008. "The New Mega-Projects: Genesis and Impacts." *International Journal of Urban and Regional Research* 32: 759–67.

Oskooii, Kassra A. R., Sarah K. Dreier, and Loren Collingwood. 2018. "Partisan Attitudes toward Sanctuary Cities: The Asymmetrical Effects of Political Knowledge." *Politics & Policy*, December 21.

Paik, A. Naomi. 2017. "Abolitionist Futures and the US Sanctuary Movement." *Race & Class* 59 (2): 3–25.

Paik, A. Naomi, Jason Ruiz, and Rebecca M. Schreiber. 2019. "Sanctuary's Radical Networks." *Radical History Review* 135 (October 1): 1–13.

Paik, Naomi. 2020. *Bans, Walls, Raids, Sanctuary: Understanding US Immigration for the Twenty-First Century.* Oakland: University of California Press.

Palmer, Breanne J. 2017. "The Crossroads: Being Black, Immigrant, and Undocumented in the Era of #BlackLivesMatter." *Georgetown Journal of Law & Modern Critical Race Perspectives* 9: 99.

Penninx, Rinus et al., eds. 2004. *Citizenship in European Cities: Immigrants, Local Politics, and Integration Policies.* Burlington, VT: Ashgate.

Peterson, Jon A. 1996. "Frederick Law Olmsted Sr. and Frederick Law Olmsted Jr.: The Visionary and the Profession." In *Planning the Twentieth-Century American City*, edited by Mary Corbin Sies and Christopher Silver, 37–54. Baltimore, MD: Johns Hopkins University Press.

Peterson, Jon A. 2009. "The Birth of Organized City Planning in the United States, 1909–1910." *Journal of the American Planning Association* 5 (2): 123–33. https://doi.org/10.1080/01944360802608484.

Peterson, Paul E. 1981. *City Limits.* Chicago: University of Chicago Press.

Pickus, Noah M. J. 1998. *Immigration and Citizenship in the Twenty-First Century.* Lanham, MD: Rowman & Littlefield.

Pierre, Jon, and B. Guy Peters. 2012. "Urban Governance." In *The Oxford Handbook of Urban Politics*, edited by Karen Mossberger, Susan E. Clarke, and Peter John, 71–86. New York: Oxford University Press.

Pittenger, Mark. 1997. "A World of Difference: Constructing the "Underclass" in Progressive America." *American Quarterly* 49 (1): 26–65. https://doi.org/10.1353/aq.1997.0009.

Portes, Alejandro, and Rubén G. Rumbaut. 1996. *Immigrant America: A Portrait,* Berkeley: University of California Press.

Powell, Catherine. 2017. "The United Divided States: San Francisco Sues Donald Trump for Sanctuary Cities Order." *Just Security.* Last modified February 13. https://www.justsecurity.org/37589/united-divided-states-san-francisco-sues-donald-trump-sanctuary-cities-order.

Pratsinakis, Manolis, Panos Hatziprokopiou, Lois Labrianidis, and Nikos Vogiatzis. 2015. "Living Together in Multi-ethnic Cities: People of Migrant Background, Their Interethnic Friendships and the Neighbourhood." *Urban Studies* 54 (1): 1–17.

Preseton, Julia. 2010. "Illegal Immigrant Students Protest at McCain Office." *New York Times,* May 17. https://www.nytimes.com/2010/05/18/us/18dream.html.

Preston, Julia. 2016. "In Debate over 'Sanctuary Cities': A Divide on the Role of the Local Police." *New York Times,* September 1. https://www.nytimes.com/2016/09/02/us/in-debate-over-sanctuary-cities-a-divide-on-the-role-of-the-local-police.html.

Purcell, Marc. 2016. "For Democracy: Planning and Publics Without the State." *Planning Theory* 15 (4): 386–401.

Putnam, Robert. 2007. "E Pluribus Unum: Diversity and Community in the Twenty-First Century." The 2006 Johan Skytte prize lecture. *Scandinavian Political Studies* 30 (2): 137–74.

Rawls, John. 2009. "The Justification of Civil Disobedience." In *Arguing about Law,* edited by Aileen Kavanagh and John Oberdiek, 244–53. New York: Routledge.

Rees, Marvin, and the Consultative Committee to Steering Committee, Global Parliament of Mayors. 2017. "Crowd-Funding Campaign to Support US Sanctuary Cities (Appendix to the Proposal GPM Support Fund)." Memorandum. Bristol, UK, February 3.

Reynolds, Eileen. 2017. "Experts Untangle Trump's 'Sanctuary Cities' Order." NYU News, Law and Policy, January 27. http://www.nyu.edu/about/news-publications/news/2017/january/marron-institute-cities-and-immigration-event.html.

Ridgley, Jennifer. 2008. "Cities of Refuge: Immigration Enforcement, Police, and the Insurgent Genealogies of Citizenship in U.S. Sanctuary Cities." *Urban Geography* 29 (1): 53–77. https://doi.org/10.2747/0272-3638.29.1.53.

Ridgley, Jennifer. 2013. "The City as Sanctuary in the United States." In *Sanctuary Practices in International Perspectives: Migration, Citizenship, and Social Movements,* edited by Randy K. Lippert and Sean Rehaag, 219–31. New York: Routledge.

Robbins, Liz. 2017. "'Sanctuary City' Mayors Vow to Defy Trump's Immigration Order." *New York Times,* January 25.

Ross, Tracey, and Sarah Treuhaft. 2017. "The Secret Trumpism of Cities." *New York Times,* June 3.

Roy, Ananya. 2019. "The City in the Age of Trumpism: From Sanctuary to Abolition." *Environment and Planning D: Society and Space* 37 (5): 761–78. https://doi.org/10.1177/0263775819830969.

Rumbaut, Rubén G., Katie Dingeman, and Anthony Robles. 2019. "Immigration and Crime and the Criminalization of Immigration." In *The Routledge International Handbook of Migration Studies,* 2nd ed., edited by Steven J. Gold and Stephanie J. Nawyn, 1–13. New York: Routledge. https://www.immigrationresearch.org/system/files/Immigration_and_Criminalization.pdf.

Saint-Blancat, Chantal. 2008. "Spatial and Symbolic Patterns of Migrant Settlement: The Case of Muslim Diasporas in Europe." *Immigration and Integration in Urban*

Communities: Renegotiating the City, edited by Lisa M. Hanley, Blair A. Ruble, and Allison M. Garland, 97–122. Washington, DC: Woodrow Wilson Center Press.

Sandoval, Edgar, Simon Romero, and Miriam Jordan. 2021. "Thousands of Haitians Allowed to Stay in U.S. as Texas Camp Clears Out." *New York Times*, September 23. https://www.nytimes.com/2021/09/23/us/haitian-migrants-texas-camp.html.

Sassen, Saskia. 2001. *The Global City: New York, London, Tokyo*. Princeton, NJ: Princeton University Press, 2001.

Sassen, Saskia. 2005. "The Repositioning of Citizenship and Alienage: Emergent Subjects and Spaces for Politics." *Globalizations* 2 (1) (May): 79–94.

Sassen, Saskia. 2007. *A Sociology of Globalization*. W. W. Norton & Company.

Sassen, Saskia. 2013. "When the Centre No Longer Holds: Cities as Frontier Zones." *Cities* 34: 67–70.

Sassen, Saskia. 2019. "Researching the Localizations of the Global." In *The Oxford Handbook of Global Studies*, edited by Mark Juergensmeyer, Saskia Sassen, Manfred B. Steger, 73–84. New York: Oxford University Press.

Schragger, Richard. 2016. *City Power: Urban Governance in a Global Age*. New York: Oxford University Press.

Sennett, Richard. 1998. "The Spaces of Democracy." Richard Sennett 1998 Raoul Wallenberg Lecture. Ann Arbor: College of Architecture and Urban Planning, University of Michigan.

Sennett, Richard. 2002. "Cosmopolitanism and the Social Experience of Cities." In *Conceiving Cosmopolitanism: Theory, Context, and Practice*, edited by Steven Vertovec and Robin Cohen, 42–47. Oxford: Oxford University Press.

Sennett, Richard. 2023. *Building and Dwelling: Ethics for the City*. New Haven, CT: Yale University Press.

Sharkey, Patrick, Gerard Torrats-Espinosa, and Delaram Takyar. 2017. "Community and the Crime Decline: The Causal Effect of Local Nonprofits on Violent Crime." *American Sociological Review* 82 (6): 1214–40. https://doi.org/10.1177/0003122417736289.

Sharpless, Rebecca. 2016. "'Immigrants Are Not Criminals': Respectability, Immigration Reform, and Hyperincarceration." *Houston Law Review* 53 (3): 691–765. https://houstonlawreview.org/article/3949-immigrants-are-not-criminals-respectability-immigration-reform-and-hyperincarceration.

Shellenberger, Michael. 2021. *San Fransicko: Why Progressives Ruin Cities*. New York: Harper Collins Publishers.

Shoemaker, Karl, 2013. "Sanctuary for Crime in the Early Common Law." In *Sanctuary Practices in International Perspectives: Migration, Citizenship, and Social Movements*, edited by Randy K. Lippert and Sean Rehaag, 15–27. New York: Routledge.

Slater, Tom. 2022. *Shaking Up the City: Ignorance, Inequality, and the Urban Question*. Oakland: University of California Press, 2022.

Somin, Ilya. 2016. "Federalism, the Constitution, and Sanctuary Cities." *Washington Post*, November 2. https://www.washingtonpost.com/news/volokh-conspiracy/wp/2016/11/26/federalism-the-constitution-and-sanctuary-cities/?utm_term=.55eb67cb9224.

Squire, Vicki. 2011. "From Community Cohesion to Mobile Solidarities: The City of Sanctuary Network and the Strangers into Citizens Campaign." *Political Studies* 59: 290–307.

Squire, Vicki, and Jonathan Darling. 2013. "'The 'Minor' Politics of Rightful Presence: Justice and Relationality in City of Sanctuary." *International Political Sociology* 7: 59–74.

Stack, Megan K. 2025. "Why Immigrants Fear Trump Even if They Voted for Him." *New York Times*, March 15.

Sullivan, Eileen. 2019. "Trump Says He Is Considering Releasing Migrants in 'Sanctuary Cities.'" *New York Times*, April 12. https://www.nytimes.com/2019/04/12/us/politics/trump-sanctuary-cities.html.

Sundaram, Arya. 2023. "The African American Exodus from New York City." *Gothamist*, February 3. https://gothamist.com/news/the-african-american-exodus-from-new-york-city.

Susman, Warren. 2003. *Culture as History: The Transformation of American Society in the Twentieth Century*. Washington, DC: Smithsonian Institution Press.

Swanstrom, Todd. 2017. "Trump and Urbanism: Defending the Unwalled City." *Urban Affairs Review*. Urban Affairs Forum's Scholar Series, February 14.

Swyngedouw, Erik. 2005. "Governance Innovation and the Citizen: The Janus Face of Governance-beyond-the-State." *Urban Studies* 42: 1991–2006.

Thoreau, Henry David. 2016. *Civil Disobedience*. Edited by Bob Pepperman Taylor. Ontario, Canada: Broadview.

Thouez, Colleen. 2020. "Cities as Emergent International Actors in the Field of Migration: Evidence from the Lead-Up and Adoption of the UN Global Compacts on Migration and Refugees." *Global Governance* 26 (4): 650–72. https://www.jstor.org/stable/27082841.

Tilly, Charles. 1992. *Coercion, Capital, and European States, AD 990–1992*. Cambridge, MA: Blackwell.

Tilly, Charles. 1998. *Durable Inequality*. Berkeley: University of California Press.

Tilly, Charles, and Wim P. Blockmans. 1994. *Cities and the Rise of States in Europe, A.D. 1000 to 1800*. Boulder, CO: Westview.

Torres, Rebecca, Rich Heyman, Solange Munoz, et al. 2012. "Building Austin, Building Justice: Immigrant Construction Workers, Precarious Labor Regimes and Social Citizenship." *Geoforum* 45: 145–55.

Tucker, Benjamin. 2020. Discussion of *"Unfinished Work: Black Lives Matter and Policing after the Protests."* The Center on Race, Law and Justice, Fordham University, September 10.

Unzueta Carrasco, Tania A., and Hinda Seif. 2014. "Disrupting the Dream: Undocumented Youth Reframe Citizenship and Deportability through Anti-deportation Activism." *Latino Studies* 12 (2): 279–99.

US Immigration and Customs Enforcement (ICE). 2024. Annual Report Fiscal Year 2024, December 19. https://www.ice.gov/doclib/eoy/iceAnnualReportFY2024.pdf.

Vale, Lawrence J. 2011. "The Temptations of Nationalism in Modern Capital Cities." In *Cities & Sovereignty: Identity Politics in Urban Spaces*, edited by Diane E. Davis and Nora Libertun de Duren, 196–208. Bloomington: Indiana University Press.

Van der Horst, Hilje, and André Ouwehand. 2012. "'Multicultural Planning' as a Contested Device in Urban Renewal and Housing: Reflections from the Netherlands." *Urban Studies* 49 (4): 861–75.

Varsanyi, Monica W. 2006. "Interrogating 'Urban Citizenship' vis-à-vis Undocumented Migration." *Citizenship Studies* 10: 229–49.

Varsanyi, Monica W. 2010. "City Ordinances as 'Immigration Policing by Proxy': Local Governments and the Regulation of Undocumented Day Laborers." In *Taking Local Control: Immigration Policy Activism in U.S. Cities and States*, edited by Monica W. Varsanyi, 135–56. Stanford, CA: Stanford University Press.

Varsanyi, Monica W., Paul G. Lewis, Doris Marie Provine, and Scott Decker. 2012. "A Multilayered Jurisdictional Patchwork: Immigration Federalism in the United States." *Law and Policy* 34 (2): 138–58. https://doi.org/10.1111/j.1467-9930.2011.00356.x.

Villazor, Rose Cuison. 2010. "'Sanctuary Cities' and Local Citizenship." *Fordham Urban Law Journal* 37 (2): 573–98. https://ir.lawnet.fordham.edu/ulj/vol37/iss2/3.

Villazor, Rose Cuison, and Pratheepan Gulasekaram. 2018. "The New Sanctuary and Anti-Sanctuary Movements." *UC Davis Law Review* 52: 549–69.

Vitiello, Domenic. 2022. *The Sanctuary City: Immigrant, Refugee, and Receiving Communities in Postindustrial Philadelphia*. Ithaca, NY: Cornell University Press.

Vrasti, Wanda, and Smaran Dayal. 2016. "Cityzenship: Rightful Presence and the Urban Commons." *Citizenship Studies* 20 (8): 994–1011. https://doi.org/10.1080/13621 025.2016.1229196.

Wadsworth, Tim. 2010. "Is Immigration Responsible for the Crime Drop? An Assessment of the Influence of Immigration on Changes in Violent Crime between 1990 and 2000." *Social Science Quarterly* 91 (2): 531–53. https://doi.org/10.1111/j .1540-6237.2010.00706.x.

Waldron, Jeremy. 1995. "Minority Cultures and the Cosmopolitan Alternative." In *The Rights of Minority Cultures*, edited by Will Kymlicka, 93–119. New York: Oxford University Press.

Walia, Harsha. 2013. *Undoing Border Imperialism*. Oakland, CA: AK Press and the Institute for Anarchist Studies.

Walia, Harsha. 2014. "Sanctuary City from Below: Dismantling the City of Vancouver." *Mainlander*, June 2.

Wall Street Journal. 2017. "Liberals Matriculate at Calhoun College." Editorial Opinion. *Wall Street Journal*, February 16.

Wallace, Sophia, and Chris Zepeda-Millán. 2020. *Walls, Cages, and Family Separation: Race and Immigration Policy in the Trump Era*. Cambridge, UK: Cambridge University Press.

White House. 2017. "Presidential Executive Order on Enhancing Public Safety in the Interior of the United States." Office of the Press Secretary. January 25. https:// www.federalregister.gov/documents/2017/01/30/2017-02102/enhancing-public -safety-in-the-interior-of-the-united-states.

White House. 2024. "Remarks by President Biden on Securing Our Border." Last modified June 4. https://www.whitehouse.gov/briefing-room/statements-releases/2024 /06/04/remarks-by-president-biden-on-securing-our-border.

White House. 2025. "Statement from President Joe Biden on Clemency Actions." Briefing Room: Statements and Releases, January 19. https://www.whitehouse .gov/briefing-room/statements-releases/2025/01/19/statement-from-president -joe-biden-on-clemency-actions-3/.

Wiesel, Elie. 1984–85. "The Refugee." *CrossCurrents* 34, no. 4 (Winter 1984–85): 385–90. https://www.jstor.org/stable/24458928.

Wild, Kara. 2010. "The New Sanctuary Movement: When Moral Mission Means Breaking the Law, and the Consequences for Churches and Illegal Immigrants." *Santa Clara Law Review* 50 (1): 981–1015. https://digitalcommons.law.scu.edu /lawreview/vol50/iss3/7.

Williams, Jason. 2020. Discussion of "*The Politics of Policing: Reform, Defund, Dismantle or Abolish*." Critical Perspectives on Crime, Law and Deviance Workshop, John Jay College, New York, June 16.

Wilson, Elizabeth. 1992. *The Sphinx in the City: Urban Life, the Control of Disorder, and Women*. Los Angeles: University of California Press.

Wilson, Elizabeth. 2001. *The Contradictions of Culture: Cities, Culture, Women*. London: Sage.

Wilson, William H. 1989. *The City Beautiful Movement*. Baltimore, MD: Johns Hopkins University Press.

Wirka, Susan Marie. 1996. "The City Social Movement: Progressive Women Reformers and Early Social Planning." In *Planning the Twentieth-Century American City*, edited by Mary Corbin Sies and Christopher Silver, 55–75. Baltimore, MD: Johns Hopkins University Press.

Wolff, Spencer. 2017. *The Valley Rebels*. Documentary film.

Wong, Tom K. 2017. "The Effects of Sanctuary Policies on Crime and the Economy." *Center for American Progress Blog*. Last modified January 26. https://www.ameri canprogress.org/issues/immigration/reports/2017/01/26/297366/the-effects -of-sanctuary-policies-on-crime-and-the-economy.

Wong, Tom K., Angela S. García, and Carolina Valdivia. 2018. "The Political Incorpora- tion of Undocumented Youth." *Social Problems* 30 (May): 356–72.

Wright, Matthew, and Irene Bloemraad. 2012. "Is There a Trade-Off between Multicul- turalism and Socio-political Integration? Policy Regimes and Immigrant Incor- poration in Comparative Perspective." *Perspectives on Politics* 10 (1): 77–95.

Yee, Vivan. 2017. "Judge Blocks Trump Effort to Withhold Money from Sanctuary Cit- ies." *New York Times*, April 25.

Yoshikawa, Hirokazu, Erin B. Godfrey, and Ann C. Rivera. 2008. "Access to Institutional Resources as a Measure of Social Exclusion: Relations with Family Process and Cognitive Development in the Context of Immigration." *New Directions for Child and Adolescent Development* 121 (Fall): 63–86.

Young, Craig, Martina Diep, and Stephanie Drabble. 2006. "Living with Difference? The 'Cosmopolitan City' and Urban Reimaging in Manchester, UK." *Urban Studies* 43 (10): 1687–1714.

Young, Elliott. 2019. "From Sanctuary to Civil Disobedience: History and Praxis." *Radi- cal History Review* 135: 171–80.

Young, Iris Marion. 1990. *Justice and the Politics of Difference*. Princeton, NJ: Princeton University Press.

Young, Julie E. 2010. "A New Politics of the City: Locating the Limits of Hospitality and Practicing the City-as-Refuge." *ACME* 10: 534–63.

Yukich, Grace. 2013a. "Constructing the Model Immigrant: Movement Strategy and Immigrant Deservingness in the New Sanctuary Movement." *Social Problems* 60 (3): 302–20. https://doi.org/10.1525/sp.2013.60.3.302.

Yukich, Grace. 2013b. "'I Didn't Know if This Was Sanctuary': Strategic Adaptation in the US Sanctuary Movement." In *Sanctuary Practices in International Perspec- tives: Migration, Citizenship, and Social Movements*, edited by Randy K. Lippert and Sean Rehaag, 106–18. New York: Routledge.

Yukich, Grace. 2013c. *One Family under God: Immigration Politics and Progressive Reli- gion in America*. New York: Oxford University Press.

Zukin, Sharon. 1995. *The Cultures of Cities*. Cambridge, MA: Blackwell.

Index

Page numbers in *italics* refer to figures.

Legal Aid Society, 14
legality, 184–85, 193n5; legal liminality of
    immigrants, 142; of sanctuary practices,
    ix, 70–71, 114–16, 120–23, 125, 141–43,
    193n5
legal services, 20, 37, 65, 73, 116, 184
LGBTQ community, 62, 68, 180
liberation theology, 138
Lippert, Randy, 68, 85, 123, 125, 169
local political leadership, 64–65, 73. *See also*
    mayoral leadership
local power, 163. *See also* city sovereignty
London, 106, 109, 179
Los Angeles, 11–12, 62, 119, 138
Lurie, Daniel, 41
luxury city, 80, 83, 106–7, 109, 111, 183

Machiavelli, 81
Mahony, Roger, 137–38
Manchester, 25, 188n4
Mapping Project, 164
Mapping the City, 165
Marcuse, Peter, 23, 32, 37, 42, 106, 188n1
Mark-Viverito, Melissa, 156–57
Marsh, Benjamin C., 24, 29, 35, 188n1, 188n7
Mateo, Lizbeth, 134
Mayer, Margit, 12
mayoral leadership, 3–4, 82–89, 97, 157, 179
McCain, John, 134
Mearns, Andrew, 27–28, 188n5
medieval sanctuaries, 48–49
megaprojects, 80, 106–7
memorials, 105
Mexico, 45–46, 73, 145, 184
middle class, 7, 32, 50–51, 107, 119, 186
migration: state control over, 1–4, 14, 20, 48,
    167–68. *See also* immigrants
Migration Policy Institute, 152
militarization of urban space, 104–5, 117
minimum wage, 35, 37, 77, 79, 95–98, 101,
    108, 163
Minneapolis Neighborhood Revitalization
    Program, 107
mobility, 143–44, 150
model immigrants, 45. *See also* deserving/
    undeserving binary
Moffette, David, 139–40
Montevil, Jean, 64
morality and immorality, 24–25, 28–29, 35,
    188n3; moral panics, 46, 104, 181
Morse, Charlotte, 36, 45, 58, 62, 73, 117, 122,
    136, 181
Motomura, Hiroshi, 48, 141–43

Muller, Floris, 5, 7
multiculturalism, 6–9, 73, 88, 187nn2–3
Mumford, Lewis, 26, 33, 35, 160, 188n4
Murray, Ed, 84
Muslims, 8–9, 68, 84, 180

National Conference on City Planning (1911),
    23–24
nationalism, 80, 84, 167
nativism, 55, 73
Nazi Germany, 66, 68
Neely, Jordan, 16–17
neoliberalism, 47–48, 73, 87–88, 91, 149, 151
New Haven, Connecticut, 87
New Sanctuary (film), 121
New Sanctuary Coalition (NSC), ix–x, 18,
    44, 48, 52–72; accompaniment program,
    59–60, 64, 71, 73, 113–14, 175–76, 180,
    184, 192n22; coalition partners, 71;
    community activism, 62–65; DACA and,
    171; emancipatory potential of, 153–55,
    176–77; enforcing immigrant rights,
    60–61; expanded sanctuary, 65–74,
    158–59; legal clinic, 113–14, 180; political
    strategies, 62–65, 113–21, 125–26;
    protests and vigils, 52, 59, 131–33,
    166–67, 170–74, *172–74* (*see also* Jericho
    Walks); resisting criminalization of
    immigrants, 54–59, 115–16; and right to
    the city, 166–77. *See also* Sanctuary Hood
New Sanctuary Movement (NSM), 43–45,
    50–52, 58, 87, 138; legality of, 70–71,
    121–23; religion in (*see* faith-based
    sanctuary movement). *See also* New
    Sanctuary Coalition (NSC)
Newsom, Gavin, 39–40, 179
New York City, 13–14, 17, 57, 99–100, 102,
    105–6, 108, 179; gentrification, 17,
    187n1; grassroots sanctuary practices,
    43–44, 48–49, 51, 115, 126 (*see also* New
    Sanctuary Coalition); mayoral leadership,
    83–84, 89; sanctuary policies, 155–57;
    urban planning, 23–25, 27–30, 188n1,
    188n7
Ngai, Mae M., 45–46
NIMBYism, 40, 97, 163
No One Is Illegal (organization), 155, 192n23
Nyers, Peter, 50, 60, 62, 65, 114, 140, 182

Obama, Barack, 2, 47
O'Brien, Benjamin Gonzalez, 51, 54–56,
    191n9
Ocasio-Cortez, Alexandria, 156

www.ingramcontent.com/pod-product-compliance
Lightning Source LLC
Chambersburg PA
CBHW031546260326
41914CB00002B/298

* 9 7 8 1 5 0 1 7 8 3 2 8 9 *